VISIONARY GUITARS

CHATTING WITH GUITARISTS

ANDREA AGUZZI

2016

First Printing: 2016

ISBN 978-1-326-58693-5

Via Passo Pordoi 13
30173 Venezia Italy

Blog Chitarra e Dintorni Nuove Musiche: http://chitarraedintorni.blogspot.com/

CONTENTS

CONVERSARE

A blind man extends his hand in the void (in the dark? In the night?)
Alberto Giacometti

Music is one of the most complex human abstractions we can afford. Within all human activities, it occupies one of the areas of greater complexity. It cannot be otherwise, because music is a space of experience and experimentation built to dialogue with the highest intricacy, the life as a whole: Henri Bergson's *élan vital* would name one of the formulas that define the need to play, to represent, to deploy forces through sound vibration that allow us to know, as tempting the smog with a stick, probing the abysmal depth and beauty of the world. Giacometti defined this human search in humility, as the effort of a blind man probing to navigate through the night.

I realized that searching was my symbol, the emblem of those who go out at night with nothing in mind, the motives of a destroyer of compasses.
Julio Cortazar

Creativity is a similar operation, to shed sounds and to sort them in search for something we never expected, so just be glimpsed, never-ending, always committed to a more movement space concern, where security is never reached... where the next step in the fog compromises each one of the decisions we've taken in the past. Each step is an announcement of the next, it is hardly possible to stop the project. From there come from the definitions of creation related to his spacial position, avant-garde, vanguard, radical, new wave, fore-guard and his bare necessity. From there come the creation of art highest social role: to take care that the languages by which we relate to and describe, report, express, present, disclose, reveal the world and by which we know, moreover, by which we *create* the world, never stop in their task of describing new and unsuspected possibilities.

True art always creates new territories.
If you must go nowhere, step out.
Jose Lezama Lima

The world is never fully described or discovered, it always turns in on itself, creating its own fog, it's always in fugue. The artist, the musician, groping through his abstractions the universe of the possible: Robert Musil is who

5

defines the artist as one who has the "smell of possibility", who is not satisfied with the presences, but seeks and provoke new ways or paths to occur, fumbling the world to seek their shortcuts or producing it by experience, walking, working, playing and tightening his rules.

One does what one is; one becomes what one does.
Robert Musil

The musician has a special role. Artists are defined as experts in construct decisions. From the biggest ones, like specialize or "falling in love" -as Deleuze would say- with a specific series of signs of the world, they're also experts in explaining the power of the signs they love, its value and beauty, empowered through small choices, microsigns, pronouncements, perspectives through the instant ability to assess and decide, making that the boring time that could elapse unchanged, becomes a dense, open, fruitful, greedy, *passional* experience. The musician decides that among all the signs that exist in the world, he will choose to play, experiment, and discover in only a limited portion of them, corresponding to a particular sensitive range, that which depends on the vibrations and echoes, on the subtle quivering of some bodies broadcasted to the air. The first technical challenge will be to tame these tremors, exceeding and endless. The anguish of the decision begins by having to choose a tool for sculpting the complexity of time.

Silence is so accurate.
Mark Rothko

Every decision made in the art world has to responsibly leave out other universes, possibly of similar intensities, which we can only recover if the asceticism of cutting -etymological sense of the word *decision*, from the Latin scire>cut - is led to its logical conclusion. The election of a **guitar** is above all a resolution continuing the logic opened by the creative urge. While we choose signs dependent of sound we leave out those born of light -in painting, cinema, space, architecture, movement drawing, dance, word literature, politics-utopia... in each tool we rejected multiple worlds of experience.

Life can only be understood backwards; but it must be lived forwards.
Søren Kierkegaard

Just to put a range of possibilities, *each instrument* concretely articulate one sound reality: it is not the same a guitar and a drums, the range of choices as to the relationship of the body with the tool is final and decisive in terms of reduction of signs and their possible recombination: that is, in terms of relating to the world, creating a regulated language and return it to combine and experiment with its borders. Each instrument is closed and open to the signs that regulates the universe. A sound tool reduces them to a scale, then, rearticulates his series to reenact the world. It's a stick, a cane, like in a Haiku, thrown into the void in search of meaning. Every decision is serious, deep and hard, since it involves neglect, abandonment. But we are confronted with a central idea, *only through the losses we can get into the extreme complexity of the world*, where everything is present at the same time. We need using the decisions to cut the reality, to stop it, reduce his dizziness movements, to understand it, understand ourselves through it, walking, even have the feeling -just a feeling- of control. *Life will always be stronger than our attempts to embrace her.*

> *There is nothing you can see that is not a flower;*
> *there is nothing you can think that is not the moon.*
> Matsuo Bashō

I must advance in the text intention, for those who have come this far. When we name an instrument like a *universe*, we refer to the Latin root of the word, *verto*, that means turn, twirl, whirl, gyre... Through an instrument, the world is placed in rotation around a series (scale) of signs, and as in a magical operation, technical control is what appears, hand by hand with the beauty and pain that every work of art makes see-through. The musician, in the act of choosing a language no other thing creates his decisions, including the instrument and technique that is associated with it- has been placed on a double perspective: the language has a history, it is there before him, or paraphrasing René Char,

> *the language knows more about us than we about the language.*
> *A poet must leave traces of his passage, not proof.*
> René Char

Many others have been before us in that position, when choosing a universe of signs we're confronting his history. Each one of our decisions is crucial: the signs to tame the sound, a no other ones, the tools and instruments, the guitar, for instance, a technique and a language... You must think in any technical label and we'll take care of the fickleness of its borders: jazz, classical, avant-garde, experimental, classical, pop or whatever else.

> *Every decision creates a border and the anguish of the frailty of his outline.*
> *I have nothing to say, I am saying it, and that is poetry*

7

Sound and music differ in this point. If the sound is an open perceptual quality, without historical boundaries, music is the deontological development of these signs: that is, what men who have lived in *certain* times defined that has to be the controlled sound in each historical space. Let us explain: if the sound is any vibration, the music creates scales through instruments that it considers appropriate. The separation of the headstock of the guitar in tones or semitones, the layout of the strings, the pitch, are *historic* decisions that the artist can take on or not, that can be present or indifferent, but they're always part of the core of their language, like the memory of all the people who have previously used the series to which we refer and which have created their particular use, his *speech acts* from general language, and belong to the heart of these relations of signs it, and as ancestors or tradition they are guidelines forms to each small movement on the headstock, as they have served us as guides, walking sticks, stands before the fog.

I can't go on, I'll go on
Samuel Beckett

Whether their name is Sor or Hendrix, Monk or Bailey, Paco de Lucia or Ravi Shankar, all these names and the set of practices that house, who have appointed and have passed accumulating personal decisions in the past, they are leaders in an ongoing conversation with the whole tradition around each of our current decisions. There is no tabula rasa, no fresh start, as each sign to which we refer is loaded with past decisions, all language is a cane full of intentions.

The journey itself is my home

Any interpretation is an intense dialogue with the past, a conversation. The author's anguish lives in having to decide and even shape its differentiating position of all that has been said, which is less a selfish need, although the need to feel like a different star in the firmament forms sad part of this game, but as the language needs to advance, conquer new routes, propose new ways, brand signs, recover others, produce new magic in worn ideas, amplify the world through all these selfish impulses tireless for rereading the tradition of the past.

The creation continues incessantly through the media of man.
Gaudi

8

All of this is built as a way in which little is known, in which doubt is one of the greatest lights. *Entrevista*, the Italian and Spanish word corresponding to the English interview, describes this same position where through dialogue is aimed to predict the fate of some signs thrown in front of his creator, who notices them like his first public, and he feels that through them he can build an own space while contributing to the enhance the history of those signs.

Conversation comes from the same root, *verto* that universe. For Epicurus, the simple pleasures of life are concentrate on the friendship that brings us the pleasure of conversation. Talking is being spinning together on something, combine perspectives, discovered through the points or visions of signs that so far had not been placed in the light. If until now the creator, the musician has been described as the result of a fraught path forks, the conversation is a form of support, a form of meeting and describe each one of the decisions he has taken to reach this point, besides the motivations behind them. Nothing else is the music, nothing but the present point in which a track record is described, made of difficulties, doubts, joys, pain, mistakes, betting, courage and cowardice, audacity and restraint.

> *I applaud the courage of he who accepts each and every one of the laws of a game*
> *he did not invent and was not asked if he wanted to play*
> Juan Carlos Onetti

If we pay attention not to a sound piece, but to their position in the whole trajectory of an author, a composer musician -that is, someone who have dedicated his life to order sound signs in music- we would read each more acutely, appreciating the effort that has resulted in the move towards a place nobody knows, with a always fake decision, always imposed by a solitary belief in their own strength, with a never guarantee success, always facing a dangerous zone, always go through tends to lead inevitably its own poison: repeats itself, which is a exact definition of boring >ab-horrere, his etymological root, means always the same, but also fear of the vacuum, fear of loneliness. Artists creates through proof and experimentation to fill the life, to avoid solitude. All the art is a conversation about this.

> *I paint and sculpt to get a grip on reality... to protect myself.*
> Alberto Giacometti

The value of a work is always relative to the risk we face when creating it, to hear it. A work of art has no value it if does not face a danger, said Rodin talking about Rilke. A dialogue with the author, the core of what ***Andrea Aguzzi*** presents, is always the story about the risks he had been taken, and the motivation to continue facing a difficult task, that no one expects and makes illuminated the art definition of Francis Picabiat: *Art is to make the useless, a must.*

The poet is a man who feigns
And feigns so thoroughly, at last
He manages to feign as pain
The pain he really feels..
Fernando Pessoa

At this point, the word of the author has had various values throughout history: the writings of artists have often been neglected: manuscripts notes from Michelangelo, to take one example, they have been slighted, like the value of his drawings and preparatory sketches for a large period of time, depending on the core value of his work was established exclusively at its greatest work: painting, sculpture and architecture made to endure, to project confidence, to cement the idea of a genius author, deified and far away from human errors and regrets.

Every author that creates is a liar; literature is a lie, but from that lie, a recreation of reality is born. Therefore, recreating reality is one of the fundaments of creation.
Juan Rulfo

But for any creator, processes in which decisions develop, crystallizing later -or not-, they are precious, an invaluable process, because they accompany, encourage, correct, support the course, one's way through a garden of paths that wind and fork, on a process led by doubt. Doubt, duda, Latin >dubius, means to be between two options, cleft for them, doubled in possibilities. The art work is a final result and how each author confronts them has since Greek times, a precise name: **poetic**, the set of decisions that underpin a human history, associated with the set of footprints that the author leaves from his steps and that anyone can read and follow, all of them, including the most committed, the more dangerous and that ones which have caused hesitation, regret and even suffering. Error and failure are great sources of knowledge in human desires and attempts, in human goals and in art categories. Perhaps, more accurate that success.

Ever tried. Ever failed. No matter. Try Again. Fail again. Fail better.
Samuel Beckett

10

No artistic field can avoid the pain, his strength comes from the way it faces all the dead roads to reach a creative position. Every word, honestly executed by the artist, has a great value in generating new perspectives on the full and human value of his work, not his herofication or deification beyond our reach. Know the processes and trajectories helps us to accompany the creator in each of their decisions, rebuild them, be creative while we hear a piece, knowing the mechanism, disassemble their strategies, arm them and recombine, offering new perspectives allowing them to go further.

> *Only in dreams, in poetry, in play do we sometimes arrive at*
> *what we were before we were this thing that, who knows, we are.*
> Julio Cortazar

To talk with the author is share the authorship and the authority of what they have made us accomplices. Nothing else requires an accomplice hearing of a work, the intense reading of all the conditions that have made it possible. For a musician, no sign of the world is alien, all of them encourage their curiosity and have value in building an open dialogue with the world, with life running through it. For a reader, for a listener, for the public hearing must be creative, and the author's words are loaded, both in their most ridiculous expressions and the most heroic, the courage to be indicators of the road travelled and the road he runs through the complex world of creation.

Michael Copón, Madrid 2016

Miguel Copón is an aesthetic private researcher.
He studied Pedagogy in Extremadura University, Fine Arts at Salamanca University and Philosophy in the Autonoma University of Madrid, when he got a Ph.d. in Philosophy about Art representation of Death. He has been researcher in University of Vigo, professor of Aesthetics and Art Theory and Director of Communication at the Autonoma University of Madrid, and professor at the Complutense University, director of Projects for the Luis Seoane Foundation of La Coruña, deputy curator at the Spanish Venice Biennale 2007, producer and curator of Nacho Criado, Los Torreznos, among others, retired painter. As art critic he won the Espais Award d'Art and has worked with media such as Diario 16, Abc, Creation, Sileno, Lápiz, Revista de Occidente and others.
He has created and directed Radio Autónoma, worked in Radio Circulo, and he has collaborated like scripwriter with the National Radio and has some sort of parallel activities within the sound design and music, art and edition.
He has published, translated or edited several books for Alianza Editorial, Tecnos, Cátedra, Comunidad de Madrid, Reina Sofía, among others.
He directed with Alberto Ruiz de Samaniego the Larva collection, about contemporary art, and Verba Volant, about Poetry, for Abada editors.
He's the chief editor in <u>preparedguitar.blogspot.com</u>, *about visionary sound aesthetics.*

PREFACE

Guitar to me has always been the key that opened hierarchies, genres, styles and that allowed me to move within time, traditions and space. Just for fun, a few years ago, I started the Blog Chitarra e Dintorni Nuove Musiche which allowed me to broad my musical horizons, giving me the great opportunity to be in touch with guitarists from all over the world. In this book I chose to interview twelve guitarists known in these eight years as a blogger, very special people that I learned to appreciate music, ideas, instinct, and in many cases their pleasant company. The title, "Visionary Guitars", reflects just their "visionary" attitude towards their music and their instruments: whether could be the kind of music (classical, contemporary, renaissance, jazz, avant-garde, blues) they play, each of them stands out for their innovative approach to guitar and their musical thoughts. To better highlight these characteristics I chose to do only open questions, leaving them the maximum possible space. All was made largely through indirect questions, such as those dedicated to improvisation (one of my personal obsessions) or cultural environment in which they live. In other cases I asked them all the same questions, such as those about musical genres, about Frank Zappa, guitar's "trans-generic nature" or about Adorno. As a result I often got twelve different answers for each of them, all equally consistent, interesting and sincere. Rereading several times these responses I was surprised to see other links and unexpected connections between guitars, personality and radically different ideas. I think that all these links and connections, at the end, help to create a book that can gives you different ways of reading and that highlights the creative thoughts of all the personas involved and not only their "simple" choices or their musical careers.

If I have been are successful in this difficult result I have to thank sincerely the patience, the willingness and commitment of Noël Akchoté, Magnus Anderrson, Lucia D'Errico, Davide Ficco, Hans Jürgen Gerung, Scott Johnson, Seth Josel, Heike Matthiesen, Amanda Monaco, Pablo Montagne, Joe Morris, Marco Oppedisano. Thanks for giving me your time, your ideas, yor music.

Many thanks to Lucia D'Errico for her great cover picture, her graphic ability is only secondary to her musical genius.

Sincere thanks to Miguel Copón for his friendship, his support and the great job he is doing with his great blog Prepared Guitars.

Finally, thanks to my family. Thanks to Serena and Nicola, realizing this book I have removed you time, smiles and attention. I think it is right that, in the end, this book is dedicated to both of you.

13

NOËL AKCHOTÉ

Noël Akchoté (born 7 December 1968, Paris) is a French guitarist mainly active in the free improvisation, classical, experimental and free jazz. Trained from the age of eight, he debuted as a guitarist in 1990.[2] He collaborated with a wide variety of musicians among which Henri Texier, Louis Sclavis, Daniel Humair, Jacques Thollot, Sam Rivers but mostly with Derek Bailey, Eugene Chadbourne, Fred Frith, Evan Parker, Lol Coxhill, Tim Berne and George Lewis.
Later in his career he began contributing on albums of David Grubbs, Luc Ferrari, David Sylvian, J. G. Thirlwell (for his band Steroid Maximus), Max Nagl, Andrew Sharpley, Jean-François Pauvros, and the band Earth of Dylan Carlson. He is the founder of Rectangle (label).

http://www.noelakchote.org/

The first question is always the classic one: how does it start your love and interest for guitar and what instruments do you play or have you played?

I guess it all started like most of us, which in fact means that I have absolutely no idea why and how. About how I have some memories. my mother is from Belgrade (ex-Yugoslavia) and as a kid I was there over a month or so for holidays to my grandparents, and their neighbor had two sons who had a hit in the 70's, they were not living there since long, but they left two very 60's solid body electric guitars that fascinated me totally, this was better than anything else (super heroes included). And this woman kindly let me to go there sometime and play those guitars. I was in heaven and could stay there for hours just playing one string at a time extremely gently, almost like some sort of ritual, or something sacramental, I would never dare to bang those strings hard, it would have been a profanation.
Later on when I lived in Paris there was a local record store with all in it, LP's and Singles, all sorts of instruments, and an electric guitar often in front. It happened that in the kindergarden and later on small classes, I got friend with the grand-son of the couple who ran that store and so after class we would step up in the store waiting for parents and that's where things got serious for me. I took my first guitar lessons in that store, with his grandfather who taught rudimentary lessons on about every possible instruments. my parents gave me a classical guitar, an Aria Pro II, that I totally worn out until quite late, I got a more serious electric guitar. I was 8 when I started, with the Carulli Method, and all those exercises to stretch your small fingers still back then, I remember crying because of the pain it did in my left hand too. After a year or so I moved to the local classical conservatory where I had a funny teacher, an amazing flamenco and

classical guitar player who went through the Algerian war and ever really came back. He had a sort of inner violence in himself, and would often be pissed off by teaching pupils, and stopped you to start playing incredible flamenco, but that was it. Next, I had classical music theory and solfège lessons with an old blind single woman who used those sad harmoniums to make you sing scales and then *dictées musicales* and so on theory, harmony, etc. Then my godfather was a close friend to Jimmy Gourley and Kenny Clarke and I was so insisting to get more lessons and jazz lessons that we asked Jimmy, who didn't want to teach me, but sent me to a very good teacher Jean-Claude André (he made few methods and some albums too, with Hal Singer and else swing on Futura-Marge Label), and took me under his arms and thought me a lot.

I had to learn a Big Bill Broonzy's blues, some Charlie Christian's lines, a bit of Freddie Green's comping, and he gave me two cassettes that I still have and that changed my life. One had René Thomas (Chet is Back) on A side, and Jimmy Raney (In Paris) on B side. The Other one had Pat Martino (Live!) on A side and John McLaughlin with Miles on B side (not Jack Johnson but those times). I tore off those two cassettes playing them from one side to the other constantly. Also in Belgrade, for some post-communistic reasons, the national recordings company (Yugoton) had just incredible licenses and those records cost nothing (for me as french), with my pocket money I got BB King, John Scofield with Dave Liebman, Sonny Terry, Lou Donaldson, Monty Alexander, John Lee Hooker but also Scorpion, Blue Oyster Cult, etc plenty of new music to discover for me. And this goes on and on, I could tell hours of anecdotes (like when my parents took me to hear first time Baden Powell's Brazilian solo in Paris club *Le Discophage,* I was standing less than two meters from Baden and it knocked me out totally after that I wanted to play Bossa Nova too, or when Castro Marin album by Paco de Lucia came out and I had seen him on TV, and I had to play flamenco, and we had an incredible Rock TV program on Sundays at that time where I saw Suicide Live (Vega/Rev) and Lou Reed live in NYC with Robert Quine which is clearly the first free player I ever heard and loved immediately, etc, but by 13 years old I was so hungry for music (reading all possible magazines, watching all gear adverts, equipment reviews, live reports, reading all transcriptions etc, taking all possible sources I had, that I came across a summer master class of all styles jazz guitar and this was: Philip Catherine and other jazz musicians I didn't know yet, including my soon to become main private jazz guitar teacher Philippe Petit (the next sessions of those master classes I also attended had Tal Farlow, Mickey Baker, Roland Dyens, Michel Haumont, Joël Favreau, George Brassens lead guitarist...). I'll stop here cause I could continue for about as long as a whole book.... and be far from finished (laughs).

So you learned the hard way...

Yes I learned the hard way and I was very hungry to learn as much as I could so I soon studied a bit of piano for harmony and voicings, I always practiced drums seriously and studied all main jazz drummers (their ride, bass tom, snare, hi-hat etc Paul Motian, Art Blakey, Kenny Clarke, Jo Jones, Billy Higgins, Shelly Manne, Big Sid Catlett, Mickey Roker, Max Roach, you name it …). Practicing guitar I went through a few major crisis, feeling I'll never be able to make it I switched to other instruments like Saxophone, Trumpet (to come closer to Chet and Miles, to feel how they did that sound), Violin, etc... everything but not vocals. Bass and Drums were longtime questions in fact. I always played bass but I hadn't any double bass so I made myself a piece of wood with a bass string on it that use to accompany with a lot records. Ray Brown and Major Holley were always Semi-Gods to me, then Charlie Haden and Eddie Gomez, then Steve Swallow and Jaco Pastorius. And many many more. When I was fourteen years old I started to gig in bars, cafés, restaurants or hotels, etc there were often better guitarists (older too) than me so I had to sit on bass. I used a Japanese Vantage[1] electric Bass (later on I got a fretless by Jacobacci brothers[2]) that I was playing upright, and I got a one meter high or so Yamaha Bass Amp t and I played all that way, standards hits that people mostly wanted and you had to play, eventually some of them wanted to sing or the boss often and you had to comp for them. At those times I felt much better since with guitar so I only kept for those experiments Bass and Drums (not enough unfortunately).

What was your musical training, with which teachers have you studied and what impression they left in your music?...

I guess I answered first half above already. My main teacher was Philippe Petit, and then I attended all sorts of master classes and I was hustling for private lessons every other artists. In those days we had plenty of clubs that would had musicians weekly, meaning the same group from Wednesday to Tuesday, and they stayed in some hotels above often so they were rather free. This is how I got the chance to study with Joe Diorio, Jimmy Raney, Tal Farlow, John Abercrombie, Dave Liebman, Mike Stern, Marc Ducret, Christian Escoudé, Philip Catherine, Charlie Haden, Richie Beirach, Alan Silva, Steve Lacy, Barre Philipps, and many more. Usually once I had met them I would follow them hardly everywhere... like Philip with Chet for example or Christian Escoudé which is to me still so incredible and I'm afraid really underrated. Christian is

---

[1]   http://en.wikipedia.org/wiki/Vantage_Guitars http://www.vantage-guitars.com/

[2]   http://fr.wikipedia.org/wiki/Jacobacci http://www.lesguitaresjacobacci.net/

maybe to me after René Thomas and with Philip, the european and french strongest player.

What did you actually learn from them?

That's a good question in fact, I don't know yet I think, I'm still trying to figure out ... maybe I looked most for a challenge, to face such incredible players with their own playing and kindness often throw me back to where I was at the time which will create an incredible and sometime painful experience that in return would make me wanting ever more to learn and progress (I'm very dubious about that word "progress" but let's say it get better at your own game here). I learned that I wanted so much to play, and that no one else as incredible as they were was going to be like me, nor that what they had found would really help me. I learned that I had to be me and that I had to find what this means and how it plays. Later on when I was in my late 20's I had the same need and this was my reason to try to confront myself with people like Derek Bailey, Fred Frith, Marc Ribot and others just to be somewhere to face my own wall. Not at all as any sort of battle cause it wasn't at all the point, but to confront myself with much more advanced players. I still have the same goals somewhere in fact. I'm thinking since long now to ask John Abercrombie for a duet, but I'm afraid to do so. I'm not really sure I can face that yet. I'd love it and maybe this is the right time for me to dare it...

I understand your feeling... I started playing when I was eighteen and I remember the first time I heard John Abercrombie's Timeless album, it was like a shock... For me he is still one of the best jazz guitar's innovators and all his ECM records are great albums, what do you think is the secret of his huge and tight tone?

I also got to hear John at very early age, like 15 or 16, and for quite long I almost got to see him live as much as listening to all his albums (really all sorts of groups, I remember a trio with Trilok Gurtu and Rainer Burnighaus mid 80's , shortly after the Erskine, Johnson trio a lot, with Kenny Wheeler's Widow in the Window, many duets too in smaller clubs ,etc. when Clubs in Paris hired artists for at least a full week). His playing immediately took me to another level, I couldn't explain or rationalize it but everything he played, how he approaches the instrument, music, even his physical position, all was talking to me, to my inner self. It actually never stopped since now, he is still one of the greatest and I absolutely listened to all his possible albums (still discovering some sessions today). Maybe his electric mandolin playing in Jack De Johnette's New Directions In Europe (Bowie, Gomez, John, Jack), was the first album where his phrasing stroke me so much. It was like "Yes!!! it's Possible, He Does it!". For long time I was sort of ashamed about jazz guitar, it was my area, my hobby, my passion but frankly I felt most jazz guitarists didn't stand half a minute on front of other jazz greats like Miles, Coltrane, Rollins etc. of course they were some incredible players but it always seemed to be a "guitarist" thing, like it didn't apply to the whole music category but like a niche, just to "guitar music". Not long after I met John in a masterclass first, then I took some private lessons in his hotel room where we played standards for long (I was close to heaven), and then Henri Texier started his Transatlantic Project with Steve Swallow, Joe Lovano, Aldo Romano, Dewey Redman, Kenny Wheeler, sometime Paul Motian and Bill Frisell joined too an I started to meet John more often then, and not long after I was part of Henri's new band, Mads Nomads, one the various Texier groups. I remember well that when I first met him he was still using picks, Copper metal picks, that I looked for long to play (I finally found on 48th Street in NYC) and the next time I saw him, he had dropped pick, and played with thumb mostly. It was an incredible signal for me to do same, I always felt better with thumb, but somehow doing this was like an absolution for me to do the same (which I still play today, I use picks very very seldom on very special sections or type of phrasing). I think I said it before: I love them all Scofield, Frisell, Metheny, Stern, Goodrick, all the great modern players of that area, but John to me is maybe the best one, always surprising. You never can tell where his phrases will go, his placement, his articulation. He seems constantly on the edge and he stretched the instrument so much. He really plays the whole neck constantly, from the lowest E open 6th string to say the highest C 1st String 20th fret ....he goes through 3 octaves in one line just taken by his musical idea, he breaks all possible intervals to avoid the position playing we all know, narrowed on four frets until next group or position. John simply is one of the greatest improvisor and musician I know. When I played with Joey Baron, he had started to play with John since couple years before, and Joey was so so enthusiastic about John's playing. For me it was so nice to hear it because I often felt that maybe a lot of downtown people never listened to people like John, I thought it's a sort of ECM-Jazz image for most who didn't actually started to listen to John's music deeper. I always looked for players that had a strong melodic sense, that played guitar but never stop to guitarist aspects, say René Thomas is an hero for his unique sense of phrasing like a Tenor, or Jim Hall for his incredible approach and open-ness, and John is one of this rare kind clearly for me (you know I love them all, and Herb Ellis in Oscar Peterson trio is incredible, but I can't say the same for example then René or John, though if I'm honest I took a lot there too). One important thing also to me is that John is such an humble human being, I've seen him often unhappy about his own playing, looking constantly for things, to extend music forever, and this matters to me a lot.

What instruments do you play or have you played? I see you have posted a lot of pictures of your guitars on Facebook .. it seems you have a... guitars arsenal!

I started with a love relation for guitars, but through the say first fifteen years at least, it slashed with serious moments of deep doubts (I still doubt and question but on a different level I guess today). A few times when I was in my 20's I totally stopped playing guitar to try to restart elsewhere. As I said before I always played upright electric bass. The next instrument I practiced and study a lot was drums, always had brushes, then a small kit just hi-hat, snare, cymbal and a mute bass drum. I wanted to be able to feel every great ride of jazz history, Joe Jones, Kenny Clarke, Art Blakey, Higgins, Blackwell, Elvin, Philly Joe, etc then Motian, DeJohnette, Baron etc. I tried to understand and sit in their shoes to see how that swing was working, happening. I did a bit of piano for harmony and when I had 3 years of orchestral arrangement lessons, then kept playing with 3 fingers more or less. I took a trumpet to feel Chet Baker, soprano for Lacy and Bechet and others too, and a bit of violin for and like Ornette mostly. I have quite some guitars indeed but I was never really a collector. I guess I am fascinated by guitars but I don't feel at all like a collector or a vintage maniac, it's really all about playing for me. I don't have really a fantasy about the object but what each of them through history brought. I mean what makes the difference between Fender, Gibson, Martin or Framus, Ovation or Danelectro? I also sold back a lot of or traded them for other models, which I still currently do. I started with an Aria Pro II Classical Nylon basic model, then I got some weird probably Italian Mustang's copy, then I got my first serious Ovation Balladeer and when I started to seriously study jazz guitar in a school I got an Ibanez Hollow Body, the exact John Scofield Model (but not because of him, I didn't knew him at that time). Then I got really more seriously involved and got a 1973 Gibson ES-175 (in 81-82?) and this went on for long until my new teacher Philippe Petit took me to Jacobacci Luthiers who did for me a Sacha Distel Archtop Jazz Model with a single neck pickup, in a sort of red brown wood. By the mid-end 80's I went to New-York and I bought a ES 335-DOT reissue blonde which also made quite a long time, it's the guitar I used with french jazz musicians like Henri Texier, Louis Sclavis or Tim Berne. In the meantime I got sometime very impressed by certain players I was seeing live and tried to see what they played further. I got that way an early 80's Squier Telecaster because of Mike Stern, an Hohner Stick because of Mick Goodrick, but that was basically it. It was only after a rather long moment of professional playing that I started to really hear and need something else. I was working a lot and I could afford some guitars easily and plenty of now *vintagery* , it was all for close to nothing by then. I was looking for the nature of the electric instrument, it's social working class 50's american way of life roots and origins. So I got a 1962 Fender Duo-Sonic, a late 50's Danelectro with a single pickup in the middle, all sorts of guitars like Harmony, Silvertone, Ibanez, all solid body. And each period of my life came with new sounds or new approaches for me, the capacity to hear and want to try further, so that I sort of tried most of possible guitars. Today besides my ES-175 I own a Charlie Christian ES-150 (with EH-150 original amp, both 1934 model). Then an Adamas 1687, a Martin HD 28, a 1963 SG Junior, a Huge Archtop Framus (I bought a lot of those for nothing in Vienna, some stayed here and there still), a John Lennon Gibson Les Paul Jr. with CC and P90 Pickups from Custom Shop, an SG Standard VOS Custom Shop, two American Vintage FenderTelecaster (a 50's and a 60's), an Antigua 80's Japan Stratocaster, an Eric Johnson Stratocaster too, but some of those will be replaced sometime too, I only keep the top of each. I need long time and special occasions (like recording for example) to know whether I like or not a guitar. My ES-175 for example I went from love to hate to need… in 30 years. I first loved it cause it was so jazz, then hated it for same reasons, then for 10 years it slept in its case until I found how to make it sound as my own. Every guitar can sound great if you give yourself to it, it's a long process I guess.

Can you tell us about the Jacobacci Luthiers? Their vintage instruments are well appreciated…

They are our D'Angelico, the memory of french guitar history. Where should I start… they were just (one brother only is still alive today), so incredible people, funny too. When I started to take lessons with Philippe Petit, he soon took me there to get my own original model from Jacobacci, they built it for me (a"Sacha Distel" model, jazz archtop, rather large, with a single humbucker on neck, red hair color… I came with that Jim Hall album were you could see his D'Aquisto and I showed them the color I wanted, they were pissed off, but it was funny). Later on I use to visit them a lot in the Ménilmontant Atelier, often came the morning and spend whole day there watching how they worked (they were born in the atelier, their Italian father did mandolins, from Napoli I think). They always had a small battery radio very loud with most commercial program on (jokes and hits), whatever happened. All Paris passed by, Sacha Distel, Jannick Top, Paganotti, etc many unknown to most people, but famous for us guitarists who did all the great albums, like Pierre Cullaz, Raymond Gimenes, Claude Engel, Jean-Michel Kajdan, etc (a lot of players you heard for sure on albums not knowing their names cause rarely credited on hits). Later on it was a guitar everyone got at some point, a Double-Neck SG type model, with Benedetti pickups, 12 strings and 6 strings, which I got them to make fretless. It weighted

21

like 9 Kilos or more, Marc Ducret got it long before, he gave it to Nguyen Lê, from whom I bought it, and sold it later to a Vintage Paris store for collectors. They were incredible funny people, but to be honest I can't say how good these guitars are today. Not bad certainly, but a bit raw, often very heavy, too heavy for me. But this is no question. I didn't really play my Sacha Distel much after my studying years, I left it to a very close friend (who now programs the Sanois Django festival, where Django lived his last years), and after 20 years having him playing it a lot, I sold it to him and it's nice cause it's still passing from hand to hand.

Talking about instruments I noticed something in the young people who want to play an electric guitar today, compared to 20 years ago it seems to me that there is less a search on tone, on instruments with a particular sound and a greater focus on pedals and effects .. sometimes I wonder if today guitars are actually becoming platforms for electronic wizardry, it's a race to the effects and pedals, I think this is fine for people like Adrian Belew and the Edge .. but otherwise aren't we exaggerating? Or is it an excuse to skip the traditional learning process based on playing the old classics?

I could probably write at least 600 pages on this what you now describe.... (laughs). Paradoxically I taught a lot when I started and since say 20 years barely never again. My first answer would be, you know, I start everything from zero again very regularly, and I did it many many times in my life and I'm permanently on re-learning basics and roots, questioning them a lot.
Where shall I start? There is no sounds in absolute. A sound is always a projection, a sound is someone projecting something that you feel like hearing weather it's true or not so true even. A sound is someone, an individual, and each individuals are different from another one. Everything else is probably what people call "noise" (there are a lot of nice noises too, but it's a different topic). I don't think there's today more people using all sorts of gadgets and pedals (I use pedals too but), I just think they're so much more visible than before. It's always been a funny question to me : why there are many people playing, and large part of them are really knowledged, and at the end there is always the same amount of (very very few) incredible and unique players? I mean why Bill Frisell uses a rather delimited, known musical material (with plenty of his own, but I mean a material you can write down and recognize if you're used to do so), and no one ever sounded like him? For me Bill's playing is almost entirely in his left hand index, in this sound he gets from it that makes you recognize him the first note and that makes you straight away enter in his whole story. What happened I think is that schools and pedagogy the last 20 years incredibly rationalized and

therefore probably narrowed the whole approach to start playing (I buy tons of methods and transcriptions, so I can see that clearly). When I started there were much much less of those books and videos, but there were still a lot of local players that almost had their own theory and solfège, by playing with them you had to ask to yourself a lot of those questions. When a pedal makes a sound, the commercial definition of the product is that everyone gets the same exact sound. It can't rely on each individual to create a new one with it. There's also another thing I find which is for example that Avant (from Improv to Experimental, Tabletop and etc), has since become a sort of mainstream niche too. I mean that if you watch The Voice or actual avant art etc scenes, they tend to work (communicate and operate) pretty much the exact same way. For example about improv-experiment I find a lot of players really started to seriously lack of background and instrumental basic roots. For me an obvious difference for example is that people like Elliott Sharp, Derek Bailey, Keith Rowe, Marc Ribot,... never started to play "like that", they looked for their own ways to play who they were as they are. I had this strong experience with Lol Coxhill and Derek, they made a strong step at a given moment of their own musical history to go to free improvised music. It wasn't always that way, it took some time to get there, they looked for it, they had a wide practice and experience of music in general (and particular too, a very advanced one). I see much less weight or sense in starting with "alternative" playing when you can't really play basics already. But I'm old school I guess, for me still the deepest minimalist player I've ever heard is Freddie Green (which to me makes Arto Lindsay a radical 4/4 rhythm alternative player in the same vein). I just don't see so much what can be transgressed if you don't have something to extend, overpass or escape. It's like saying your playing "out" when all is anyway out and none quite "in" (can be great too but it's something else).

This "pure tone" thing is not about how many racks you use between your guitar and your amp but something like a "moral" question. What is unique about guitar for me is the fact that it's a rudimentary simple, popular, cheap and affordable instrument to start with. It's not about what instrument, type or brand, but really deeply about what each individual, each of the millions of us, will pull out of it. From Herb Ellis to James Blood Ulmer, Link Wray to Pat Metheny, Albert Collins to John Abercrombie or Pat Martino to Robert Fripp, etc. I guess that's what learning the instrument is about, you only can learn it for yourself. I mean here that whatever applied theoretical material from each great player you like you study, at the end it will always and only be you playing, nothing nor no-one else. It's a matter of literally incarnating and inhabiting your instrument and your speech.

So ... all the methods and technical book or studies?

23

Every technical book or studies is another challenge about how I'm playing, partly my abilities and lacks of (that's practice), but mostly what I use of it in my own musical speech. It's funny you mention US players now, my Gesualdo project has a concrete specificity which is that ideally I'm looking for unique voices that can also sight-read naturally (as opposed to rather learn the parts by heart, but just read). In this particular regard, it was pretty brutal that most "different" players (avant or not), where clearly located in the US mostly. I can hear for example what originates in most classic jazz guitar (swing to bop) in Keith Rowe's playing. With 1000 other tablet-op players I can't at all (I can hear visual arts backgrounds, or conceptual studies or etc, but not much of any instrumental approach). This prepared guitar approach also is something pretty symbolic for me (I skip here the original need to do that which fully made sense and was a great move or say a great window opened), but why would you in the hell so much need to look for what the guitar doesn't really do, or has been designed for as opposed to all you could do with it? As a source of sounds I find prepared guitar extremely limited in fact, it's always the same 3, 4 objects one uses because that's the ones that really do something obvious (therefore more or less unconsciously repeating the whole history of instruments... bang, pick, blow, etc). It's the same for graphic scores for me, it doesn't really show much more than how vague it is or can be (again here it has nothing to do with its first original attempts which were totally contextual, and to be seen inside at least 300 years of musical notation history and the politics of music, why did we come to such a class division between players, conductors and composers). Isn't it interesting that all avant people who come to the point of wanting to play or compose scores (for social reasons as there is an obvious social *plus-value* about producing scores) need mostly to find the few graphic or non standard notation ones, just because they do not read ? I tried to read Riley's "in C" last month, and frankly for me it's mostly a downtown peace of exotica. But more or less anyone can read and create that, whereas it would be really close to impossible for the same people to interpret Ligeti, Stockhausen or Nono's pieces. I also think the technical aspects of instrumental playing is a lifetime process, and therefore the earlier you get set in front of it for what it really questions and needs you to position and solve (that permanent balance between what you hear and how far you can play it), the more chances you give to yourself, to be able sometime around the middle of your life to come closer to it. Some people always played the way they started, or say started straight away at full intensity and understanding of their art (I guess Derek Bailey didn't change much his approach and practice of improvised music, though he played and dialed for long before with idioms), and I'm not talking of "geniuses" like Christian, Django or Hendrix, who come from another planet to me. I can see in my forever heroes for example a sort of serious moment where things came out more clearly deeper or more themselves around their 40's (clearly with Frisell, Abercrombie or Scofield). It's interesting to hear for example Frisell playing fast and fusion with Mouzon in the late 70's early 80's, to come today with "Space Guitar" playing only the 2, 3 notes that says it all. I wish to write some day about this particular topic, I started a book in fact but I still need to find how to approach it, not a method, rather a novel that could be read by anyone, not just guitar players.

That would be very interesting, you talked about improvisation, what does it mean for your music research?

Hum.... that's another whole full question. Genres and Categories are to be filed under Beliefs or Wishes I guess. Now if you face musical facts and practice just for what they are, say, do, show you that all those categories are maybe sociologically valid but musically irrelevant. From a pretty orientated background maybe Derek Bailey in his Improvisation book, stated that basically the first musical gesture ever and since ever is to improvise. Improvising is a term I don't like to much because has a kind of negative assumption, like "as opposed to not". To me the main line in music is about being played or not totally played. It's close to what classical music uses as interpret (and not classical music only but as I'm talking instrumental music here). You can play many type of texts in one's life. You can play your own text and therefore not need nor want to score it for example. I play my own text since a while now, but as I want to discover it further I do not state-write it. You can play someone else text too whether by accompanying he or she, by playing in someone's band, or playing with someone, in all those cases it will be you playing the others approach or pace, or area. But it'll remain you playing. Then you can play-interpret a score and depending on what's the score, about which style, period of musical history you will face, a rather open but precise score (say medieval to baroque) or a fully framed score (say romanticism and further since). Such a predominance of the written object (call it scores) is historically a rather small moment of the whole musical history (though not minor at all). I'll give you an example: I do not think J.S. Bach did really wrote any scores in his life, he mostly notated music. I mean that his head was full of very precise musical lines and ideas and thoughts that he daily practiced and played, but notation was just a data there. This emphasis on notation is basically a XIXth century thing that ends with the next century (to me 70's). I do not think it will stay in future, and if you look at it, writing-reading is under 5% today of the whole musical daily practice and production. It's a western thing too mostly (this even when non-western cultures trying to westernize it). If you look at it every serious players since the last 3000 years at least was always a serious improviser as well. And this isn't

25

anything particular, it's to make an image a side effect, the same as all serious chefs have incredible instincts to pick up what's most interesting daily fresh product on their local markets at 5 o'clock in the morning.

So we arrived to Bach, I try to risk a reckless question... Bach composed sometimes without specifying instrumentation... maybe... maybe he wasn't interested about the "Sound of Music"... I mean maybe could be possible that his music was hidden into a scheme, a structure capable of several realizations, several possible and different sounds? And the moment when the music reveals its true nature is contained into the exercise of its variations? Bach at this point would have composed something like jazz standards or pre Cage scores?

Absolutely Yes ... by all means, yes. A classical and early music close friend mentioned to me recently that Boulez probably secretly was totally obsessed by a life and work structure close to the one of Guillaume de Machaut. If you read Machaut (and others around and after him), you come to that incredible and somewhere vertiginous impression that he did it all since start. You can have this same feeling with other pioneers I guess, like if you think about what was before and after Stéphane Grappelli in jazz violin? I feel strongly that music has its own language, I mean today I hardly read anything else than music itself (or hear too of course). And we all know that you practice an instrument to be able to somewhere make people forget about it. What you're talking about here is something I deeply experience those years in fact. Through my own instrumental moment, but in resonance with other experiences. For some reasons my girlfriend and I (she clearly), decided to try to see for real most of great historical art pieces (but art is always at present, and whether produced hundred or thousand years ago, makes no difference). In front of Michelangelo, Raffaelo, Tiziano, Da Vinci and others, Brueghel strongly for me, you immediately see where lays the "problem". Art isn't, was never, about esthetics, but about a message, and a message delivered in a universal form that only arts can materialize, symbolize, produce. I guess this is why I never stopped to style, in music either. I always heard "pure playing" (Is the Media the message as said McLuhan later?). Music produces more music, I guess Bach achieved that level like few did. It's not about beauty or pleasant or etc, it's physics, meta-physics, alchemy. And I play all these composers on guitar simply because that's what I do, my own voice is playing guitar. I've never seen arts as a matter of beauty really, but opening something in you that none else does. What you mention is just a fact, if you take Bach, the whole idea of compositions, interprets, pieces and so on, were radically different than what we understand of it now (and that has been since confusingly filed under classical music, whereas it's just a XIXth

26

century approach). It's also only very recent that the player is not also a composer of his own, an interpret and improviser of most others, and his own interpret. In his book Derek Bailey totally pointed out this intimate close relation between playing and improvising. I also never really understood (coming from early jazz especially, where you had a lot of collective improvisations too), that "free improvised" music. It meant somehow that all the past jazz history wasn't free really? I've seen like Chet Baker taking twenty or more choruses in a clubs on a blues, in small combos often trios, and this sounded like ultimate freedom to me. Bach now to me has something hidden I have to find, whenever you play him you feel the process of playing this music is just a step in a much higher wider labyrinth that will reveal if you let it happen, just playing this music. I can't even tell what yet, but it feels like transcendental, or a perfect balance between mathematics, physics and a "of a third kind" spiritual order of some sort. I'm sure he was extremely conscious of this nature of his work, this incredible capacity to move minds and souls. As for Variations... well I see everything we play as a variation (a slice, a moment, a piece) of a whole life thematic of music.

Do you think it's possible to talk about improvisation for classical music or we have to turn to other repertories like jazz, contemporary music, etc.?

I only reject one thing and probably it's this area that has solidify in the last thirty years and that claims to be specialized about improvising, which to me isn't factually true. What happens is a lot of people started to make awkward noises, or reject (but also ignore by all means) any of the standard musical elements such as harmony, rhythm, functions, etc. and developed a new style-genre-area, which works as any other styles and social groups today (hip-hop or metal, jazz or electronica etc.) and today is known as "Improvised Music" (often melting with experimental music). Those do not improvise more than any others really but found and fixed certain musical elements and facts that makes them recognizable to themselves and circles around, like any other genre.
There were some small arguments when for example Jim O'Rourke tried to pin down Evan Parker or Fred Frith that for example Evan doesn't "improvise" that much (and would be dixit a common jazz player). I liked the question but not the answer in fact. I think Evan is just an incredible Evan Parker and no one else would ever play like he does, and I put him very, very high in the instrument and even on jazz history. But I don't take one thing, it's this moral value put into improvising.
Improvising is a normal thing that we all do, or should do. As I told you before I heard Chet Baker taking thirty choruses in clubs on a blues and I played and listened a lot to Evan too, and they both play incredibly but have their own and

differently rooted maybe languages. They both play variations of their own. If we need any values I would put it on the subjectivity, on how someone plays his own, how deep he found his own voice. Whether a classical music interpret, a traditional player, an electronic artist or any. I like a lot (and generally I think Derek in his own words said it so incredibly clearly and simply), Derek Bailey's answer to what is improvisation for him : "More Playing per m2".

Talking about him, in 1968 Derek Bailey asked to Steve Lacy to define in 15 seconds the difference between improvisation and composition, the answer was "I" *In 15 seconds the difference between composition and improvisation is that in composition you have all the time to decide what to say in 15 seconds, while in improvisation you have 15 seconds.[3]"*. **Was the Lacy's answer a little too much ironic or is it a true one?**

It reminds me a Steven Bernstein story where he met Lacy and told him how much he loved him and that he played with so incredible trumpet players like Don Cherry... and Lacy : "no fucking Don Cherry, I played with Rex Stewart!" (laughs). Back to your point, I don't see that has a difference because I've never seen Composition as the opposite of Improvisation. Charlie Parker never wrote a tune and all were variations on standards and known harmonies, for example. It's the same you find with some great teachers who never wrote a book but were transcribed from their lectures. It means nowhere that they didn't have their own concepts (Saussure for example, Nietzsche too, his writings are less finished than his thoughts, using only short forms as aphorisms). And on the other side I know too many people who can write music, who do compose, have all the technics for it and write endless variations based only on that knowledge which are just rather decorative than really needed. It's funny, it's probably the only price I ever got, a composition one, and I stopped writing music after more or less. I didn't see why to write music that wasn't original enough to me, I prefered to play it first and see if I real need to enter into a compositional process with it since. In some ways I see composition as an accessory to playing rather than the other way around (I'm not talking in general here of course). Derek did variations from the same for all his life, I don't see where is the opposition to written studies for example. Now being a composer is socially a different story, and I guess in some cases it's more what people want to achieve socially, than strictly musically. There's always a certain age where like improvisers want to become a touch more respected or seen as more serious maybe, and start to be active as composers, even if that resumes to a weird black spot on a white page with couple haikus aside, known as graphic scores. Also Lacy did compose a lot of tunes that could have longer

---

3   Derek Bailey, Improvisation It Nature and Practice in Music, Da Capo Press, 1992, pag. 141

forms but where people would later on blow on, the same way you do with all other jazz tunes, which I assume for a composer isn't a really advanced form. Again it's a wide world, there is endless space for as many approaches, practices, desires, thoughts as individuals to bring music in. I thought I should try to compose again music lately but each time I really don't know what or why, whether when I record daily I never ask myself such questions, I just play. Also legally I register all I play (at Sacem, the french Authors rights society) as compositions, never as improvisations (because they have those ratings based on what I said before where a composer is higher in % than a player).

Shall we enter a bit 'more into the technical details of your playing? Listening to your solos I don't think you're a guitar player tied to "lick", what kind of "vocabulary" do you use in your music? Do you use special scales? Do you ever find that you use a phrase that you've played before? Do you ever feel the need to stop using something you already know that would work? Do you ever use some "filling phrases"?

No I don't lick much ... (laughs). Generally all I practiced since ever was meant for me to be useful (which means heard deep inside) and forgotten technically after, once digested (I can't think of this and that scale when playing, it has to be fluent). I barely don't use any phrase "licked" because I haven't really learned any as I can remember, I sometime think about other players (it's almost a private code from myself to myself), in given context (like I have a "Martino", an "Abercrombie", a "René Thomas", etc a Sharrock or a Swallow, a Coryell or a Bern Nix, etc.) but this relates not much to any given lines but to an approach. We could say that Martino would be a G-Minor type of intervals on a pretty straight phrasing, Abercrombie a way to expand intervals, etc. Consciously I use very simple materials, like the C scale mostly, its derived arpeggios in all sorts of orders, Dominant 7th notes (blues or not) that are like hooks to me, a generic "altered" type of phrasing which contents a bit of every possible known material (from half-step-whole step-half step typical Dizzy Gillespie scales to all the Minor Melodic or Altered possible main scales) . I know all those things, I practiced them a lot, I still do some time, but I mostly play by hear since long now. What is most important for me when playing is what I hear and how I developed some "different" spots inside. For example I use a lot something I would call the "Wrong Note Theory". This is something that comes back to the days where I could hit wrong notes by mistake and started to think about it. I also use a very shaped type of phrasing in which you could possibly use any notes, any tonalities over whatever and it would work. The only difference is today I really hear that, it became natural to me, I can totally solo with an A Blues tonal center over someone playing say a G or Eb blues and you may not find it that out

29

in fact cause it's natural to me. I use more Symbolic or Colorful references for example if I think "Larry Coryell" I may start to use pentatonics in a certain way (too fast, messy, but also lyrical) and this would be a whole area pretty defined for me because I practiced around such people a lot. I think morally I could never use obvious licks and even worst obvious other great players licks. I only probably had one moment where I really sort of step into someone else shoes and this was when I was around 18 or so and I met Marc Ducret. His approach, technique, style was a strong influence for me to get out of how I was playing before. This is how I think, in terms of people much more than scales or this or that. I really can't think "let's play an A arpeggio over a F root that will make us a smart F major7h #5"... that just wouldn't produce any sound and even less music in me. But I can strongly think about Bern Nix, or Elliott Sharp, or Arto Lindsay, or James Burton and B.B. King or Johnny Guitar Watson or Cornell Dupree, etc. etc. this is something that really comes to my mind a lot in what I play today for example, but I guess no one would be able besides me to recognize it in relation to what's being played when it happens. When I started it was that big fantasy of scales, so I tried hard all those scales in all tonalities, all positions (all fingerings, here 3 notes a string, here 4, here drop etc), but this never made any music for me until I decided to continue practicing all those things but totally stop thinking to apply them concretely. What happened is after maybe like 20 years of hard playing and practicing something opened in me which allows me today to just play and not think of what it is because I can hear what I play and vice versa, as simple as that. I remember a master class where I accompanied Sam Rivers and he first started with a C Scale unison altogether and he brought so much music out of it, I was totally on my knees after it. Proving possibilities to create new music with most simple materials will never end. And this because the main difference is made by Who Plays. Much more than What in fact.

You named Marc Ducret. For me is one of the most talented French guitar player, I love his solo records, when I listen to them I hear everytime something new .. they sound always fresh... how is to play with him and what do you think are his music bases?

That's I guess a long and pretty intimate chapter for me. Marc's basis and roots are various, a lot of rock guitar in fact but like Duane Allman for example, or Jeff Beck I guess. He played also Oud for long time, only for himself. I guess a lot of jazz from his times like Pat Metheny, other modern players, someone less known he started with unique guitarist like Malo Vallois (and of course the whole history, Marc is a sort of living library, there's very little he doesn't know or at least didn't give an ear once). At some point I became like part of the

30

family, I played for a while in Hélène Labbarière's band, the great bass player with whom he had a son. We met a lot, he was a strong influence in music, guitar, lifestyle too. His generation (people like Yves Robert, Dominique Pifarély, some others too), wanted hard to take this music out of the smelly jazz clubs and usual clichés, opening to contemporary life, like any other artists would do, but jazz didn't yet. They felt this music is for everyone, is art as well, it needs to participate the same world as our actual world. I'm afraid that twentyfive years later, it didn't worked out in fact, and I feel many of them totally withdraw, some started to close themselves, to rely only on their music, make it sometime really hard or hermetic for other audiences, maybe some got bitter underneath, I can't tell. Marc's playing when I first met him was probably the most advance since long in whole world of guitar music. Really totally new, using radical different types of approach, from chords to lines, place of the guitar in the group, questioning it all, functionally, harmonically, melodically, rhythmically, up to how he dressed, lived, etc all was very, very different. It was fascinating to me, it was difficult not to step in and sometime even clearly borrow. Also with Marc there was these incredible expectations from all over, the music world, the press and labels I guess too, many people wanted to see him as a sort of "New French Metheny" or something commercially and artistically "Successful" (you know... Grammys and Awards etc). But he started to meet Tim Berne and played with everyone in Europe of the big names, and obviously was looking for something else than become just a succesful famous guitarist, not trying to use "grand public" forms either. I remember one breaking moment for me, when Naked City first played in Paris, and sometime later when Marc Ribot came to play his "Don't Blame me" solo, I tried to share with Marc but I could feel this wasn't really happening for him. He wasn't listening to Derek Bailey at all by then (he did a bit later I think), he wasn't too keen on people like Elliott Sharp or most of the avant of the time I think, which for me were major. Maybe I got it totally wrong but it felt like a sort of "moral" judgment on his side about such approaches, like maybe these people couldn't "really play", as they say in jazz. Then I felt a bit uneasy because I started to grow in my own career and got to play gigs he played before, and it was no question for me how such a master he is, there wasn't any sort of comparison for me but outside people did. Things like he left Winter & Winter, and I came in shortly after, etc, people like to comment. Then my own stories took me to pretty far away from the music he played (UK improv, Chicago Post-Rock, Electronica), I had left euro-jazz scenes, we lost track a bit, didn't see much. He moved to Denmark, I was living in Vienna etc. it's a bit of a painful story to tell today because I don't know... I only have a huge respect for him, I owe him an incredible lot in so many ways, but if I'm honest it's really hard for me listening to his music sometime. Maybe because I know him too personal? In the last years I found his projects and playing sounding like someone hurted inside, someone who closed something intimate inside. Other people may not see that, but I only feel this and it's hard to see or hear for me. Something like a wall somewhere, some sort of stigmatas, something in fact really dark. There is something for me in his music lately that is about "refusal" (a refusal to joy, or simple things, or just what people may want to hear too). The weird thing is when he started there was a lot of controversy around him, some more straight people had their problems with his playing, and today it feels like a sort of sect for me, some people that wouldn't like it at all before seem fascinated now. I regularly get some of his fans a bit aggressive with me. Anyway, much respect and love, Marc!

Talking about interpretation, sometimes ago Elena Càsoli[4] said to me "I improvise the interpretation of what you call encoded. Scored music requires an ethic of respect, attention, closeness and knowledge of its aesthetics, looking at the sign left by the author. But it's a moving, alive, elusive, intangible subject, which awaits the encounter with an interpretative act. And this meeting, in concert, has a space for improvisation, every evening new and different5". What do you think about these words?

Well I'm sure it's truth for her, and to what she does and is dedicated to, but for me all what matters is how she will herself sound at the end, and not too much about the text she picked up to interpret. In my early music recordings, I deliberately "punk-rock" for the area, I also would never call this interpretation, because besides the composers I play, it's really me playing, it sounds like me in this context before all. This's not orthodox for sure, but when you know the history of church you can witness how much "canon" radically changed through the last 2000 years. Let's say all those written scores are only a rather small moment in music history, it starts with Beethoven to make it short and somehow stopped in the 70's. Today's interpretations are also subject to a lot of trends and fashions, to nowadays and what happens around us, it was very different 30 years ago, much, much more wide and raw 80 years ago, it will change again many times, so why bother? I love Alfred Deller, Scott Ross and Glenn Gould's music, but I never ever thought of or even looked for any sort of other truth in their interpretations than their own. I also think that way because I don't believe people ever played so differently music though the last 6000 years. I think the relation to instrumental music was more or less the same, from Greek Polyphonies to AC/DC and all you want in between. Classical music doesn't

4   http://www.elenacasoli.com/

5   Andrea Aguzzi, Chitarre Visionarie Conversazioni con chitarristi alternativi, 2014, pag. 53

really exist to me, it's an idiom based on texts but having the same exegetic problems as any other holy texts (or considered as such). Today Wahhabism[6] can't be possibly more radically opposed to Sufi's traditions, but they are both centered on Islam. Interpretation is something you do each time you play, but whatever type of music you play, for educational reasons classical people are very framed by it, but this is more a collateral damage than anything else to me, In heavy experimental music you find same approach without any real text but with same position to produce sounds. You could say Derek Bailey was the main interpret of a music he composed himself all through his life in slices and variations, and it wouldn't be wrong. This may not be the reason why people would like to hear him, but you could superpose that frame and it could work too. It's just words, and music doesn't use much words in fact. When I lived in Vienna, inside the Opera house there is an incredible record store that reissued all sorts of shellacs of Classical Music interpretations from the beginnings of recordings industry, and you could hear so much different approaches by those players that would be totally shocking and rejected today. Mozart sung as Offenbach for example. Another famous Vienna story is about a conductor who takes the Vienna Symphonic in the early XX[th]century and they started rehearsing Wagner, and in the orchestra is a pretty old strict French Horn Player. And they go through the piece once (can't remember which one), and suddenly they hear the french horn blowing like you do hat huntings, a quadruple forte, so the conductor stops all and asks him why and who told him to play this that way: the old man stands up and says it was Herr Wagner .... he had created the piece with Wagner and kept original notes where he asked for it. Music has changed so much and at the same time the fact of playing never really did I think. Older bass players use to say (some of them) that the day they invented pickups for basses, they acoustically killed the rhythm section. It's something you can still hear in recordings, this old school of playing together in large bands without any amplifications and it had an incredible range of dynamics. OK it's true, it's lost today (but it's lost everywhere, listen to most actual string quartet and then play the Busch Quartet and you will see), but a lot of new things came as well. For example I'm sure that this double kick speed metal drumming was existing over 1000 years ago very similar. We need to link generally, see what is common rather than what is opposed. People in Jazz today see sometime other music as really hard to swallow, but the jazz they play today is for me a negation of jazz as I heard it played by its creators, etc.

---

6   http://en.wikipedia.org/wiki/Wahhabism

If you listen to a different interpretation of a music you have already played and you want to perform this again do you keep it in mind or do you prefer to proceed in complete independence?

In fact I record all this music to hear it, literally. I barely never listen to other interpretations before except in some rare cases (and not anymore today I found my own scales for the moment at least) just to see what tempo they use. I started to read a lot about musical notation history and it's very interesting because basically most we have is guessed but rarely certified. The other thing is that most of actual early music's recordings are pretty disturbing when not really annoying to me. I don't see what they play anywhere in the scores (I mean the tones, the dynamics, this and that). A lot of early music recorded today is suffering a very strong fantasy about what it should sound like. I like people who play this music for today, not thinking of what it was and should be, but let the music speaks for itself. And you really can honestly sincerely play this music today as you are with what we have written out and let the rest happen. I know it's stupid to say but all shows that if people like Machaut would live today, they would probably use IOS programs on Ipad and certainly not Gut Strings and real Church Reverbs. It's an actual disease to want what you don't have, a definition of happiness is to desire again and again what you have. For example having played with Rolf Lislevand[7] (Jordi Savall Ensemble founder), I could really see why I like their approach a lot, because it has a fusion-jazz-rock aspect totally assumed to it. This is how they are and how they play, its coherent. But in 2014 someone dressed in fake medieval clothes, singing in latin, and having a bad tempo when playing in rhythm it's just circus to me. Hopefully new generations are totally passionate with this music but totally of their times listening to Lady Gaga with pleasure, going out, dancing, living their own life and this is what music needs first.

I agree with you, I have seen your concert with Rolf Lislevand and your music was so beautiful! You had an amazing interplay even if you were playing different instruments with different styles, how have you been able to create such an intense relationship?

Because he is a great guy! An incredible player but also a fantastic human being. If you're going to play in such a duet with two rather radically different worlds, music, instruments, you need to first see all you actually have in common, and we do have a lot.

---

[7]   http://www.dailymotion.com/video/xv1fp8_face-a-face-rolf-lislevand-noel-akchote_music

For me it's maybe to take a parallel like when you play live on a movie, one rule us never to watch the film while playing, the only chance to go through is to have two parallel compact coherent lines. If I play what I really play and go through a story next to a film that is edited thought framed etc, the two distant lines may create a gap of poetry (if you follow the film you may enter into a bad circus). Maybe it's a more generic thing with Rolf too, I always loved and did a lot of duets or encounters with other people that come from total different worlds and work pretty differently (with writers, authors, singers, actors, scientific people, any sorts of different music, flamenco, metal, country etc). If both are able to sustain the difference, because anyway each is each already, then a lot can happen. Rolf is great master, he has nothing to prove so for him it's I guess simple to try. With more weak people they would get very worried, afraid to sound bad in a context not totally framed as they usually do, worried about what their usual audience will think, etc. With Rolf we barely didn't talk before about what we will play, we enter studio first day, went for a nice lunch, then came back and noodled around just playing, seeing what would be the areas to go deeper with and after 45 minutes we both knew it I think. I had for example to get used to Lute acoustic volume, but it came pretty fast and on the other side it made me feel like pushing my Martin Acoustic guitar playing in his area. Very simple, really. It's my old adage that you should better play first and rehearse after if needed only ....

I know that you like very much Sonny Sharrock, to me Sharrock is one of the most underrated guitar player, but his music was so great and records like "Guitar", Black Woman, Faith Moves and Ask the Ages are simply great, I really enjoyed your tribute "Sonny II" for Winter&Winter .. have you ever met him or played with him? How much did he influenced your music?

Sonny was an incredible natural born player to me. Also somewhere he incarnated the whole american music history (from Rag Blues Pickers to Evangelists, To Swing, Free, Bop any and all 20th century Music and Guitar Music). Sonny is the first and last Free Jazz guitarist I ever feel. By Free Jazz Guitarist I mean someone next to Albert Ayler, Cecil Taylor, Sunny Murray or Pharoah Sanders (and others of course). Someone who freed the instrument like no one else did before, and probably due to historical moment. To me Free Jazz means not so much playing outside of all rules until then, but Freeing the Jazz literally. Questioning where jazz had arrived at this point (hard bop more or less), and bringing it in a same move to its next chapter, while returning to its roots. Most free jazz greats had a very rooted approach, in some ways Ayler is like Buddy Bolden, Ornette, Don Cherry, Shepp, Cecil they all played a freed version of earliest swing & New Orleans jazz in fact. A very common move in fact, to jump to next, you better root yourself to before and make the big step above today's situation. I take a lot of my influences in origins in fact too, for example the strongest minimalist player I know is clearly Freddie Green, the first avantfree- rock "downtown" guitarist maybe Slim Gaillard and so on. With Sharrock questions about skills in jazz totally blew away, those are not only technical questions but often moral ones. He literally freed the instrument from absolutely all before common usage and approach of it. He just played, with such a force and intensity that you thought his guitar would implode and disintegrate any moment. I've seen him live first time with his band (the more pop-rock one with two drummers like on **Live in NYC** album or **Seize the Rainbow** and **Highlife**[8]), they played two nights in Paris *New Morning* Club, it was close to empty, very spare audience but I came both nights and literally swallowed every single second of it, like a fan basically, coming there mid day seeing if I had any chances to grab a sound-check or talking to them.

On Stage he had Two Les Paul and a Marshall, I soon understood the other Les Paul was in just in case he broke strings in fact. I told this many times I guess before but he had on top of amp a box of standard Fender Picks, in Heavy and X-Heavy gauge, that he regularly took a handful and put in his mouth, and every maybe 20 seconds the picks were torn apart, like stroked by a shark or something totally incredible, almost like a hurricane .... as he threw out all around those picks, I grabbed about 10 of them in the pause and put them in a frame. Each of them where damaged differently, like each one was a different guitar stroke or line. Those picks had a strong influence on me, yes and so Sonny did. In totally different way but that has somewhere similarities some years later it happened again to me with Derek Bailey who also was incredibly rooted in Guitar Origins.

I try to ask you a little bit 'provocative question about music in general, not just about contemporary or avant-garde. Frank Zappa in his autobiography he wrote: "If John Cage, for example, said, now I put a contact microphone on the throat, then I drink carrot juice and this will be my composition ", then his gargling would qualify as a COMPOSITION, because he applied a frame, declaring it as such. "Take it or leave it, now I want this to be music.[9] " It's really good this statement to define a genre of music, just say this is classical music, this is contemporary and it's done? It still makes sense to speak about "genre"?

---

8   http://www.discogs.com/artist/282987-

9   Frank Zappa Peter Occhiogrosso, Frank Zappa l'autobiografia, Arcana,1990, pag.111

Hum... there are a lot of sub-meaning in here. Let me be provocative too, I love John Cage the human being, and his music was totally him. But him gone, I don't think this music stays very much and sustains well the compositional process of others playing it without his presence to it. I could say the same for Zappa in fact, I really love his guitar playing, I think his compositions are pretty dull though, it's basically bad jazz-rock with college jokes (Ok I provoke openly here but). You can call anything "anything", all is possible (all has been done already even), now whether this will be a strong work is another story. You can read interviews with Cage and probably get even more than by listening to his music, but I can also say that for example Pierre Boulez's texts and scores are really more interesting to read than to listen to. It's not true with all, for example I think you can really listen to Stockhausen, to Xenakis you can both read or listen, to Ferrari you need to listen. Luc Ferrari whom I was very close to, told often this funny story that always non classical composers wanted him to listen to their compositions, and for him having the strong classical background he had (a Messiaen's student in his famous courses times), it wasn't at all this side (rather poor for him) that he was interested in. He liked Zappa's playing but not his scores so much, they where like student studies. Same with Zorn and others. But I have no ears for concept until it comes as music or arts really. When Onkyo started, I played with almost all of them (Sugimoto, Otomo, Sachiko M etc at least once), and my problem was never that they played one note per 20 minutes, but that I could tell exactly what would happen and worst, what could never happen. You knew the plan already, it was no point for me. Very few of them had a strong speech with this context. With my label we released a duet album of Otomo Yoshihide and Taku Sugimoto from the late 90's, all acoustic improvisations, which was a step towards silence, not yet totally silent but going there, this is very strong musically because again very coherent for that time. I liked that a lot, it was fully music to me[10]. What came after (and I lived in Vienna by then) was just often getting pure empty gesture for me. I don't think it's no point to do what people like Jeff Koons are doing, I just don't find such works interesting at all for arts. It's maybe much better as design or fashion, and I like a lot of great fashion designers. As I said before avant arts became the biggest mainstream today, anyone can put something inside something else, or use neons to write anything etc, it's fine, it's not very demanding. Also for me such arts are technically poor, it's like 2 dimensions, whereas art is for me always at least 3D and mostly way more. I'm a player, I like crafter arts I think and performing arts are very demanding, I like that.

---

[10]   https://itunes.apple.com/us/album/untitled-1-4/id455326881

Yes .. I understand your point of view (even if I'm a Zappa addicted): I like Yoshihide things as a turntablesist and a guitarist, I saw him playing with a jazz band here in Venice and I enjoyed his creativity .. I listen to Sugimoto things ... but I have to say I don't understand his music and his idea of silence .. when I want to hear some "Japanise silence" I prefer to listen to Takemitsu music ...

That silent thing came in a special moment also. There was this huge fed up of the classic free jazz thing where people played too many notes all over loud and fast. Derek had a great expression for it he called it "Sweaty Bollocks Free Jazz" (laughs). This were like mid 90's a lot of incredible new music and approach was coming from all sorts of sides. For me it was the first time people were doing great experiments and improvisational music outside of jazz scenes. In Chicago there was a lot going on, people like David Grubbs or Jim O' Rourke were opening a lot, others like to Tortoise, Steve Albini, in NYC as well with Sonic Youth. In Cologne there was incredible electronic music with Sonig A-Musik, in Vienna with Mego or Fennesz, Polwechsel, Malfati, in Japan, in Berlin etc. I'm thinking of people who influenced me a lot like Markus Popp and Oval, Bernard Günter, Gunter Muller, Voice Crack, Roof with Tom Cora, Stock, Hausen & Walkman, Fennesz, Riyoji Ikeda, ... people like Grubbs and O'Rourke were digging history too with Luc Ferrari, John Fahey, people less heard like Loren Connors, Arnold Dreyblatt, ... so that's how it started mostly in Tokyo and Vienna and Berlin, with people starting to play as less as possible, to remove the need. The speech going with it was to cut with intention, let the silence show what there is, impose yourself new forms, new approaches, etc. All this is of course like always also very trendy and theoretical but you know... when I moved in Vienna it was the peak of it, but it was already a bit long since it had started, It was already pretty rotten for me. It already was taken upon by arty areas, Wire magazine, the coolest thing to do. I remember going to shows where I couldn't stand it anymore. I went to see Martin Siewert Trapist trio and the whole show was like an audio wave, never starting for me, but for them it was the whole point. I love Martin's playing I want to hear him play some guitar, but he spend whole show head on his table with a million pedals turning knobs with not much difference, eventually going back to laptop. I think the peak of the farce or the taking the arty piss, came with that MIMEO orchestra which was supposed to be Keith Rowe's band, but Keith always denied it was, and it was I fact launched by Hans Falb who runs a festival in Austria. Pita (Peter Rehberg) would come half an hour in the show with a huge Döner and eat it while opening his laptop, there was this joke that people did their emails during the show, which you could verify if you knew some of them in the band, you'd get emails during show time etc. It's all over now since long thanks god. Silence is death for me. I thought Cage's"4'33'" was a clear statement on these areas, but it seems not at all. There was something esthetically Nazi in this music (not at all ideologically but just playing with those esthetics) that was really disturbing for me, also knowing that Berlin-Vienna-Tokyo had a strong past with it. Anyway....

You talked about "Wrong Note Theory" before... I'm very interested about errors and their role into music evolution, so what's the role of the "Error" in your musical vision?

Sonny Sharrock was maybe the very first player that strongly questioned me about this error topic. When I was in the learning process I wanted to watch how every single guitar player that I liked was technically holding his instrument, pick, right and left hand, body position, fingerings, hands etc anything clothes and pedals, cables and gear, strings and picks shapes, and so on. I took as many LP's as I had with close pictures of guitarist and put them in my room like a gallery, like staring at you too, which made a sort of judgement-picture. At this time I was mostly trying to control a C Major Scale in its 7th positions from low to high on the neck, meaning also looking all possible ways to finger it, how to group and split the G/B strings change of interval etc. I was working hard and pretty desperate I would ever be able to do that fluently one day. And then came that Sonny Sharrock Monkey-Pockie-Boo album[11] where basically Sonny was doing everything but NOT what I was trying so hard to master. That was incredibly transgressive and even disturbing to me. But it teach me incredibly well somewhere unconsciously, it made me aware of the error as not just something wrong but a open window on reality and somewhere truth too. It opened my ears to the whole 360° of the guitar, it pointed out the mental gap between your own moral idea of the good note and the reality of the playing. I had already questions and doubts about certain players playing amazing lines but with sometime a real harsh unpleasant sound, like people having a too strong pick or heavy right hand and pushing too much, this creating a pretty noisy or ugly sound.
And I wonder if they were even really aware of that. Certain gipsy players for example in France or even my teacher, had sudden moments where they wanted to stroke hard and play fast and this would result not in a fast line but in some kind of very harsh muddy loud noisy piece of cake in the middle of their solos, that to me was pretty much ruining it all. Jack Wilkins for example has this still (no offense at all, I really love them all). Anyway all that made me strongly aware of sound and how sounds live. For example if you play a C note (say D string 10th fret), you cannot think of just a C, because where this one is placed

---

11   http://www.discogs.com/Sonny-Sharrock-Monkey-Pockie-Boo/release/530623

on the neck, on which chosen string, with which finger you will lay it (will make a difference if index or pinky), will not only produce a C but all sorts of adjacent wanted or unwanted noises, sounds, resonances. You will also have to start to think about how long, how modified (tremolo, short, long, vibrating etc) you want it, how loud, how much weight etc. which will end up if you're strictly objective in a concrete fact that your C note will trigger at least more than half extra sounds or noises to the whole result. I got aware of that and of more as I practices and studied later on, like for example there is still today this strong fantasy or expectation in scales for many younger or beginner players, almost like a religious belief that scales are the clue to playing well. But scales do not produce any music until you do make them sing or play. A scale is a just a commonly agreed data file in a given (our western) system. I got aware of that pretty early: the best choice of notes on this or that changes, would be ruined if not properly articulated rhythmically. Say a 9th on a 7th chord can be nice color but if you missed that 7th chord by one bar and your supposed to be a 9th falls on the next chord it may just turn totally else and totally wrong. So that I got soon aware that things weren't so much about their maths and theories but about what you were going to hear and play out of it. And from that point, this idea of error started to turn into another idea: it's only you playing (no one else ever will play you, this even if you're the biggest Pat Metheny or Alan Holdsworth dedicated fan).Today after close to 35 years of playing, I came freer with many technical aspects so that I can just play and not think anymore, so that error idea is irrelevant, but is always probably an unconscious proposal trying to come through. There is no error. There are unclear or undecided enough ideas maybe. A Mistake only comes when you're unclear about what you hear, and come to a crossroad and didn't really decided where to go, then you may end up in the middle, or in the woods. There is this kind ancestral saying that I heard many people telling (Joe Diorio in a master class first time), which goes: when you hit the wrong note, repeat it twice, it will become a style. What makes the difference between a noise and a sound is its source. If you hear noises as sounds, an other one will hear sounds only. A Sound is always and necessarily a projection from someone (or something at first if you're more into experiments, but the source will have to be handled by someone at some point to come alive). Human produces both noises and sounds by nature, even not being musicians at all, it's our choice to hear them or not.

You named my favourite guitar player: I'm a totally devoted Allan Holdsworth's fan, the Metal Fatigue and I.O.U albums blew my mind when I listened to them more than twenty years ago. I think his improvisations and his tone is so unique, what do you think about him?

I totally love Holdsworth, he is someone I started to listen also very early age. And I love all his various periods in fact, from Lifetime to IOU to any projects or sessions he played on, you always get it in the face really strongly. I put Holdsworth very very high in fact, and not just because of his Paganini aspects, but as a sort of unique great Renaissance-Baroque master. Not far from Kapsberger for example. Someone who invented his own total world, and who's music and message is permanently an "Art Total". He is not just playing fast, his music is that way, it's his music who developed it, I'm pretty sure of that. There are a lot of fast players, later on with metal especially, from which a lot are not questionable but not exactly interesting and often not having much music really. It's different of course but when the golden trio of Eddie Van Halen, George Lynch and Randy Rhoads started to create this new approach it was the same unique historical moment, totally Baroque again, also in each of these and in their concrete playing you could hear the whole music history behind. Holdsworth is very very rare unique player, in the sense of those who make you think a lot because they question a lot, on the same level as Derek Bailey or Mick Goodrick, and such people are extremely few in history.

Talking about music history I have the feeling that in our times it flows without a particular interest in its chronological course, in our discotheque before and after, past and future become interchangeable elements, shall this be a risk of a uniform vision for an interpreter and a composer? The risk of a musical "globalization"?

You're talking about politics in fact here. Where Art is always an exception. There are indeed 10, 20, 3000, more... players today. But maybe not.... Maybe today, what you call Globalization (I don't have better word either), is only the fact that social networks, internet etc. allow them to be visible where they would remain private before. I have a strong sense to history maybe because I also found out that history repeats constantly: "New is an old thing". We had (my generation and I guess other ones around) that incredible fantasy of "Year 2000", we went through it and nothing happened and so after a bit of time will probably come out with the 3000's fantasy too. Although I have to be careful with one thing which could also come from aging (can't say yet, I'm 46, born 68), and that is: the more I enlarge my historical horizontal knowledge (the more I experienced different and else musical moments through the last 3000 years), the more I have the tendency to think we're only going through a fatal regression. When you read De Machaut, Binchois, Chantilly Codex, or you visit Michelangelo, Caravaggio, Gesualdo even who's pretty much a modern young man already, etc. it's getting hard to point out what our last 500 years really brought as new. It takes us close to probably how I see and feel about things. I

41

said above I love so much John Abercrombie, and I really so much do, but not because John would be such a unique radical creator, BUT because he really is such an incredible incarnated variation of a lot of materials we know from history already. It resumes to life in fact, how one makes the same absolutely unique and his own.

James Burton isn't playing anything new on the paper, but no one ever did it before that way. The same for all, Jaco and so on. I see in fact Globalization as the best antidote to niches. I guess I'm a liberal in the original sense of the term (something that has been pretty rarely tried since). I prefer Market to Culture. Market got people like Scofield or Frisell to play the essence of themselves in a form that is clearly framed, where Culture never had clear goals besides their political usage of arts on short terms. I know I'm talking something pretty out and that will be argued if not just harshly rejected by the most of "our" friends but here I stand (get back to me, if not just for insulting).

Market challenges creativity much more than Culture which often kills it in the egg. If you think (and it's very easy to doubt about), that globalization (it's again such a vague term), ruined certain hierarchies of knowledge, I think facts are against us. Today I have access to much more than when I was looking for it back 30 years ago (and I know and understand the usual comment to it that when you have to look for it you learn way more than when it's all freely laying around as today, ok I take this point but I think it's just us, a one way, and many other ways are... as they say: all roads leads to Rome...). What I started to experience with younger people, say between 15 and 25 years old, today is that because so much more (really 98% is) is around today, by some unknown to us *logos*, the ones who want to look for whatever they ignore still will actually crush by "chance" on way more hyper-linked series (series of musics, videos, links etc.). Internet and Globalization did not invent anything, what they did was to hyper-show things that were always around us. I'll tell you an anecdote. When Minimalism came back in improv' scenes during mid-end 90's (call it Onkyo or Lower-Case or etc, all post AMM), I had a real difficult moment with it (obsessional or personal too probably, though I still think it's really bad, just hope it's been useful for some), I got quite concerned about it and the messages I was perceiving of it (basically linked to what will solidify in 90's and it's total shelving) Anyway, I was so pissed about all that, that I tried to find clues and hooks to get out of it, and I once asked to (we were touring in japan, I remember well we on a quay waiting for the train to Osaka) David Grubbs about:"how do you feel historians and musicology will remember this moment in say last 30 years from now ?" David's reply is still ringing in me, he said:"they won't be any need for history to be made by then because all will be available constantly and therefore any need to file or select will be pointless." True I guess. Today it's incredibly positive to me. It wasn't back then at all (lost a lot of angst in general).

You named the Market, so let's talk about marketing. How much do you think it's important for a modern musician? I mean: how much is crucial to be good promoters of themselves and their works in music today?

I'm going to be probably pretty paradoxical here. If I had say 200,000 $ to spend on promo, I feel I could make some sort of semi-hit of mostly anything, and I would love that (René Thomas for example). Now I only believe in content on the other side (one clearly not excluding *de facto* the other for me). I really feel that whether you get known, coverage, get media and networks promotion, makes no difference at all on a midterm. What does is content only. So if I had those 200,000 bucks I would promote incredible and underrated contents (don't laugh at me now – lol). I made quite serious amount of money doing things you never heard of, but I never enjoyed myself so much as now, while hardly not making a living on it. Times have changed that's an obvious thing but not the only one reason for that I think. It's true that when I started you could always easily work a lot and enough to sustain yourself without needing much if not any promotion or visibility at all (loads of local gigs, lot of anonymous gigs too, jobs, functions... but nice ones). Today it seems you need to be much more visible and you can be quite visible but it will necessarily affect your condition, and not really change your situation (there's an evident link to Gesualdo here that I should not forget to develop later[12]). Basically creating and its needs and daily life will never make possibly a job. Market or Culture are, creation never will be. So that you swing between those two. Yes I guess the days where Freddie Green could be the incredible artist he is spending all his life and career (died on stage even) during 52 years in the same Count Basie Orchestra (he even survived Basie and continued after Basie's death in) are obviously gone but... Art has no price. It's not a cheap line, when I started to record Gesualdo I had no money, no Label, mostly no one understanding it, but I had to do it. So I did. When I started to arrive in the French jazz scene as a sort of young "modern jazz" guitarist, I remember well, there were hardly 5 to 6 people in (Philippe Deschepper, Gérard Marais, Claude Barthélémy... Marc Ducret, Nguyen Lê, then more avant would be Jean-François Pauvros (my hero), Jean-Marc Montera, maybe some more or contemporaries but hardly not 10 altogether). Today it's about 50 in working top shape just in France, and if you open up to people with talents but still learning or developing their things, you'll reach 300 easily. If we wanna talk worldwide I would say 300,000 invested knowledgeable people, 10,000 serious players from

---

12   The Gesualdo point I made is that due to his condition as noble folk he couldn't really be a artist and his works remained intimate somehow, and not dressed to its times and functions as they did often for official composers.

which close to 100 are struggling for the top 10 (and we're only talking a niche area like avant-modern-jazz-improv guitar, that sells at max 1,000-2,000 copies when full worldwide promotion).
Yes I invested in myself the last decade or so, and I'm my own self promoter. I guess it's like people making cheese and selling it from milking the cow to sticking the etiquette. What Globalization made possible is that everyone do it, but the cake didn't grow. It's like 10 000 people on the same cake that did not really feed 10 to 15 individuals 20 years ago : yes. Ideally (business-wise talking), I'd wished I'd be alike Bill Frisell, yes. The freedom to be your own and be respected for and given enough simple opportunities to work for your living as such. On the other side I've noticed that for such people it came rather late, I mean being established enough to be just able to name your next project and hope for it to be viable financially. I'm "only" 46, they are between 65 and 70 (some just turned 60). I get a lot of reactions and feedback to my work since sometime. Especially since I started my own Downloads Catalogue and my way of working. Maybe in the word Communication there are two sides, one being the marketing term we all know, and one meaning just communication: share, exchange, learn, give, take, give it back, pass it on etc. I'm probably between it and working spending a bit of time trying to let my things be known publicly. I would only stick to works, but I somehow like that aspect too, talk to people, share, etc. It's generally a question for me at the moment whether try to re-socialize and play gigs in the existing circuit, or leave it totally and go into some far away castle just work and not communicate anyhow but through strictly works (and no comments to it, or open e-door). I don't know, we will see.

Your musical career has been going on for several years, how have you seen the musical world changing? Do you note differences between the students you teach and you taught? How new technologies (new musical instruments, midi, social networks, forums) have influenced your choices and your musical form?

Well it's close to 35-40 years of playing now so yes I've seen various periods through. It's difficult for me to judge them in terms of better or weaker in fact. I don't suffer any form of nostalgia I think. I enjoyed a lot of times before where a lot was different I think, then it moved on to sometime great, sometime slow and floppy, sometime totally new... today is in some ways really different, but humans are always the same. For example I think it's objective to say that in the mid 90's there was a moment of rare density and opening from all sides which totally went on the other way after 1991. When you started at a given time (which you always do) you raise yourself with values of that moment, which are intimate to you I guess, then times continues to roll and you can decide to refuse that or to accept it, you don't know yet and you let it happen to see where it takes you. I guess also because I always did what I wanted each day, I'm mostly interested in what is coming next. I believe in time a lot too, it's very interesting to see (read, experience, learn) an artist over 50 or more years for example. Today obviously Internet makes things very different, on one side. On another it made all the same but more too. I mean when I started you had to look hard for information, I used to walk every shop to find old magazines issues, scores if any, LP's etc. Today you can access all this in a click, but the same small amount of people want it too, and this was the same before. There's a very interesting critic from the 80's (died not long ago, of course a bit fashionable now), Philippe Muray, he wrote criticism of arts since those years, pretty brutal but very visionary too, he wrote a line I like a lot:"I don't think it was ever better before, I think it was ALWAYS better". So that today I don't see massive changes in real. There are today maybe 300 different distortion pedals available from any brands, all types, all prices, from which I haven't really heard any new one for example yet. But maybe all this agitation will bring something new. Like in music maybe only Metal had a new formal structurally approach in music lately (and I don't listen to metal much but each time it happens I can hear new things). It is maybe a progress that people like you, Miguel (Coupon), and few others who share and enjoy a passion and knowledge get connected, I appreciate that a lot really, but is it that new and how many people in real talking are into that kind of vast interest in guitar and music? Not much as we would be before, where we would meet in a different way. What I'm interested really now is that I start to see really young players who were born in all this, who never even could imagine a non connected world, and for whom all is "post", I like to see how they go through all this and how they find what it's clearly more particular than other things (not by tastes but by content or density say). Today you have 100 times more methods and transcriptions than when I started, but I think it didn't really help the young players much more. It's good in many ways it shows human has his own pace and path. About new technologies I'm really excited about, but because of concrete reasons, that it allows you to do things that would be more complicated before. It would be difficult for me to record the way I do before for example, but I would still anyway. Before all this I always recorded a lot of music aside in studios, just for myself, not to be released. And this while being on labels, like a private secret garden.

Talking about innovative composers, what do you think about John Zorn and the New york musical downtown scene, so ready to get and recode every musical language, improvvisation, jazz, contemporary music, cartoon music?

45

Those people where very influential to me, I went to Knitting Factory to see some of them in 1987 (playing in front of no-one, I can remember Frisell with Don Byron, Lonnie Plaxico, Marvin Smith. I came 3 hours before and we were 4 in the old Knitt). Elliott was very important also to me, when I first seen Carbon live it was a revolution. I think Zorn did an incredible work for our music, he really is an example by all means. Then Naked City was a clear line of division in France, I remember I took all sorts of jazz people on their first show in Paris and people like Ducret and other jazz players didn't like it at all. For me it was an incredible new moment opening. Now about Zorn works I can't tell so clearly, it's more complex, it's very much about the people around him I think as well, and that's why they are like a family. Tzadik wasn't exactly new music, those tendencies had started before (like Parachute label, etc.), but the label strongly united them all and opened for a lot of people clearly. You see through my answers "New Music" isn't really a term I use. I'm rather into daily music. Day by day. One thing is also that this downtown music scene is now 60 and since not much really came anew I must say. You will always find the most and top incredible players in NYC, but as for a new movement since the last 20 years I can't really tell. It's rather young and there are new players playing music that has been created before. We'll see, I'm ready for more.

One of the things that I can honestly say about guitar is its ability and capacity to change its shapes a musical medium over the centuries and between the various musical and social forms: we can choose between classical, acoustic and electric types suitable for different musical and social cultures. You have followed a very personal path inside the guitar, how did you develop this path and how are you developing it?

Our chance with the instrument is really that it's never been anyhow orthodox. It's a popular instrument (still today how many kids everyday buy their first guitar for 99$ or 59$? A nylon Korean, an electric copy, a folk etc). Which means that anyone can play, and anyone does and did. Each one brings its culture, and Guitar is the perfect instrument to mix and melt all sorts of traditions, from West-Africa to India, Bali to Detroit, Italy to Germany etc. whereas a lot of other instruments have been more or less set since before (let's think about piano, violin, or reeds and woods). Maybe only drums has this universal approach that leaves us plenty of space to continue, because every new musician brings along a new technical and individual approach. I started with jazz guitar, my heroes were people like Herb Ellis, Barney Kessel, Tal Farlow, Joe Pass, Jim Hall etc. and for years I did not question that particularity, I was trying to learn it for long that way. I was feeling a lot of problems but I couldn't tell where it was coming from. On the other side I always listened to other music, and other guitarists, like Blues, Rock, Funk, Reggae etc Brazilian or Flamenco. Until I realized quite long after that as a jazz guitarist I was running after saxophone players or trumpet players that played all in flat notes (Eb, Bb etc), and this was making me totally blind avoiding guitar's nature which is E, A, D, G not Db ! This was a major change for me I started to relearn the instrument totally differently (learning fingerpicking, open tunings, any guitar music in its own natural tonality). It's weird somehow because as a kid and continuously I always loved other guitar music, Baden Powell was a strong influence, Manitas de Plata, Paco de Lucia, then blues a lot, B.B. King which I also saw live many times, Johnny Guitar Watson was as important René Thomas for me too, Keith Richards of course, many other E-A-D players. I realized that and started to look for any natural keys for the guitar, I opened a new page. In old jazz tradition, people like Tal Farlow showed me this, it was common to play phrases or tunes and play them in all keys, a famous game was play the blues starting in C and every chorus moving up or down (could be half-step, or in fourth, or etc any intervals, but each new chorus a new tonality). So that after some years of playing a lot of open D, or C or G my bebop background started to come out again in any context or keys. This is the moment where I started and had a strong need to explore totally different instruments. Playing 50's rock guitars like Harmony or Silvertone, or Framus Solid. My sound started to open a lot. And things came way more clear to me. Also in all those years I always sessioned in different styles, more rock or pop often. But it wasn't yet a natural interest. That's the reason why I started again to look for different instruments doing different things, huge archtops like Framus or Hofner, Noisy Solid Body Rock 50's 60's guitars, Martin Flat-top, anything went, Charvel metal with Schaller Vibrato, Effect Pedals, etc I already knew players like Eddie Van Halen or Tommy Iommi, George Lynch, Randy Rhoads, but suddenly it came clear to me that all those players were just the same tradition as what was before. What's so different between say Slim Gaillard, Chuck Berry, Charlie Christian and Eddie Van Halen? Maybe also because I started with Swing there was a lot of those mixes already, from Blues to Swing, Mambo to Gospel and etc, all coming from the same root, you can call Jazz or Blues, or Great Black Music as Miles did. Before I started my ongoing early music series, I had a new moment of strong practice, and decided to re-enter classical guitar which is an area I didn't knew well enough (although I started with rudimentary of Classical guitar, the famous 19th century methods and studies we all know, the Carulli was my first book in fact). I knew there was something I didn't like so much in it, I couldn't tell what yet. For example the Studies (Sor, Carcassi, Coste, Giuliani, etc Pujol), I always thought were genius, incredibly well thought instrumental approach. For the instrument by the instrument. But then their own compositions were always a bit cheesy to me, always very decorative, too technical and too many notes, lots of arpeggios to describe the sea, the landscape, the mood, but rarely like in jazz a one note speech. And doing so I came to the Lute transcriptions, and there it was. Lute is just the missing link to later on Blues-Rag guitar. I really see a direct link between Lute music and Charley Patton, Blind Blake, Big Bill Broonzy, Robert Johnson, etc the guitar Evangelists, Country-Rag. When you ask me how I developed it, I can't answer because I made everything possible so that it happens but never really worked it out. I have interest for all guitar music and I started to practice all of it and things came naturally in my playing without trying to force it into. Generally I never practice what I play, I always practice what I don't play naturally or still ignore. I always choose music books of players that I naturally don't feel close to, I mean technically. Like my playing is really different from Ted Greene, George Van Eps or Johnny Smith, so this is what I will study.

Do you think that the guitar, with its presence of virtuoso very personal musicians at every musical level and genre would be a viable alternative to the now tragicomic distinction between high culture and popular culture and Schoenberg's affirmation " if it is art, it is not for all, and if it is for all, it is not art [13]**?**

Well as you know "Artist" is a term that rather didn't exist through art history. It's a pretty recent thing, and there is a reason to that. What matters are works, not the person so much. Most artists have a very boring life, working, working and working. Soon this life takes you to a particular social life, keep good distance from a lot of things cause all your time goes into your works. Art in that sense is always present and universal. Otherwise it's what you call Hobby, or Group of Interest, or Clubs and Niches. Now maybe I have special ears or eyes that make me see through things and nothing is a problem, no dressing or form will stop me from experiencing a message. Most of the people today tend to stop into labels and there is always a strong social side about music, so that people want to listen to this or that first because its image they want to embody for themselves, ignoring often many other areas that may be much closer to them but are not dressed socially a way that is giving them a good enough image for that moment (this is why medias tend to serve much more exact than originals, because they can shape it). When you're deep into it, you stop asking all those questions, about arts and artists I think. Artist became a social naming for someone doing something that is related to a lot of fantasies for people not doing it (it's the same as Porn Actor, it's more about what people think they do, than what they really do, it's obvious watching such films where all is fake and

---

13   "New Music, Outmoded Music, Style and Idea" (1946), in Style and Idea (1985), p. 124

Guignol, but people want to believe in it so...). All the movies on artists are totally made up because no one would see someone in a room sitting for 18 hours not moving much. As I said before there are two things, Art and Culture. In my eyes it's all very clear and you can resume it as Culture Vs. Arts. Art is a danger to all powers and it always has been. So culture now invented the complete chain to be able to control it. In France you have now a whole cultural chain of people who went to the same schools, work the same areas, are promoted by people who did the same, playing in venues that are same crew, etc, critics part of it the same way and so on, the whole complete chain. By hazard with French jazz I went through it shortly in the 90's and left very quickly because it was so clear what the deal was and what it would kill me. All those words on arts and artists are systematically coming from outside. Like people want tragedy, hard lives, ignored artists, violence and despair, the Van Gogh syndrome. But this is for people working on it, absolute bullshit. I don't play better if you pay me very well, I just feel better. There is an incredible book by Thomas Bernhard on it, released recently named "My Prizes". There are many other examples about what an artist real life can be, like John Fahey's "How Bluegrass Music Destroyed My Life", or Nietzsche's Posthumous Notes (16 volumes in French), or many correspondences of artists published from Céline to Sade, Kafka or Flaubert, and many others, all is always about how dull the society is and when will they get paid finally. It's the same as since I moved to downloads, traditional press here doesn't want to see it at all. It's not like they don't understand, they understand quite well I think, but they fully refuse to understand and show it. It's dangerous somewhere that someone step out totally of all those systems, they reject it because in that new approach you do not need any of them by principle, unless they write something that really would make sense (which tends to have totally disappeared, everything is about following the market today, but claiming their freedom). You asked me before what changed lately, well this has clearly changed for example, through internet. There are whole worlds of people who know a lot and want to explore further and skip totally all those traditional circuits because they stopped writing or thinking since long. It's the same with what they called Music Industry, the crisis is in the system, not in the music. Anyone bringing incredible music and works will always find its way a way or another.

We have talked about avantgard, impro, etc... do you think there is a music genre easiest for the non-musician listener to appreciate?

You may divide music in two parts, some say good and bad, other this or that, I think that the two main parts are music that can reach anyone whatever their forms are, and others that are directed to groups of interests, club members and niches who wants to firm their difference using music for it. But this applies to any époques, style, moments in fact. Monteverdi until say 6th and more seriously 7th madrigals, is maybe not flashy but arse-licking-power openly. It's all written up to please and shine, there are a lot of cheap repetitions and cheap tricks etc. I have some people like that I never really got, where my question to its supporters would be : why in the hell should I listen to that rather than other more direct versions of the same ? I can think of Frank Zappa or Robert Wyatt for example. I sometime think that John Cage is more interesting to non-musicians than to players, and Pierre Boulez too but in a different way (his texts and scores are often deeper to read than to hear). But it's a lot of paradoxes too. Some people think that this and that is vulgar but none of them sets vulgarity in the same place. I don't find Céline Dion vulgar at all (nor actually Paris Hilton although ok it's a more dangerous line to go with her but), and I find total porn a lot of experimental-improvised music in the last 15 years. Who Am I to judge? Virtuosity always had its fans for example and not all is really worth. I remember in Austria amongst cool people seeing themselves as really special and tasty were so in love and found themselves so mirrored with deep fried American Country, and the same people would kill if you played them their own country music like Tyrol and Schläger, but objectively, both versions are 99% the same. Same over conservative, misogynist lyrics, same "a man and his gun" things, same racist things (past my valley are all foreigners who don't get our heimat-love) etc. It's not because it's fast and flashy that it's bad in fact.

Allan Holdsworth isn't flashy I think but he's dead-fast. It's very difficult to tell what I really think. So I really think that there is music than can speak to all people at any time and others who needs your agreement before you even heard it. Sonny Sharrock always got a wider audience than free-jazz or even jazz areas whereas maybe Derek Bailey did less even his audience is not strictly improv'.

It generally takes a long long time to hear things I feel, I need to listen again and again the same because the more I do the more I hear anew. I'd give you a counter example now, for some reasons I came in music at a time where Fusion and Jazz-Rock were all over and big (Paco De Lucia, Meola. Coryell, McLaughlin would play still in huge theaters), and I have a real taste for it (I can go really deep, as deep as Uzeb and Yellow Jackets, not stopping until you reach maybe Kenny G., and even, I'm not sure of that). For me I can agree of a special esthetic there, than can really be repulsive to many people especially today (it wasn't back then, FlashDance was top cool and hype), but I really love it, and I assume it's really corny cheesy but still. So for most cool people this is openly what they call (I don't) commercial crap (you selling yourself to a fantasy they have of the bad nasty capitalist). Well I'd love to have a real fusion band today (I mean muscles rhythm section, 6 strings bass, percussions, 2 keyboards and an Alto Saxophone) and play very very smooth music, some kind Barry White Jazz

… and if I would do this supposed to be easy listening music would probably be a real scandal for most critics and jazz audiences. So what to do?

Please tell us five essential records, to have always with you .. the classic five discs for the desert island …

01 – **René Thomas** w. Chet Baker – *Chet Is Back* (recorded in Roma)[14] He is probably the most incredible Jazz Guitar Player ever for me. His voice, flow, freedom and intelligence of speech never ceased to not only amaze me but teach and open me. With his own *cuisine* of Django and Raney, he really opened the instrument, and particularly the presence of guitar in jazz, to one of the strongest voice in jazz. Generally certain european players had a strong influence on, probably too because I asked myself early about jazz and being a european. To name a few People like Eddy Louiss, Daniel Humair, Jacques Thollot, Jean-François Jenny- Clarke, Christian Escoudé were and often are still an influence today.

02 – **John Abercrombie** (in fact almost any album with John teaches and moves me but for example: **Witchcraft** duet w. **Don Thompson**[15]. Its almost pointless to try to explain but Abercrombie is really the modern jazz guitarist that touches me the most deeply and intimately. John is someone that each time (and I do very regularly, never stopped to since 30 years), surprises me totally. How he goes through music, the neck, how he phrases and paces-pulses, his dynamic and shape of phrases, how wide he made the range of the instrument, which also means how he fingers and physically places himself.... I love them all Scofield, Frisell, Goodrick, Metheny etc but John has something that speaks to me like none else. I don't know a single album with that will not return me in the next 10 seconds of his playing.

03 – **Bill Frisell** w. **Jan Garbarek** – **Pathprints**[16] (in Fact I went back through all early ECM catalog last couple years from Metheny to Garbarek, Weber to Rypdal etc that unique moment and sound in music) I have a strong moment with early Frisell lately (and I love his actual works too), I've first heard him live with Paul Motian first 5tet (w. Ed Schuller and Jim Pepper), and his playing changed our ears totally since. But that early 80's Moment where he Played his SG Jr. with Pro-Co Rat was very unique, again I love beginnings.. Bill is also someone that has this extremely rare tone in the finger. One note of Bill Is complete Frisell each time. He uses rather simple materials in fact, based on

---

14 http://www.discogs.com/Chet-Baker-Sextet-Chet-Is-Back/master/284251

15 http://www.discogs.com/John-Abercrombie-Don-Thompson-Witchcraft/master/525123

16 http://www.discogs.com/Jan-Garbarek-Bill-Frisell-Eberhard-Weber-Jon-Christensen-Paths-Prints/master/108083

classic guitar voicings sometime stretched or very focused like his three notes famous cluster-voicings. But his playing is always rather simple theoretically (I mean as oppose say to Scofield's alterations). He opened all of us incredibly, and somehow he helped us through the journey of the end of jazz guitar, if I may say so. To me one side of Bill is that he is obviously the "last great jazz guitarist", in the vein of the Freddie Green, Charlie Christian, Jim Hall, Barney Kessel, Larry Coryell and Pat Martino (and many more), like he closes that long slice of history and therefore I guess opened to another one where all your influences can be equal, whether country music, blues guitar, folk or rock, or any other that build you. His original 4tet (Baron, Driscoll, Roberts) was a major break in Music, alongside to Paul Motian Trio which also is
probably the last Historical group (again to me here, i'm not interested in talking the end of this or that, but just watching at the transitions between historical moments, objectively I guess).

04 – **Johnny Guitar Watson – Love Jones**[17] – This is the very first album that made me aware I was so attracted by Guitars, I bought the 7" when it came out late 70's early 80's – before my father played a lot of classic swing jazz at home and this this album I came clear to me all this music was from the same root. Johnny Guitar Watson is the first one for me, but I could have named others that rings in me a lot still like James Burton, Clarence White, John Fahey, Albert Collins, B.B. King, Bden Powell, and so on and on.....

05 – **Philip Catherine – Guitars**[18] I got to meet Philip when I was 13 years old in a Summer Masterclass sessions over a week with my soon to be teacher Philippe Petit, and Philip's playing was just so so incredibly sensitive, emotional, strong and soft, also resuming our european approach like rarely. I talked to Philip long for the Gesualdo project trying to convince him to join, but he turned 70 and wants to improvise mostly today, more than just read music. Philip is one of those forever influences for me that I need to dive in and then forget to better come back again later, like maybe René Thomas, Derek Bailey, Larry Coryell or Jaco Pastorius. I could have name many other albums but this is an evident side of me : jazz guitar.

What are your five favorite scores?

This in an interesting question, because I don't think I know what as Score really is yet. I've always been reading a lot of music daily and scores too but generally any notated music in any styles and sometimes formats or forms (from Tabs to

17   http://www.discogs.com/Johnny-Guitar-Watson-Love-Jones/master/102330

18   http://www.discogs.com/Philip-Catherine-Guitars/master/227197

Standard Notation, Beginners Methods to Studies, Transcriptions to *Fac-Simile*, Jazz, Fingerpicking, Rock, Blues, Metal, Baroque, Country etc All Guitar Music, or Bass too). I have a sort of fascination for Methods and particularly Beginners ones, always very excited to see how one approaches the fundamentals of the instrument. It's difficult for me to tell you what's my favorite score because I never used so far any scores as an interpret in the classical sense of the term I guess. All I do is read music, sight read music, and this even (especially I should say) when recording early music lately. To me a score is a tool basically and nothing else, the finality, goal of it is to recreate this particular music notated, but the notation is just a convenient common *accessoire* in the this process of playing music. It's the same way that I never really understood the division made between Composed or Improvised. I see only one division and that is between Played or Not (How, How Well, How Subjective, Incarnated, Made Alive etc). But OK, at the moment my favorite scores are of two kinds : one is 14th century music (Machaut, Binchois, Cordier, Ars Subtilior etc), because I found in this writing all answers I probably was looking for long. This music isn't classical music at all, it's somewhere "Pure Music", very alive and incarnated on one side and extremely symbolic, loaded with signs and universal symbols on the other side. Maybe the same way when you go to Vaticano museum and visit all the rooms until Capella Sistina, the works there are not about esthetic beauty but about the power of their messages. A time where art meant something ... had a strong metaphysical function too and not an isolated niche practice. The other scores that I read a lot at the moment are double bass transcriptions from Ron Carter, Ray Brown, Wilbur Ware, Steve Swallow, Jaco Pastorius, Jerry Jemmott, etc.

With who would you like to play? What kind of music do you listen to usually?

Hum... I have a very particular way to listen today, and MP3 and Ipod have been incredibly useful for that since. I concentrate on details, lines, sounds, moments in complete works of a given artist and mostly guitarists. I have certain all time favorites list of players that I dive into complete recordings and listen again and again same slices (often same as when I started music), a bit like a philologist or librarian digging details into collections and archives. Otherwise I listen to Pop mostly, for many many reasons, one being that Pop music often resumes our times the best, swallowing all other sounds in the air plus being an incredible team production a bit like Hollywood movies, a collective work from extremely achieved people each in its own area. I do sort of go through new music around just to inform myself, but I need some distance often to hear it. As for people i'd like to play with, in fact I should say people i'd like to play more with. I've been blessed to be able to play or study or meet with most of my heroes in fact. I could have said Miles and Ornette like many but it's not even really so true today. I think today I would like to play with people I didn't already meet and know, younger players like the incredible 15 years old Augustin Brousseloux for example (but we play together already and share a lot[19]). Or Charlie Rauh whom I feel very very close to even we have different stories but we can share a lot of basis and views[20]. I come from early jazz and know that music really well and deeply, but until my late 20's Jazz guitar had sort of shadow my whole global guitar views (even though I always listened to all sorts of guitar music from rock to pop, classical to world). It's only by then that I fully got aware of the fact I had because of jazz phrasing quite ignored the fact that Guitar is an Open E Natural Instrument. And after that I sort of went away from my actual jazz scenes, I felt it wasn't really happening anyway, and started to play and look with all sorts of different artists and music traditions, which got me a bit in conflict with the jazz scenes. People didn't got it I think there, my whole range of interest were rather a negative hard to get thing for them, but it's only since some years that younger generations came to me for whom it was not only normal but rather very positive. There are people I'd love to play more with like Joey Baron, Kenny Wollesen, Bradley Jones, and one forever hero, Bern Nix. Many others too I guess. For many reasons (one being that I started to gig when I was 14 and did intensively for close to 20 years), I stopped touring much and doing all sorts of live collaborative projects in the last decade, wanting to only concentrate on my own works (and not always play live also because for one hour of playing live you need to give away 23h of your whole day and I have a lot that I want to be done in a day). But time may comes sometime soon that I set again 2 or 3 live projects and want to tour more again. I would like to have 2, 3 setups or groups that would be with people I love and that would allow us to construct on longer terms, not in one genre or style or context also but like a base, some sort of homeland. It would take I guess too long to express here but i'm really very excited about present times, probably also because I came with a sort of real good feeling about my own, having done a lot until now that sort of raised like my own world-home-house, it frees you a lot. And since some years I see a new chapter of the world map and music that starts to raise. Something finally Next and not Post anymore like for example has been most of the jazz scenes the last 15-20 years I feel. Really looking forward to that coming-up. I think I can contribute something there...

Your next projects? When we will see you playing in Italy?

---

19   https://itunes.apple.com/us/album/dark-dingdong/id893897111

20   https://itunes.apple.com/us/album/frets-olaep/id893779852

Well a lot lot lot as usual and more... definitely a lot of early music more to continue, and the 5 Guitars project also with more repertoire that I want to be played. One obvious all ready is to play Machaut in Reims (Champagne and where he was from and wrote the famous Messe de Nostre Dame for). More Guitar Duets series to be recorded soon, more loops and samples funk-fusionelectro- dub too. Some albums in preparations like a Tribute to Masayuki Takayanagi for New Atlantis Records[21] (I only started and as for every single tribute album I want to go through all existing materials first, it helps me a lot see angles not from darkness or blindness). Our duet with Hans-Joachim Roedelius[22] to be recorded again and anew as soon as possible I hope, Our Last Tour Live and Studio Recordings with Polish Duet Mikrokolektyv[23] to be released.

And many many more that I can't tell because I work very fast so that I often can't tell from a day to another. As for Italy well... I'd come when you like me to (laughs).

---

21   http://newatlantisrecords.com

22   http://en.wikipedia.org/wiki/Hans-Joachim_Roedelius

23   http://mikrokolektyw.com

MAGNUS ANDERRSON

Magnus Andersson has long been active in the contemporary music field, and has played a significant role in the creation of the modern guitar repertoire. He studied at Trinity College of Music in London, and at the Viotti Music Academy in Vercelli,Italy. In 1984 Magnus Andersson founded the guitar class at the International Summer Courses for New Music in Darmstadt (Internationale Ferienkurse für Neue Musik), where he taught until 1996. He teaches at the Royal College of Music in Stockholm and is a founding member of the innovative chamber music group Ensemble SON and was artistic director of the 2006 and 2008 Stockholm New Music Festival.
Magnus Andersson received the Swedish Gramophone Prize in 1985 and 1986 and was nominated for a Swedish Grammyin 1992. He was awarded the Composers Union Interpreter Prize in 1983 and the Kranischsteiner Prize in Darmstadt in 1984.
He has performed the premieres of numerous important contemporary works including works by Ferneyhough, Sandström,Dillon, etc.

https://en.wikipedia.org/wiki/Magnus_Andersson_(guitarist)

The first question is always the classic one: how does it start your love and interest for guitar and what instruments do you play or have you played?

My earliest memory of the guitar is hearing the electric guitar tune "Apache" over the radio. However, not in the famous version by Hank Marvin of The Shadows, a hit in 1960, but in a version by the great Danish jazz guitarist Jørgen Ingmann[24] (1925–2015). So, this must have been in 1961. I was then 5 years old. My parents then bought the record, a single or perhaps it was an EP, Ingmann playing Apache. I absolutely loved it. I loved the cover too. This was a portrait of Jørgen Ingmann wearing on his head an impressive Red Indian war bonnet. At that age I adored the red indians and hence my respect for Ingmann and the guitar was firmly consolidated. In 1963 Jørgen Ingmann won the Eurovison song contest with his wife Grethe with the song "Dansevise", surely one of the great winners in the history of that contest. In 1958 my father bought a television set. That was the year of the world championship of football took place in Sweden. I was two years old and have distinct memories of watching games. In fact football became such a strong part of my identity when I grew up that many friends and associates were very surprised when I in my teens I decided to retire from football to dedicate myself to music. But, apart from seeing football for the

---

24   https://en.wikipedia.org/wiki/J%C3%B8rgen_Ingmann

first time on television, it also gave me my first encounter to the classical guitar. I must have been around 8 years old. Magic! I asked my parents for a guitar and they bought me a classical guitar. Unfortunately I was not exposed to any good teaching from the beginning, so all I did was to play around with the instrument mainly improvising until the age of 14 when I began to practice and began studies with Roland Bengtsson[25] (1916 – 2005). He was one of the pioneers of the classical guitar in Sweden and very versatile musician and also successful as a double bass player. I found him to be a very good musician with a very sensitive ear. I admired him and his total unwillingness to compromise with his views on what was good about music and musicianship. At 14 I also started to play the double bass for Henry Lundin (1908-1999), a legendary musician and double bass player in Stockholm Philharmonic. He strongly advised me to leave the guitar and focus on the double bass. "You will never be without work". I am grateful for my studies with these two musicians, so obviously even then, from another time and another outlook on music. The outcome was that I never became entangled in pop music nor electric guitar. Although the fact that I heard both the Who and Rolling Stones in Stockholm around 1965 left a strong impression. Energy and anger were impressive.

When I began to study music at Trinity College of Music in London I also started to take piano lessons. At times I did actually practice the piano quite a lot a few hours a day. Since then I have retained my interest in the piano, its music and its interpreters. The piano has a rich and complex tradition that gives a valid perspective on the culture of the guitar.

So you don't receive any musical training until you were 14 years old, what impressions did Roland Bengtsson leave in your music? Have studied with other teachers?

One thing I would like to add is that Roland Bengtsson had been a student of the great Spanish guitarist Angel Ferrera Iglesias[26] (1917 – 1977). Just a few years ago some people in Spain approached me about my studies with Roland Bengtsson. They had figured out that I must belong to the lineage of Iglesias through my studies with Bengtsson. Well, I don't want to make any point of this detail, but I have had the great fortune to meet teachers that in one way or on other were part of a tradition that were larger than their individual concerns. In 1973 I had a scholarship in Santiago de Compostela and "Catedra de Segovia". Segovia didn't come that year, but Jose Tomas was there and so was Jose Luis Rodrigo. Santiago de Compostela was my first international experience and

---

25   https://sv.wikipedia.org/wiki/Roland_Bengtsson

26   http://www.aguicex.com/Angel_Iglesias.html

students from all over the world were attending. One of the students there, an oboe's professor at an American university and on his sabbatical period, advised me to go to London and Trinity College of Music. He had been there for a few months with William Grandison. I had no knowledge whatsoever, but I took his advice and applied to Trinity College for 1974 academic year.

I was accepted and I took my diploma in 1976. To be in London at that time was an overwhelming experience. The guitar was at its peak of popularity and I lived just a few blocks away from Wigmore Hall. In those years there were an abundance of guitar recitals, so I heard John Williams, Julian Bream, Alirio Diaz, Narciso Yepes and many others, but I also got in touch with much everything else that a city like London offers about museums, art and so on. London was for sure then the center of classical music and I was an omnivorous consumer of a wide range of music. Of particular importance for my own development were more marginal concerts in small places for the London's vital improvisatory scene of free improvised music with musicians like Derek Bailey, Evan Parker and Barry Guy. An experience that certainly was fruitful for my later development as an interpreter of new music. My teachers at Trinity College suggested me to remain and continue my studies at the school, but instead focusing on music theory and conducting. My guitar's teacher, William Grandison, was a keen promoter of new music and he really led me into it as he believed in my capacity to actually develop something worthwhile in the field of new music for guitar. It was also William Grandison who drew my attention to the Italian pedagogue, guitarist and composer Angelo Gilardino[27]. He said that Angelo Gilardino must be quite a thinker about music and he judged this solely by the quality of Gilardino's fingerings for the red cover guitar series of Berben edtions. So, at the end I decided to not stay in London, but to continue my guitar studies with Angelo Gilardino in Vercelli. But, before I actually moved to Italy I had an intermittent stay with the German guitarist Sigfried Behrend[28] (1933 – 1990) in Hausham, Bavaria. He was Germany's most important guitarist at the time and also active in what was called avant-garde music, working with composers like Xavier Bengeruel, Sylvano Bussotti and others. He was also an enthusiast for Bavarian folk music and I had quite a lot of exposure to this type of music while I visited his home. He was also a keen trout's fisherman, so I also experienced many beautiful streams, of which there were many in due to the closeness to the Alps around the countryside of his village. Behrend was an interesting teacher and quite a complex man. He kept a log of our lessons. After a period of not seeing him he would take out his binder with annotations. One

---

27   http://angelogilardino.com/

28   https://en.wikipedia.org/wiki/Siegfried_Behrend

lesson he noted: you are still not cutting off the loose ends of the strings at the machine head. Since then I am always careful about this.

In the fall of 1976 I began my studies with Angelo Gilardino in Vercelli. He completely changed my life and his complete dedication to pursuing his vision of what the guitar should be, and this in a most logical and severe way, was a total revelation to me. There was also, in his teaching, a sense both of the aesthetical and ethical side to music and art that made him a true representative of what is the most impressive aspect of Italian culture; that the aesthetical aspect of life is closely connected with the ethical qualities of what you do. In fact, that's what Dante teaches and says. As you can understand I am also immensely grateful to what Italy has given me, Without this experience I would have been a different person.

I must finally end with some words about my no less important teachers in theory, orchestration and conducting. In Stockholm I lived very close, just the next block, to a legendary teacher in Sweden of Palestrina and Bach counterpoint. His name was Professor Valdemar Söderholm [29] (1909 – 1990). An extremely knowledgeable man. With him I did both fugue and Palestrina counterpoint, but also some pastiche writing of sonatas in the style of the classics. He was very supportive. At the same time I also went every Saturday for four hours to classes in orchestration with Professor Gunnar Johansson [30] (1906 – 1991). He was a former horn player at Royal Opera Orchestra and his knowledge of the orchestral repertoire was huge and he knew it all by memory. He wrote music to more than 70 films and had been professor of orchestration at the Royal College of Music. He somewhat disguised his broad musical background and he told me he did some studying with Carl Nielsen [31] and even visited Schoenberg in the late 1920s. Both Valdemar and Gunnar were of a stock that is no longer made. I also had some years of study with the Swedish conductor Claes Mehritz. He was a great pedagogue and a true enthusiast whose love of music was very invigorating.

Talking about Schoenberg do you think that the guitar, with its presence of very personal musicians at every musical level and genre would be an alternative to the distinction between high culture and popular culture and Schoenberg's affirmation: " if it is art, it is not for all, and if it is for all, it is not art "?

29   https://sv.wikipedia.org/wiki/Valdemar_S%C3%B6derholm
30   https://en.wikipedia.org/wiki/Gunnar_Johansen
31   https://en.wikipedia.org/wiki/Carl_Nielsen

I am not quite sure what you mean with a viable alternative in this context. The guitar is for sure an instrument that is unique in its way of easily adapting itself to various cultural contexts, from local folk music cultures in Vietnam to highly complex music of western art music and everything in between. But, I think that the fundamental problems around high art or rather the dissolution of high art as it was understood in the 19th century is something worthwhile to reflect upon. Schoenberg was extremely concerned about the ethical aspects of doing art, but we must not forget that he was also very capable of writing music that was both light and entertaining. But, he came from a tradition that also includes Wagner and Brahms and Nietzsche too, for that matter. In many ways that period in our history was a very happy one for music, in the sense that high art music also could be a statement in a larger social context that meant something also as a public statement. This is true for the music from the time of Haydn, Mozart, Beethoven, Wagner, Brahms, Verdi to name just a few. But, the problems that art and society were going to face were already part of the content in what they said, or to speak with Marshall McLuhan: what we have here, in particular with Wagner and Nietzsche are "early distant warnings" from the past. I think that art as such is, under threat in the present situation as everything is, in one way or another, forced to be part of the entertainment industry today and hence be treated as a commodity. I cannot see anything positive coming out of this in the long haul. The general blurring of distinctions does annihilate differences and hence inhibits articulation of thoughts. At the end no one knows what he or she wants to say in a broader sense and we get a life that becomes too individual even egoistic and more like a private venture. To expect the guitar to be a viable alternative in to this is hard to see and perhaps is asking too much to the guitar.

Berio in his essay "A remembrance to the future," wrote: ".. A pianist who is a specialist about classical and romantic repertoire, and plays Beethoven and Chopin without knowing the music of the twentieth century, is also off as a pianist who is specialist about contemporary music and plays with hands and mind that have never been crossed in depth by Beethoven and Chopin.[32]" You play both traditional classical and contemporary repertoire ... do you recognize yourself in these words?

Yes, I do agree with Berio. But, I would not say that it something that applies in all cases. The truth is that the music of someone like Berio for example has become more marginal. I remember Hopkinson Smith, answering a similar question, said that there was no real need for new music. He was, as is often the case, regarding his relationship to this issue. But, his answer is partly true even if

---

32   Luciano Berio, Un ricordo al futuro, Einaudi, 2006, pag. 54

it is somewhat ignorant and limited in scope. However, an admired pianist like Radu Lupu and others has more or less said the same too. Personally I do not in music adhere to the somewhat restricting linear description of music history that the establishment promotes. A more interesting position is to look at history as something existing in space and hence acting upon us at the same time as it was. It opens up many coexistent tracks and helps us to make associations in way that more corresponds how our mind actually works. This standpoint has helped me greatly in understanding music better and to communicate what I feel better too. In other words, music can work on us figures of thought to help us think and feel and a broader culture does help us in attaining such a goal.

You talked about 70's London impro scene, what does improvisation mean for your music research? Do you think it's possible to talk about improvisation for classical music or we have to turn to other repertories like jazz, contemporary music, etc.?

In general it is, of course, a fact that improvisation in classical music has become virtually non-existent, even if we know that all of the classic composers, from Bach, through Haydn, Mozart, Beethoven and further on were good improvisers and someone like Haydn tells us how he used improvisation to find new ideas. Today we cannot quite re-live the context of a former age, so it becomes a subject of study. At least if we think that improvisation in such a context must have some philological truth to it. However, if we compare music with what is fully accepted in classics performance in theatre, where the truth about a play almost always demands a more radical approach to textual issues, well then music is obviously far behind. In any case, it is, of course possible to approach classical music in a more radical way, but there are many ontological and epistemological problems to relate here and I am not sure they could be solved in a satisfactory way. But, I think, to give one example, that Peter Sellars[33] has done some remarkable readings and stagings of central works in western canon of music. I also think that Chaya Czernowin[34]'s use of Mozart's opera Zaide in her own opera Adama/Zaide was an interesting way of relating to the classical tradition. As regards myself improvisation has been a part of my music activity, but then solely with musicians that partly comes from Jazz and Contemporary Music and then moved into what is sometimes called free improvised music. This is a style and those that I have worked with the names I mentioned earlier as part of my background: Derek Bailey, Evan Parker and Barry Guy. The latter I have even performed and worked with quite a few times. Recently I also

---

33   https://en.wikipedia.org/wiki/Peter_Sellars

34   http://chayaczernowin.com/

interpreted the artist Chris Markley's Black Board at an exposition at the Artipelag in Stockholm. In performing an "installation" like this, is built upon the idea of a huge pentagram covering a large wall. On this pentagram visitors can write or draw whatever they want, with the intention that this later, after a week in this instance, will be "interpreted" by a visiting musician. In performing something like this one has to, of course rely very much on some sort of interpretation as improvisation. On the other hand, I did hear a few performances and could observe the fact that musicians that improvise as a profession more or less play what they always do while I think, on the other, that I was perhaps able to refer to a much broader repertoire of sounds and ideas due to my "cultured" background. So, I would definitely say that in this case I did something in which my classical training was an advantage.

Sometimes ago Elena Càsoli said to me "I improvise the interpretation of what you call encoded. Scored music requires an ethic of respect, attention, closeness and knowledge of its aesthetics, looking at the sign left by the author. But it's a moving, alive, elusive, intangible subject, which awaits the encounter with an interpretative act. And this meeting, in concert, has a space for improvisation, every evening new and different" What do you think about these words?

It is truism that has been said by many performers in the past - easy to say, but less easy to realize. To be spontaneous in performing a score demands a thorough knowledge, imagination and a sound technique. It was clearly a more obvious part of the style of earlier performers from Liszt up until Vladimir Horowitz, well Gyorgy Cziffra and Shure Cherkassky has to be included in this line among pianists as well. Performers today are more anxious about technical perfection in a more restricted sense. To approach interpretation in a more improvisatory way means that you have to allow for chance as a part of the performance. Chance is, as Carlos Fuentes said (and many others) the mother of invention. But, chance is very hard to deal with for most classical musicians as the demands are so high and the ambience is not always a model of generosity.

Shall we talk about "Chance" as an "Error"? For "error" I mean an incorrect procedure, an irregularity in the normal operation of a mechanism, a discontinuity on an otherwise uniform surface that can lead to new developments and unexpected surprises...

Well, this again is partly answered in the previous question. What you do refer to here is possibly what we think of as a mistake. A mistake is simply a deviation from what we planned to happen when we play a piece of music. Mistakes are almost impossible to completely avoid, if you are not Arturo Benedetti Michelangeli. I am sure he found he made mistakes, but he was also obsessive in taking heroic precautions to avoid them. But, at the same time many performers are appreciated for how they deal with mistakes. One such performer was Alfred Cortot, who many would say made interesting mistakes, although for many he stepped over the line for what is acceptable. In the history of conducting there are also those that rely on inspiration and atmosphere rather than discipline, such as Furtwängler or Knappertsbusch, with amazing results. So, certainly errors can lead positive surprises, but it is important to know that mistakes has to carry, in order to be interesting, a certain energy that is both informed and culturally burdened.

If you listen to a different interpretation of a score you want to perform this do you keep it in mind listening or do you prefer to proceed in complete independence?

I do not mind listening to various interpretations of pieces that I am about to play or study or have studied. I have no naive notion of that one can start with anything without knowing anything or start off by being completely blank of any prejudice. To act towards a piece is also an act of self-reflection and self-criticism, a fundamental aspect of western art. Of, course there is many imitators around who really do not present original ideas, but to assume that staying away from exposure will give an original view is hardly plausible. But, as Paul Klee said at the beginning of last century, in searching for a pure beginning he wanted to erase all cultural varnish, is still true for all of us. Finding strategies for seeing things in a fresh way and to re invent the child in us is an ongoing process as well.

I try to ask you a little bit 'provocative question about music in general, not just about contemporary or avant-garde. Frank Zappa in his autobiography wrote: "If John Cage, for example, said, now I put a contact microphone on the throat, then I drink carrot juice and this will be my composition ", then his gargling would qualify as a COMPOSITION, because he applied a frame, declaring it as such. "Take it or leave it, now I want this to be music." It's really good this statement to define a genre of music, just say this is classical music, this is contemporary and it's done? It still makes sense to speak about "genre"?

The Frank Zappa story you refer to in your question is really (and I have not read the book) an example that belongs to some fundamental questions on art that Marcel Duchamp posed. One of Duchamp's most famous works is "Fountain", which simply is a urinal given another name and then exposed as a work of art. Zappa's example of an imaginary (I assume) Cage piece is basically the same. You just do an activity that produces sound and then you call it a composition. Mostly Duchamp was extremely careful with how he did his objects and at times he was quite demanding in an artisan way too, but the main concern in these actions were to draw our attention to how we look upon art and that art in many ways is a social construct that only has to fulfill certain rules to be called art. Cage is somewhat similar and when Cage is successful, which he not always is, then the outcome is mostly a result of complicated and carefully executed strategies that uses chance. The problem with Cage, and there are many, is that I find it quite oppressive and not very free. On the contrary it is too rigorous and the musician is basically seen upon as a passive doll or robot. There is also a contradiction about acting upon sound as though you cannot own it or you want to liberate it and at the same time both giving works titles and demand legal rights of authorship. As regards belonging to a genre it is clear that Cage now belongs to the canon of classical contemporary music. Which means he is established and he is part of the institutional world. But, speaking of Zappa and Cage in conjunction with each other, it is illuminating to compare two films, one of Zappa playing the bicycle and Cage performing his Water Walk. Zappa is obviously the more playful of the two with a twist of protest (not aggressive at all), typical of his generation at that time. Cage is quite rigorous in his humor, not unlike a Presbyterian pastor.

Nadia Boulanger said that a great artist is defined by what he or she says not to. The abundance of possible choices can be overwhelming or even terrorizing for the modern man.

Cage made an important contribution in showing a way of how get free of choice, as it were. An interesting question, I think.

Your musical career has been going on for several years, how is the world changed around you? How new technologies (new musical instruments, midi, social networks, forums) have influenced your choices and your musical form? How?

There has been an enormous change throughout the 40 years or so that I have been active.

When I started, art music or classical music had much more attention than what it has today.

Just a couple of years ago I was invited to a dinner at the Italian Embassy in honor of the conductor Riccardo Muti[35]. At the reception was a music critic for

---

35   http://www.riccardomutimusic.com/ita/index.asp

Dagens Nyheter[36], the largest newspaper in Sweden, or rather; he used to be a music critic. Now his task was to cover all sorts of things, but not music. He told me, that when he started off, there were an abundance of concerts he was asked to write about and sometimes even up to three recitals a day. This is how art music was dealt with in media when I got involved in music. That has gradually changed and today there are no employed music critics at any of the newspapers anymore and art music receives much less coverage. Popular music on the other hand has moved on from what was called entertainment to the same pages where art music were used to be covered. I have seen the same thing happening throughout the industry of culture and it evades the mentality everywhere. If we look at the Swedish Radio for example, they used to produce a lot of studio recordings when I started. As being part of public service they also were expected to, in a way, educate their audiences and to present new music. This has completely changed. No productions and the daily tableau gives no timing for when pieces are going to be played. It has become an outlet mostly for mediocre presenters that just transmit a kind of stream of classical muzak.

In the past I have been working as an advisor for the local authorities in Stockholm and Gothenburg regarding financial support to artists. In this environment it is very clear that there are many that have pretensions of doing art, but fundamentally no one wants to define what it is or what it should be. So, gradually I have seen an increasing space given to forms of music that originally were part of the entertainment industry and popular culture. Selling becomes also the prime judge of quality. Certainly this sector also wants more money, so it is not surprising that more and more of public funds for the arts are going in this direction. I know this from my own country, but I think it is a tendency elsewhere. When I started what I did this was, just as today, a fairly marginal activity, but I never had the impression of that it was not considered to be something important and worthy of support. This is not the case anymore. The other radical change in music life since I began is what the personal computer has done for simplifying and spreading musical production. No doubt this can be seen as clear democratic move that is dissolving the traditional centers of powers. Just consider, for example, the crisis of the traditional big record companies. A part of the same complex if also the dissemination of music through streaming and what this does to our way of listening recorded music. As a sociological phenomenon what we see here is also a gradual dissolution of respect for elites and knowledge. No one really listens to them anymore.

On the other hand, I have, of course, been confronted with all these changes in my musical activity, but there are aspects of what it means to be a human being that have not changed since the beginning and human needs are much the same

---

36   https://en.wikipedia.org/wiki/Dagens_Nyheter

throughout the ages. Hence, it is not all negative, I think, real art has to retire to a kind of underground context.

If you had to choose, who is your favorite composer to play?

As regards favorite composers, none of them has written for the guitar. That is why I have been involved with creating a new repertoire. Needless to say I try to find a favorite in every composer I have played. Those I have worked with, Donatoni, Clementi, Vacchi, Ferneyhough, Dillon, Barrett, Riehm, Estrada and many more has given me more than I could have asked for from music.
Needless to say, the guitar has had a wonderful increase in qualitative repertoire in recent years and includes works by composers such as Helmut Lachenmann, Elliot Carter and Giacinto Scelsi. All names that belong to my favorites in contemporary music

I have, sometimes, the feeling that in our times music's history flows without a particular interest in its chronological course, in our discotheque before and after, past and future become interchangeable elements, shall this be a risk of a uniform vision for an interpreter and a composer? The risk of a musical "globalization"?

It is probably true that the understanding of music history is vanishing as a living thing. That is, music is something that was made by human beings with the same concerns as we have. We have to define though what we mean with understanding. Something that is very difficult to say what it means with certainty. There are also many types of understanding. The question of chronology only helps with this partly and then in a very basic and somewhat crude way. I have touched upon this earlier in our conversation, but the musical globalization is part of the commodifying of music and of the human subject, as it is exposed to commercial interests and certainly, more complicated issues are less commercial. We must here also consider about tradition, which concretely is the handing down of craft from one generation to the next one. A slow process that is not easily adapted to a life that moves faster and faster.

Let's talk about marketing. How much do you think it's important for a modern musician? I mean: how much is crucial to be good promoters of themselves and their works in music today?

Media today is a sort of God. Somehow it seems that everything can be solved through marketing. In Sweden most artists are forced into seeing themselves through marketing. If you do not succeed you are having a marketing problem.

66

But, it is important to understand that certain things are not always marketable and some processes in art needs time develop. The important thing is to have, in a developed and civilized society, institutions that can, in responsible way, read and communicate to broader public interesting artists. In the art world this works slightly better, but this is partly an effect of the incredible economic growth we have seen in art. Art music hasn't all the same economic muscles, as there are no objects to buy and sell. Money in music is basically part of mass culture. Without masses of money we have no real marketing. But, to answer your question more direct, there are, of course, many musicians in new music that are concerned with marketing themselves to festivals and promoters. To promote yourself is without doubt necessary and even more today than before.

Which composer (or which historical movement) do you think is easiest for the non-musician listener to appreciate? Do you think they enjoy pieces that are more technically difficult or just more "flashy"?

One has to acknowledge the fact that a large part of the music history consists of music that belonged to an elite. As the middle class grew in power from the end of the 18th century and into the 19th century, music became also public and we built concert halls that were temples to the glorification of music. This had an effect on the structuring of music in order to make it more popular and easier to understand. Music became a commercial enterprise already with Handel and to draw audiences also the virtuosic soloist became part of the fabric of music as an enterprise. For the non- musician listener this is music that is easy to understand, but, mind you, also for the musician it is easier to understand. The music from this time is often of a very high quality, but there is also a lot of crap. This is an outcome of the mechanization of the product line.

Do you note differences between the students you teach and you taught?

I have been teaching students from children to adults. Children are more or less the same, but they have more to do than when I grew up. In Sweden their free time is very regulated with, it seems almost every minute planned with various activities. This does not help to stimulate neither patience and imagination. As regards older student the difference from my time is perhaps more pronounced. Students are more anxious to fit in and to adhere to the rules. This is probably due to the fact that prospects for the future are less positive.
I have also noticed that less students actually end up with a musical career.

I try to risk a reckless question... Bach composed sometimes without specifying instrumentation... maybe... maybe was he not interested in the "Sound of

Music"? I mean maybe does the music in this case is hidden in a scheme, a structure capable of several realizations, several possible and different sounds? And the moment when the music reveals its true nature is contained in the exercise of its variations? Bach at this point would have composed something like jazz standards or pre Cage scores?

I am not sure I completely understand the question. Bach belonged to a speculative tradition in which ideas of numbers and hidden meanings in music were both an important and a vital part of his composing methods. We must not forget that he came from the same soil that saw the birth of Johannes Kepler. This probably made him sensitive to the idea that music was something that went beyond sound as such and pointed music to realms beyond here and now. These ideas are an important part of the spiritual history of mankind in general and not only related to the culture from where Bach came from. Bach's music keeps its identity in whatever mode of sound you realize it. I think Bach found this very satisfying. It is not much point in trying to speculate in what Bach would have been like if he would have lived today. He was a product of his time and you cannot just use this context as a matrix on our time. A product like Bach is a result of many trajectories coinciding in him. I am sure there are many musicians with the same extraordinary gifts that Bach had, but this sort of gifts need a particular milieu to blossom. Do we have that today? Not really, I think.

Please tell us five essential records, to have always with you the classic five discs for the desert island....

I have a large selection of vinyl and CDs and I use it a lot. There are some recordings that I return to quite often, but I am not sure if it means that they would be my favorites if I made a more considered selection. In a list of many options some will be missing. However, among my most played 5 records (only vinyl) are:

Billy Holiday	Songs for distingue lovers
Monica Zetterlund /Bill Evans	Waltz for Debby
Alfred Brendel	Haydn Sonatas
Artur Schnabel	Beethoven piano sonatas
Otto Klemperer	Mahler Symphony no 2

What are your five favorite scores?

Arnold Schoenberg	5 orchestral pieces op 16
Anton Webern	5 orchestral pieces op 10

68

Alban Berg	3 Orchestral pieces op 6
Beethoven	Piano sonatas
Bach	St Matthew Passion

With who would you like to play? What kind of music do you listen to usually?

Those I play with are also those I want to play with; Rohan de Saram, Pascal Gallois, Mats Gustavsson, Raymond Strid and others.
I have played what I want to play on the guitar, but I am always looking for new scores.
I listen to music everyday and a lot of new music too. But, as you can understand from the list there is a fair amount of jazz music in my diet too and certainly not only those two singers mentioned above. I do regularly also return to the classic recordings of Sonny Rollins and sometimes also Miles Davies.

Your next projects? When we will see you playing in Italy?

My next project is to finalize a residency at York University with the trio I have with Pascal Gallois, bassoon and Rohan de Saram, cello. Later this month we will perform several new works for the trio by young composers studying at York Univerity.
I will be in Italy in early September 2015 in Macerata in Basilicata. An initiative by the Italian guitarist Carlo Bruno. Who is now living in Sweden

LUCIA D'ERRICO

Lucia D'Errico is an artist devoted to experimental music, performing on plucked strings instruments. As a performer and improviser, she collaborates with contemporary music groups, and with theatre, dance, and visual art companies. An artistic researcher at Orpheus Institute Gent, she is part of the ME21 research project. Currently, she is working on a doctoral research (docARTES programme at Leuven University) on recomposing Baroque music. She is also active as a freelance graphic designer.

http://luciaderrico.altervista.org/luciaderrico/Home.html

The first question is always the classic one: how did your love and interest for guitar start, and what instruments do you play or have you played?

My interest in music started very early. Quite the opposite happened for my interest in musical instruments, despite their abundance in my home, my dad being an amateur guitarist and my sister a dedicated piano student. I started playing the guitar at the age of twelve, to reproduce some sounds I heard on a tape of the Beatles, and since then I never stopped. My focus on guitar has been an episode of a pretty crooked "age of reason" that fortunately is coming to an end, together with my instrumental specialization. I enjoy not so much mastering many different instruments, as multiplying my sonic horizons virtually onto infinity. Even inside the guitar I look for a multiplicity of ways out. I could call myself an escaping guitarist.

Being an escaping guitarist you have a huge arsenal of string instruments, can you tell us about your gears?

Differentiating my instruments is an important part of my escape plan. My companion for many years has been a classical guitar made by Mario Novelli, which I still use. But now my favorite playthings are a Music Man Sterling bass guitar, incredible source for prehuman noise, and a Fender Road Worn Stratocaster guitar. Besides, I enjoy oud, and I have just ordered a chitarra battente, a steel-string guitar typical of the South of Italy. But I've also had fun with mandolin, toy sitar, balalaika, charango, tar...

What was your musical training, which teachers did you study with, and what impression did they leave in your music?

As a teenager, I followed the academic studies in classical guitar. In parallel I led an intense composing, arranging and studio activity together with my sister Anna and my cousin Matteo. I think that was a crucial period in my musical formation, bursting with creativity and especially with listening experiences. In my conservatoire education, Tommaso De Nardis occupied an important place especially for his ability to connect music with potentially every field of human knowledge. I am happy of my schooling, nevertheless I am lately getting my academic training into perspective: I got from it as much as I lost – a lot in both cases.

One of the things that I can honestly say about guitar is its ability and capacity to change its shapes. Its incredible ability to spread is due to several factors, not least the fact that it can be realized both in industrial and artisan forms, and the fact that we can choose between classical, acoustic and electric types suitable for different musical and social cultures. You have followed a very personal path inside the guitar: how did you develop this path and how are you developing it?

There is no such thing as a perfect instrument. Even in the world experimental music, which I have been attending quite a lot, musicians tend to take too many things for granted. Every instrument is not only historical, but political as well. Take the piano: we still have difficulties in problematizing many aspects of it (if only its being a product of equal temperament) even if the musical and social context has completely changed from the period of its glory. The guitar, despite the incredible malleability you rightly speak of, does not escape this lot. It has a huge diversity of backgrounds, but each of them carries some historical and social implications. I try to keep that in mind in my musical activity. Instrumental specialization can be a very risky tool, narrowing down the possibilities of a musician rather than enlarging them. I am not afraid to give up guitar completely if I am ever to find out that its possibilities are limiting my creativity. I always try to remember what went on in times such as the Middle Ages or the Renaissance: the degree of experimentation on the side of musicians was vehement, to the point of having no fear to discard instruments that had ceased to be interesting. The fact that we are trying to retrieve them nowadays sounds pretty funny to me!
Sometimes we are in the same bowl as that fish which, being used to take water for granted, is not even aware of being immersed in it. It is very interesting, playful and healthy to try and discover as many layers of water as possible before reaching a deadly nothingness. Once you have played with them and selected the ones you can renounce, and taken your risks, you gain awareness and creative energy.

Do you think that guitar, with its presence of very personal musicians at every musical level and genre would be an alternative to the now tragicomic distinction between high culture and popular culture, and the affirmation of Schoenberg: " if it is art, it is not for all, and if it is for all, it is not art "?

The opposition between high and low art is grounded on a fundamental misunderstanding of the role of art itself. Art should highlight things that normally happen in everyday life. Its only utility lays in the fact that it gets – or should get – more attention than what is normally dedicated to each moment of life. I wish that art were totally useless in this sense. The problem with artists is that normally they are afraid to be useless, instead of wishing they could be so. In this sense, I find Schoenberg's quote as problematic as the idea of a "culture for everyone". In addition to that, the very idea that one has to support culture – be it high or low – sounds a bit underhand. I would say culture is meant to support people, and a person that does not feel the need to be supported at all might not just be the worst of brutes, but the most advanced of artists. Do not forget that every revolution is the ideal substratum for the restating of a new form of power. I am not sure that the nature of an instrument so manifold as the guitar is by itself a sufficient tool for what you are envisaging.

Berio in his essay "A remembrance to the future," wrote: "... A pianist who is a specialist about classical and romantic repertoire, and plays Beethoven and Chopin without knowing the music of the twentieth century, is also as off as a pianist who is a specialist about contemporary music and plays with hands and mind that have never been crossed in depth by Beethoven and Chopin." You play both traditional classical and contemporary repertoire... do you recognize yourself in these words?

I have a problem with the very idea of repertoire. The notion that the larger our knowledge is the better is quite repulsive to me. It is like capitalizing culture. Actually, I think the very notion of culture is quite repulsive to me too.

What does improvisation mean for your music research? Do you think it is possible to talk about improvisation in classical music or do we have to turn to other repertories like jazz, contemporary music, etc.?

When I think about improvisation, it comes to mind that we improvise each and every day without realizing. In many different ways, but most notably in language: there are extremely few things we say, even in the most formal of conversations, which are not improvised. I do not think that classical musicians

72

have ever achieved the naturalness of a conversation in their practice. In the context of contemporary music, or of free jazz, it happens somewhat often that improvisation is confused with *alea*, and in the worst of cases with chaos. Probably we can talk of improvisation in whatever practice has the humility to handle few and very interiorized tools, in order to use them as in a speech, independently of the musical milieu in which this takes place.

What is the role of the "Error" in your musical vision? For "error" I mean an incorrect procedure, an irregularity in the normal operation of a mechanism, a discontinuity on an otherwise uniform surface that can lead to new developments and unexpected surprises.

If an error occurs, in life as much as in music, the most productive thing I can do is try to listen to it. I have a penchant for errors, as for crises, and when I manage to make friends with them I am never disappointed.

Sometimes ago Elena Càsoli said to me: "I improvise the interpretation of what you call encoded. Scored music requires an ethic of respect, attention, closeness and knowledge of its aesthetics, looking at the sign left by the author. But it is a moving, alive, elusive, intangible subject, which awaits the encounter with an interpretative act. And this meeting, in concert, has a space for improvisation, every evening new and different." What do you think about these words?

Something strange has happened during the last two centuries, and it is even stranger that the majority of classical musicians overlook that – including myself until very lately. The score, initially used simply as a mnemonic tool in support of a sound tradition, has become a "thing", an object such as a painting could be; and an object of devotion as well. I respect very much the work of *interpreters*, that is of people who manage to regard musical notation as a trigger for an increased performing energy. Nonetheless, I can relate to a score in a fruitful way only considering it something to be completely obliterated by the time of the performance. Musical notation started as an aid for memory, now it has become a hindrance for oblivion! Absentmindedness is for me an essential requisite for a creative performance. Few things are more counterproductive to musical energy than the huge effort it takes to remember, read, and even respect a score. Whoever manages to relate to the score in this sense (I mention Gould, at the risk of being banal) has found a way. For all the others, I put forth the scenario of abandoning musical notation – it is rather old and tired after all. I hope that the excellent composers among my friends will not be mad at me after reading this, but that they will respond creatively to such a provocation.

Ok, so if you listen to a different interpretation of a score you already played and you want to perform it again, do you keep it in mind listening or do you prefer to proceed in complete independence?

This entirely depends on how the interpretation is!

I try to ask you a question a little bit provocative about music in general, not just about contemporary or avant-garde. Frank Zappa in his autobiography wrote: "If John Cage, for example, said, now I put a contact microphone on the throat, then I drink carrot juice and this will be my composition", then his gargling would qualify as a COMPOSITION, because he applied a frame, declaring it as such. "Take it or leave it, now I want this to be music." Is it really good this statement, to define a genre of music, just say this is classical music, this is contemporary and it is done? Does it still make sense to speak about "genre"?

It has never made sense to speak about genre, just as it will always be the case that one has to speak about genre. Even contemporary music is a genre, willy-nilly. It is a genre whenever musicians try to adapt themselves to a standard and to a taste that can allow them to access recognition, power, money, etc. And this, believe me, happens a lot. But there are cases in which it does not happen, and these I call the masterpieces: when people find a way to face the chaos of nothingness starting from the very edge of a preexisting codified system. A diver plunges into the ocean. In this fragile and potentially fatal trajectory is the power of those who try to renounce to be labeled as "genre". Whenever there is a genre, there is a superimposed We. Whenever there is such a We, we are dead while we think we are alive. Let art extract the difference present inside each one of us, not reinforce the presupposed identity between diverse people. It is really the only way I can conceive for equality, not the violent throwing of pre-constructed categories over autonomous and unassimilable experiences. In this respect, art *should not* communicate, but elicit the incommunicable.

Your musical career has been going on for several years. How have you seen the musical world changing around you?

The world never changes, but it changes continuously! The only thing that never changes is change. If we manage to adapt to that, we will be always new and always old. The means through which this happens – Gutenberg's printer or Twitter – are irrelevant.

74

So... the medium is not the message?

It is. But ultimately there is no message, or if you want the message itself can be just a medium. The interesting things are those that cannot be mediated and communicated.

If you had to choose, who is your favorite composer to play?

My answer is at the same time the most pretentious and the humblest that I can: myself. I do not believe in the supposed humility of the interpreter who brings the message of a great composer from the past. It is just a different way of prizing oneself: "I shine because my surface is so bright that it can reflect the most beautiful stars". I am on a much lower level: I trust only what can belong to me, acknowledging my limitations but also the infinity of what is contained therein. Doing this, I do not need anyone to impose his or her authority upon me, recognizing at the same time the capability of every single person to do the same, to find all the richness that is needed within oneself. I really hate names.

I have listen to you playing several times... as a player would you define yourself as a virtuoso?

I do not appreciate virtuosity, even when I want to be entertained. There are circuses for such things; the problem is I do not even enjoy circuses that much.

I sometimes have the feeling that in our times music history flows without a particular interest in its chronological course; in our discotheque before and after, past and future become interchangeable elements; shall this be a risk of a uniform vision for an interpreter and a composer? The risk of a musical "globalization"?

It is not a risk, it is an expectation. I have already mentioned my suspicion for culture, now I add that for music history. Chronology is just another way to accept an external authority that has little to do with our own experience. Knowledge of music history leads us to bring in music what we already know of it and through it. If I could just be perfectly ignorant, musically aphasic... but these days it takes a huge effort, a huge knowledge to become ignorant. If the phenomenon you are talking about can help us along this route, be it welcome.

Let's talk about marketing. How much do you think it's important for a modern musician? I mean: how much is it crucial to be a good promoter of oneself and one's work in music today?

This is a very difficult puzzle to solve. I have already mentioned the need to adapt to certain standards in order to attain a position, money, power, and so on. The fact that being a musician is also a job is in itself problematic. Being able to occupy a position in order to destroy it from within is a delicate, demanding activity. Music history is packed full of shining examples in this sense; but also of people that were destroyed by the impossibility of matching expressive eversion with social acceptance. Schumann, most notably. We might want to consider the possibility of separating money from music completely, in order to avoid a cold plunge into the Rhine.

Sometimes ago in an interview Carlos Santana said "Some people have talent, some people have vision. And vision is more important then talent, obviously.[37]" I think you have a great talent but... what's your vision? You have said before that you are an escaping guitarist... are you going more into compositions?

I agree with Santana. As someone said, talent does what it wants, genius does what it can. What trivial results can come from talent. If you are right and I have some, I cannot decide whether it has been more a help, a ladder through which I managed to climb to a certain height and that I am free to throw away, or rather a hindrance, a prosthesis that helped me walk like everyone else but that I am afraid of throwing away. In art it is wiser to crawl with your own legs than to run with someone else's.
As for my vision: if you escape somewhere to enter some other place you had better stay where you were before. My hope is to keep escaping, to avoid building myself yet another label. The separation between composer and performer is itself something that does not belong to my vision, something made up and whose meaning is not very clear to me. What is a performer to do if not to compose sound anew every single time? Musicians or parakeets?

I try to risk a reckless question... Bach composed sometimes without specifying instrumentation... maybe... maybe he was not interested in the "Sound of Music"? I mean maybe the music in this case is hidden in a scheme, a structure capable of several realizations, several possible and different sounds? And the moment when the music reveals its true nature is contained in the exercise of its variations? Bach at this point would have composed something like jazz standards or pre Cage scores?

---

37   Bill Milkowsky, Rockers, Jazzbos & Visionary, BillBoard Books, 1998, pag. 29

The age of musical recordings has brought a big potential to us: that of questioning the need of notation. What Bach was making, the apotheosis of music notation, relates to a historical phenomenon, and the fact that it was born leads us to suppose that maybe it will die. What you call variations I do not see as such: they are a set of prefigured conditions under which the performance of the *score* happens. The fact that these conditions are potentially infinite is not a good reason for considering the so-called faithful rendition of score a source of infinite possibilities. In my view, music has very little to do with optics, and what Bach did had a reason in the opticalization of sound. The problem is much wider than Bach's avoidance to specify the instruments for some of his scores. The problem lies in the fact that the parametrization of sound through a written score has radically changed the way of thinking about music, and of composing it. This has made possible the making of incredible masterpieces; but perhaps nowadays it is more interesting to look for alternatives, to bring music back to its starting point: sound.

Please tell us five essential records, to have always with you... the classic five discs for the desert island...

I dream of a desert island with no CD player…

What are your five favorite scores?

The ones that escape the possibility of being written. I am on the lookout for them.

With who would you like to play? What kind of music do you listen to usually?

I am really at odds with classification. My YouTube account is going crazy when it comes to suggesting some clips to listen to. I do not have a line of consistent listening; I rather go through a series of singular musical objects that are inspiring from a merely sonorous point of view. This might include techno, hard core, hip hop, Southern Italian folk, Bulgarian folk, trip hop, *liscio*, ambient, grunge, classical… and the list is much longer! Maybe I can tell you more precisely what I do not listen to: I do not find much delight in most kinds of heavy metal and of jazz. And no, I do not listen to contemporary music if not for work. But I am in constant mutation…

Your next projects?

I am working on a three-year-long project for the team Music Experiment 21, a research group in the center ORCiM, in Gent (Belgium). Starting from the concept of empty center, and from some observations on the music between the 16th and the 17th centuries, I am going to develop ideas and sounds that question what it means to be a performer nowadays. As for my activity as a freelance, I want to get rid of the idea of repertoire as much as possible, and I started to do something concretely about it with my solo project *The Waste Land*, a musical dramaturgy dedicated to the death of the repertoire. But there is much more cooking, you will be my guest for the next blowout!

DAVIDE FICCO

David Ficco was born in Turin in 1962. He graduated with honors in 1982 (class of Guido Margaria, Conservatory of Alexandria), he studied with John Williams, Jose Tomas, Betho Davezac, Jakob Lindberg, Oscar Ghiglia and Alain Meunier, resulting from these last scholarships EEC and diplomas of merit at the Accademia Chigiana in Siena (1982-85). In 1989 he received the title of Guitar Performer at the Royal College of Music in London;. He has recorded for Naxos, Stradivarius, Amadeus, GuitArt, Moisycos and Oliphant repertoires dedicated mainly to the '900. As the author has composed music for guitar mainly, part of which were published by Gendai Guitar (Tokyo) and Carisch (Milan).

http://www.davideficco.com/

The first question is always the classic one: how was your love and interest for the guitar born?

It started when I was nine, in 1971, when my brother was given a guitar for Christmas. My brother, who was a lover of music and opera, gave us the opportunity to have guitar lessons: of the two of us I was the one who accepted and that's how it began. Guido still sings and plays today, but only for fun.

So he didn't become a musician?

No, he graduated with a Master in Physics at Turin University and then completed a special course in Computer Science at Harvard University in Cambridge (MA). He's been living in the US for 30 years, now working in a large computer systems corporation and living near Newport in Rhode Island. He is what we in Italy would call a "runaway brain".

Let's get back to you. What instruments do you play or have you played in the past? What's your musical background?

I studied in Turin with Silvio Costa who is an old-style teacher of many instruments; Luigi Borghi, a classical guitar teacher to many guitarists in Turin and Luigi Locatto, the guitar maker himself, a former student of Borghi, but at the time a pupil of Notaro and Margaria, then I spent six years at the Conservatory of Alessandria with Guido Margaria, and finally, I took individual courses with John Williams, Jakob Lindberg and José Tomás. Meanwhile I studied with Oscar Ghiglia for four summers at the Accademia Chigiana in

Siena. All different people obviously, but from each I received a great deal and I'm grateful for that.

As for the guitars, leaving out some initial instruments of less value, I had one of the first "Sakurai 5" that ever arrived in Italy (I think it was in 1976), moving on to a couple of "Ramirez Class I" guitars around the same time as I took my final diploma in 1982, followed by two more made in the early 70s. To tell the truth I had the chance to play a Locatto in 1978 (his third guitar, for the final concert at one of the Varallo Sesia summer courses). He had been, as I said earlier, also my teacher for about a year, and since 1988 I have always used one of his guitars. At first a 664 in cedar, and from 1995 a diapason 650 because my left hand had been a little bit damaged by the reckless use of the long fretboards. In 1994 I bought a cedar Fleta directly from the maker, but my youthful impatience clashed with the proverbial unforgiving nature of the still green instruments of the Barcelona Master hence I sold the instrument after a few months. From 2009 and for some years after, I had the pleasure of playing some antique instruments, sharing the passion with my friends Diego Milanese and Umberto Piazza, excellent connoisseurs: Arias, Fleta, Galan, Orange, Simplicio and Friederich guitars, ranging from 1874 to 1959. While I would think of myself as a "mono-guitar" and prone to choosing an instrument that doesn't require too much looking after, I've been through the prestigiousness of the tone and sensitivity to the vibrato of these instruments in order to learn to recognize and use colours and shades that were still missing to me. However, knowing the undeniable charm of the past and after many years being faithful to a Locatto, since 2010 I've been playing a Fleta, custom built made in spruce with the handle measures derived from Garcia, and for his special availability I'm obliged to thank the Maestro Gabriel, now sadly deceased, who honoured me by giving me a label with a personal dedication. From the original concept linking Torres-Garcia-Simplicio of the Locatto to the Fleta the technical approach to the sound has changed with some advantages and disadvantages. In the future we'll see what happens.

Moving on to my musical background, I'd say that I've always been very curious and sensitive to "quality" music in general, although I focused mainly on classical music. As for my jazz playing friends, I always appreciated their freedom to shape the musical speech extemporaneously and think in a more analytical and conscious way compared to classical musicians. I always listened to beautiful, well written songs, but when I was a teenager I loved listening, in the evening, with friends, to Stravinsky's Le Sacre or Pierrot Lunaire or Verklärte Nacht by Schöenberg, or Berg or Bartòk, I was a very strange kid! Anyway, I listened to a lot more music for instruments other than guitars, ranging from the ancient to electronic. What strikes me in a piece of music, of any kind, is the quality and the intensity of the content, the stylistic perfection, the emotion that manages to inspire me regardless of the media that it employs: I think you can enjoy very different music without feeling yourself less "pure". What is important to me is to feel that in that piece "there is a lot"; a lot to receive and if you are willing, a lot to learn. I like to emphasize the affinity and the similarity between the condition of the end user and the performer, because they intertwine. I listen almost solely to what I like and to what excites me and I play, if I can, what excites me and what I like to listen to.

How did your interest in the contemporary repertoire start and what are the stylistic trends with which you mostly identify?

As I said, as a kid I enjoyed unusual musical atmospheres, angular, taut and lunar: they touched parts of me that otherwise would remain silent. After all, this is exactly why I still play a certain kind of music and I promote the practice of it: if you want to express the colour blue, you need to play blue music. Other music has other colours. In our guitar class, led by Maestro Guido Margaria, it was the norm to review new music: I've listened to Mosso, Margola, Viozzi, Brainovich, Marcianò and other "ink fresh" composers and as students, if we had the chance, we would play their music for the "premiere". In the early years whilst in a trio with Carmelo Lacertosa and the mourned friends Alberto Cogo and Domenico Gandini, and with the extraordinary voice of Luisa Castellani or alone, I had the chance to play or ask for new compositions. We received, for example, compositions by Daniele Bertotto, Giulio Castagnoli, Felice Quaranta, Gilberto Bosco and several others, which I had the honour of playing. But the event that immersed me in non-guitar contemporary music was, just having graduated, entering both the prestigious Contemporary Music Ensemble of RAI[38] and the Symphonic Orchestra of RAI in Turin, where I collaborated continuously for thirteen years playing the work of many important authors. Occasionally I used the electric guitar (I remember with nostalgia my black Gibson Les Paul Custom... although, once, I had to play it with a saucepan...), bass, acoustic guitar and banjo. The orchestra was joined by the occasional chamber formation. You asked me about styles and trends: we have to distinguish between what we're asked to perform, which goes beyond our tastes, and those that we choose. As for the latter, I've seen languages or styles prevailing in my choices that are not unstructured or borderline - evidently my desire to communicate needs the presence, although diluted, of intervals and harmonical sequences in which there is still a shadow of consonance. But, of course, I am not afraid to provoke nor I am afraid of a completely revised guitar.

---

38   Italian National Broadcasting Company

As well as being a guitarist you also have an intense activity as a composer, do you want to talk about it?

You are too generous in calling me a composer! I would rather say that I've simply written music for guitar and other instruments. My activity, due to time and other reasons, is not as intense as I'd like it to be: my writing has accompanied my journey as an instrumentalist and it's been satisfactory, in ways that are even a little difficult for me to define, especially my emotional side, as well as representing sometimes the answer to a contingent professional need . It's my intention to continue to compose, but extending it beyond guitar work because this is really what I feel the need for. I haven't followed any academic course on composition (apart from some lessons in harmony with Aldo Sacco, Felice Quaranta and analysis with Daniele Bertotto, Maestro whom I remember with great affection and gratitude) and I'm not tied to a particular compositional style. When I write I decide what I want to say and I try to find a structure and language that are responsive, according to the means at my disposal. Until today I've not moved often from writing in the tonality, although understood in its wider and free use, but I experimented with forms of serialism, polytonality, while in ambient music I gave free rein to each area of experimentation. I started to write for guitar in 1988, when I found myself almost by accident (although I don't believe at all in accidents) forced to do it and accepted the challenge. In my hotel room and on the train I wrote frantically for Valeria Moriconi, an extraordinary actress who I had the good fortune to be on stage with in Jesi with her Garcia Lorca, and so the Sette Frammenti were born.

From that year, every so often I had the thrill of composing. When I write, I try to be convincing with myself first, passing on the ideas through very strict censorship. I have to hear that the notes I feel playing really belong to me. It's a demanding journey and-I must say-even emotionally exhausting. Consistency of language, which is important for me, has to be subservient to the message. I'm not interested in knowing whether I'm "ahead" or "behind". If what I write is convincing, it's fine by me and I don't set myself limits, I'm like a painter or a poet who experiments continuously. But there is one aspect of composing that still intrigues me: when I re-read or even listen to a song of mine I'm never able to rebuild anything of the creative process, although the drafting at the time was weighted and rational: it is always as if it was another person who wrote it and I often wonder what it is that I am listening to. And afterward, I have to study my pieces always with great care, because it's as if they were not technically mine.

How do you deal with the difficult task of composing for instruments that you don't play or for an ensemble that you don't know? What's your approach to writing as a composer? Do you use your computer or do you prefer a more "traditional" approach? Do you write on score paper or do you employ other systems such as diagrams, drawings, etc.?

When I composed with electronic instruments or audio material processing - almost always with a very tight timescale imposed by events - I exclusively and pragmatically worked on getting the final result, trying various means, with great openness and freedom, as long as it was useful, ready to welcome ideas related to the nature of the instruments themselves, provided that they were consistent with the idea of the piece that I had in mind. It comes to my mind that apart from the usual magnetic tapes, I've used synthesis software and MIDI sequencers, the ARP Avatar or an old MicroMoog that I used in the 80's, plus the Roland 707 guitar synthesizer, not perfect, but interesting nevertheless. I often let the end result drive me and not vice versa so allowing the piece to grow by itself... The approach was very real but hybrid, handmade, written reports, diagrams and spaced out grids, ideas continuously being defined, experiments, yield tests. For the guitar I prefer using paper and pencil. Audio and MIDI tracks for electronics. I'm planning a piece for piano and the master keyboard is there waiting for me. As for other instruments, I will look into everything that might be useful to know. The most difficult aspect for me is to not divert from the deep, emotional impulse which kicked off the composition. This is the most important challenge, to steer ahead, knowing that an excess of melodic inventiveness, the inconsistency and superficiality in lexical thematic development (if you try it) are the traps that too easily a guitarist-composer can fall into... It's a very narrow road. The biggest work is to trim, reducing to the essential the amount of notes created, and sometimes, frankly, it is above me and it irritates me somewhat as well ... (smiles).

It seems a new small classical guitar music scene has emerged, one dedicated to innovative and contemporary repertoire, apart from you the names Elena Càsoli, Arturo Tallini, Maurizio Grandinetti, Marco Cappelli and David Tanenbaum, David Starobin, Marc Ribot and the studies of John Zorn come to mind... can we speak of it in terms of a music scene? Are there other guitarists moving along these musical paths that you know and that you could suggest?

I've known Elena from many years (we were classmates at the Chigiana) and the others through their work, and I think that - for all of them - their commitment to contemporary music is an inner need, an extension toward languages and techniques that can express things too heavy to be ignored. To me it isn't a binding professional placement in itself: there aren't any moral obligations and duties towards this music, but it's certain that it conveys strong and deep feelings, a more complex and articulated concern compared to previous music (to

83

which, however, I am deeply attached). The imperishable discourse of what music represents, whether it's a medium that, in itself, conveys nothing but itself, or whether it's a representation of "something" that always accompanies the music from his own creation, is well known. I've decided however, to lean towards the emotional, regardless of the philosophical position on what music is: music is music. And as for myself, it must be emotion and abstraction, like any art form; otherwise it has no meaning or interest in my opinion, it's only the craftsmanship of sound materials.

Speaking of innovative composers, what do you think of John Zorn, of his studies called Book of Heads and the New York downtown music scene so ready to appropriate and to re-encode any musical language, improvisation, jazz, contemporary, noise, music for cartoons?

It's a way to think the guitar with a very wide extension, indeed: a guitar that finds its meaning precisely because it's immersed in something outside itself. Very interesting, but I come back to what I have said before: an expression which collects and witnesses contemporaneity is something significant in itself and should become the habits of those involved in today's music, but it is equally permissible to make a selection and present works that, for structure and content, may go further and remain over time. An interpreter can then easily "sing the present" and select a more grounded course of action: both roads are accessible and sensible. Staying with Zorn, let's go back to today's musical world: entering a "pop" (popular, i.e. widely shared) vision of contemporary music, it's almost impossible not to get into a fusion of musical elements and so this is significant precisely because music runs concurrently with time, reinventing itself in real time. A different proposition is a distilled and structured work, perhaps intended for fewer people, but able to convey a message of a more profound and less experimental substance. Even today we remain amazed listening to works by Cage or we wonder about the meaning of Marcel Duchamp's urinal, though it is likely that, having to listen to music or in buying a work of art for our home, we would choose something that it is already inside of us, finding confirmation and reassurance in the meaning which already exists within.

You have made several monographic records with music by Carlo Mosso, Franco Margola, Claudio Mantovani, Manuel Maria Ponce and Lauro, why have you chosen these authors and their works? To whom do you feel more closely connected?

My monographic works on contemporary authors were motivated by an almost emotional bond, due to the personal knowledge of the individual composers: I felt compelled in myself, to bear witness to their work. Today I don't agree with many things that I recorded on those records, my interpretive evolution is constant, but I'm glad to have been able to record them. For example, I started working on Bruno Bettinelli after having had the good fortune to talk to the Maestro himself over the phone and hearing his ideas and concerns about the fate of contemporary music in Italy; the Maestro has since passed away, but I had within me a promise and I tried to honour it in the best way possible. The Cantico by Claudio Mantovani is a very evocative piece of work, in which I only recorded some guitar parts. While in Ponce and Apasionata, on the other hand, I paid tribute to the repertoire of my training years, especially the Authors of the 1900s which I didn't and I don't want give up. The records were recorded in different ways and at different times: for example, Mosso was done entirely at night to avoid ambient noise, but constantly struggling against my ever slowing night clock, therefore nowadays I would only accept recordings that are done in the daytime and which are well focused, with direction.

In your "contemporary Italian Authors" album of 1993 you also played Serenade for a Satellite by Bruno Maderna, this piece of 1969, written on a large manuscript with several staves not placed in a horizontal position and out of order, is a game of combinations that lets the performer have free range, making it one of the more famous examples of random music. What choices did you make in order to play this piece? Did you have in mind the musical path chosen by Claudio Ambrosini in his 1985 transcript?

The execution with the guitar solo could have been carried out structuring the material in many different ways, but I thought of something that would have been short and clear to those who would have listened to it, making the score accessible with a certain simplicity: I exposed the material in a progressive and complete manner and then proceeded to read the sections all the way back to the beginning, varying the dynamic according to the written directions: first one way and then the other. In practice, a very simple pyramidal structure: the piece ended where it had started.

I sometimes feel that in our time the history of music is flowing without a particular interest in its chronological course; in our music library concepts such as before and after, past and future become interchangeable elements. Can this not involve a risk, to an interpreter and a composer, of having a uniform vision, having a "globalization" of music?

A musician must make choices and the listener too, and even more so today. As you say, the 1900s and our times are characterized by osmosis, a kind of musical macro-metabolism always in the making, in which it is not easy to figure out where to stop if not for assonance within ourselves or because of an exegetical requirement. Making a choice is fundamental for everybody: for the listener and the composer alike. As for writing, if I may venture a comparison with the human psychological condition, we can talk about constraints and frustration or, on the contrary, the absence of boundaries and anguish by omnipotence. Once there were very precise constraints, taste, form and technique, and the composer felt the frustration of having to express everything and beyond, according to these limits, to push ahead without incomprehensible constraints for the public. Nowadays there is a sea of musical substance and the social and cultural constraints are much more lax than in the past: it's almost normal to accept osmosis, except in certain areas of natural resistance, and this causes a sort of distress from lack of boundaries, almost like an Artistic Endlessness: the feeling that everything has already been said by somebody else. The focus should be on ourselves, in my opinion, choosing to face a sort of vertical inner work, the only one that can withstand once it has become a piece of music, then eventually being able to distinguish itself, for intrinsic interest, in the global sea of supply.

Luciano Berio wrote that "the preservation of the past has also a negative meaning when it becomes a way to forget music. The listener gets an illusion of continuity that allows them to select what seems to confirm the same continuity and to censor all that seems to disturb it ". What kind of role can music and contemporary composers take in this context?

The same as in the past, but today with a much more complex task, given that the 20th century has not been single-stranded and progressive, but articulate, complex and at times extreme. Today, more than ever the listener might look into the past, and to its recognizable parts of modern music, in order to compensate the frustration he feels at the abundance and variety of what is on offer, the sense of alienation. This, indeed, may confirm even more what Berio says on the instinctive channelling that users of music do towards the "known". Their resistance, in fact, faced with the free evolution of making music, to the creative act in itself, which probably they should somehow be able to disregard from "a priori" placement. It's up to the individual listener to give himself this freedom and up to the composer to be able to defend their art, their creative freedom, making these acceptable. I am referring to the quality of the content and to the force of imposition.

How important is improvisation in your musical research? Can we talk about improvisation in a repertoire so encoded as the classic one or do we have to turn to other repertories like jazz, contemporary, etc.?

Now, for various reasons, I haven't especially developed the art of improvisation, though my nature would be extremely close to that of an improviser. By the way, I have always had jazz musicians as friends. Answering your question, however, I want to focus the discussion on a very precise framework, one that involves more closely the classical guitar; the classical-tonal improvisation, which in my honest opinion needs to be closely studied, cultivated and taken up again both for the guitar, and classical music in general. If this technique were to be revived, it would give a different meaning to the entire classic-romantic repertoire, it would open new creative and interpretative horizons, or even just give a technically logical meaning to the reading of those repertoires. This revival would complete the musical framework related to our musical instrument, which is already widely enriched by jazz, blues and more sporadically, from Renaissance-style improvisation or linked to contemporary music. The absence of an 18th-century-style improvisation is due undoubtedly to the extreme specialization, which the musicians underwent from the late 1800s onwards, as performers. Extreme specialization has become overwhelming with the development of the electro-mechanical sound reproduction: the "performer-priest" has since performed the music as if being invested of some sort of mission, which subsequently became more and more neurotic. We'll see what will develop, if this aspect interests an audience, as we've already said, always in need of confirmation, in substance. As for me, finally, although I am very fascinated by the act of improvising (which I cultivate, privately and in my own way), I note that the execution and composition aspects have probably filled my whole world connected to my six strings.

In 1968 Derek Bailey asked Steve Lacy to define the difference between improvisation and composition in 15 seconds. The reply was " In 15 seconds the difference between composition and improvisation is that in composition you have all the time to decide what to say in 15 seconds, while in improvisation you have 15 seconds.". Was Lacy's answer too ironic or does it relate to the truth?

It's just like that. The better and cleverer the improviser is the better he can in 15 seconds offer a meaningful and structured discourse, even if, in this extreme case, in a microscopic size. The composer has the advantage of being able to think for six months ... Geste vs construction: they are both the result of expertise and extensive sedimentation.

What is the role of error in your musical vision? By error I mean an erroneous procedure, an irregularity in the normal operation of a mechanism, a discontinuity on an otherwise uniform surface that can lead to new developments and unexpected surprises...

If we talk about composition, if the error is surprise, a diversion of a stream, a signal of an underlying disorder that needs to be expressed, an involuntary sneer to the rules, it's welcome: it will always be a source of construction, a small shoot of something else to come. After all, we're going back to what we said earlier: error ... for whom? To confirm what and why? As in people's lives crises are sometimes the only opportunities for change, in composition the error-deviation may have the same function. Speaking instead as a performer, the error is a sign of my humanity, surely, from my point of view, it disrupts the flow a bit, creating a crack in the building and it hurts my ideal of continuous speech. But I must quickly accept to have fallen into my imperfect dimension, focusing then on the many things I want to say, that is on the authentic essence of playing.

How do you view the current crisis of the music industry, with the transition from digital media to mp3 downloads and this all new scenario? This whole passive tendency to be updated and having large quantities of MP3s that can hardly be listened to carefully, does that not involve the risk of neglecting the real assimilation of ideas and creative processes?

The excess of the supply, which feeds a superficial and uncontrollable bulimia, has become a serious problem. We moved from being bloodthirsty for 78/33 rpm records freshly released ...to that of being drowned, as far as the new generations are concerned, in a sea of non-discernment. Anyone can record, without selection, and everybody can acquire. While the great supply on offer and the ease of access to music apparently encourages cultural enrichment, on the other hand it is drained of strength if not dealt with carefully, sparingly, in the presence of a guide to develop the critical skills for choosing, and this is the real problem. We go back, basically, to what we were saying before regarding the composers: they also are often victims of an excess of input. As for the discography in mp3, I have the soul of a lover of old Hi-Fi and of beautiful recordings (including the equipment they require). I feel quite disheartened and I understand that to a kid today to spend time to understand if a recording was performed with the "ortf" technique or another, by this or that capsule, is almost ridiculous. And I understand that being able to listen to them (as I do with dozens of mp3's) in order to be up to date is a tremendous benefit ... but I am afraid that something big and important has been lost: a love of quality, uniqueness, slowness. Maybe I'm getting old ... Maybe there is a place for everything, and I welcome the large amount of free music, but if we also preserve firmly the little amount of music at a price ...

Can you suggest five records that are indispensable for you, to always carry with you, the classic five records to take to a desert island. What kind of music do you listen to?

As for the music I listen to, I answered that earlier. In the classical world, it's very difficult to answer. I would say, without having to specify each issue and knowing that within half an hour I might rectify the choice ... the Chopin Etudes op. 10 and 25 by Pollini, Verklärte Nacht and Pierrot by Schoeberg, The Sacred and the Symphony for wind instruments by Stravinsky of 1920, a Cantata by Bach and Sonatas (and here I would find it hard to choose just one), the K550 of Mozart (But I would choose at least three ...) and the Requiem; the Mottetti by Costanzo Festa or Monteverdi's Vespers. I mean ... it is a very wide choice: a back up question? (smiles)

What are your five essential scores?

Another big question, and now we are obviously talking about the guitar. I would say Quatre Pieces Breves, the 998, Nocturnal, Homenaje and a chromatic fantasy by Dowland. Ah... Takemitsu In the twilight. But in half an hour I could reconsider... (laughs)

What advice would you give to those who, after years of study, have decided to start a career as a musician?

To believe deeply and work hard with a great teacher, and evaluate themselves and allow others to evaluate them, thinking exactly what kind of figure within music and the guitar world you want to become. Always make sure to adhere to their true nature and not to be attracted by other things, changing pointlessly. I must say, I was not always capable of doing that.

Who would you like to play with and who would you like to play? What are your next projects? What are you working on now?

I have no idea of what kind of partner I would prefer, definitely a musician who enriches me and shares the interpretation at a deep-level and in tune with me, I'd be grateful. I wouldn't want a confrontational relationship, because the ensemble in music is also the sublimation of an act of love, or at least a deep sharing of the senses.
Currently I would like to revisit some of my past work in order to give completeness and usability to the music and then I would like to create some

89

short pieces for guitar different from previous ones, something that says more, and differently. What I would really like, though, it is to write for other instruments: I have in mind to write something for the piano, for example: I'd like to work on that... or a concerto for guitar, but such work is so time-consuming and I frankly, find it hard to make my life and the role of a performer compatible with that of somebody who writes music, these activities take a long time and a mental effort which is entirely different. It's not easy.

We leave you with one last question ... which is actually more of an afterthought: Luigi Nono said "Other thoughts, other noises, other sounds, other ideas. When people listen, they often try to find themselves in others; find their own system, mechanisms, rationalism, in the other. And this is a wholly conservative violence.[39]"... now ... is experimenting free from the burden of having to remember?

To hear echoes of ourselves in the other is reassuring and human. Accepting the novelty and the breaking up of that known order is vital and innovative. Experimentation is looking inside ourselves with different eyes, more candid and open to the new, the unexpected, without preconceived notions: it isn't the denial of memory (if for memory we mean the vast sedimentation largely unconscious that lives within us), but a different use of it, less codified, less obvious. It's like writing "back soon!" with ever shifting letters, horizontal, dynamic, at the door of codifications, so to speak ... no? It's trying to propose and hear a different response to inner contents different from the past. Even Mozart experimented and he went a little further (for example in instrumentation), but to our ears his music seems to be a perfect and an untouchable monument made of bricks of known matter: at the time, though, maybe someone did not agree with everything... Even Stravinsky was booed after the premier of The Sacred and that piece, is now considered a classic, it still keeps us glued to the chair. And then it all depends on the context: in the past the linguistic-formal possibilities were very well defined and experimentation was represented by small strides, by lexical or formal developments which, received at first with surprise and sometimes disappointment, would then have made history. Today, as we said, the echo of the music explosion of the last 150 years (starting from Wagner, Liszt and Debussy) still hits us and is not completely metabolized and the opportunity to hear today "absolutely everything and now" unheard of until a few years ago, makes choosing at minimum complicated. When dealing with experimentation, basically in the cultured world, the vastness of opportunity requires even more trimming work, a search of an essence, of an inner

---

39   Luigi Nono, La Nostalgia del Futuro, Il Saggiatore, 2007, pag.243

enlightenment of intent, to get what the experimentation (albeit self-referential and misunderstood) should always achieve; a real step forward for those who express it, that for those who observe; something that somewhere will stay "stuck", multiplying then in turn for germination, independently. In this sense it would undermine that conservatism inherent in people who would like to hear the echo of themselves in the expressions of others, as we were saying earlier. We could consider the electronic music of the 60s and the use that the Weather Report made of it, for example, in "I Sing The Body Electric" in 1971/1972 : I don't think the first people that experimented with the magnetic tape, run in a loop or on unstable and primitive valves synthesizers, imagined that those sounds, bizarre but suggestive, would be heard on a pop music stage, but it happened, even if the pop group was not what we could call mainstream, but without a doubt accomplished and not afraid of trying. We are primordial animals and at the same time sophisticated and complex: we must choose what to say, how and to whom, to respect the need for reassuring sedimentation and how forward to run in the research. That's what makes us different and unique.

Optimization for translation: Dores Causetti

English translation by Elisabeth Lucy Gabbiano

HANS JÜRGEN GERUNG

Hans-Jürgen Gerung, studied physics from 1983 to 1984 at the University of Technology of Munich, changed in 1984 to the Leopold Mozart Conservatorium in Augsburg and studied guitar with Franz Mayr-Musiol and trumpet with Wolfgang Siegert. The study ended in 1988 followed by an even longer, more intense period of study focused on the lute music of Johann Sebastian Bach; aim was the development of a suitable guitar instrument for the faithful representation of these works on a modern sound-tool.

After numerous attempts a complete edition of Bach's works BWV 995 till BWV 1000 and BWV 1006a arranged for 10-string guitar of the novel bass register tuning: G; F; C; D; E, A; d, g, b, e' for which the Johann-Sebastian-Bach-Institut-Göttingen pronounced their respect. In the years from 1994 to 1998 his studies followed the interpretation of contemporary music with Prof. Christoph Jäggin (Switzerland). Through his mediation Gerung began studying composition as a student of Hans Ulrich Lehmann (Switzerland) In 1999 he presented himself to M° Sylvano Bussotti and remained his student until 2005. In the summer of 1999, Sylvano Bussotti wrote for Gerung, the piece **Ermafrodito** for guitar solo and in that same year it came within the scope of an advance presentation on the occasion of a conference in the Conservatorio Luigi Cherubini in Florence. In 2002 Luca Veggetti choreographed the score and together with the Balletto Teatro di Torino it premiered in the Teatro Carignano on the 10th of May, in Turin.

An international concert activity led among other things to cooperation with artists like Arturo Tamayo and the Orchestre Philharmonique de Luxembourg, with the singers Sarah Leonhard, Ian Caley and Daniel Gloger, with the ensemble cantissimo under Markus Utz, the Schola Romana Ensemble and the Stadler Quartett. Premieres of his works were to be heard among others at the Contemporanea di Udine, at the ECLAT Festival Stuttgart or at the Festival Internacional de Música Clássica Contamporánea de Lima.

In 2006 Gerung founded the International Festival Forum für Neue Music – Oberstdorf.

http://www.edition-gerung.de/

The first question is always the classic one: how does it start your love and interest for classic guitar?

My first encounter with the guitar came early, when I was just 6 or 7. My father loved it very much and I remember every time we had guests he would start playing and singing. Therefore I had a strong experience in what it means to make music. And so, my father became my first guitar teacher.

What instruments do you play or have you played? I know you play the ten strings classical guitar too ...

Yes that's true; I also own two 10-string guitars. The first one, constructed in 1990, by the Spanish luthier Pedro Gonzalez (Pamplona) I use nearly exclusively for contemporary and experimental music. The second, built in 1992 by the German Luthier Andeas Dill (Weingarten) has a declining tuning in bass-register and it is a perfect fit for baroque lute-music, especially for Bach.
Further I own a beautiful French lute (9-course), constructed in 1974 by the famous Dieter Hense; a Liuto-forte (10-string), constructed in 1998 by Prof. Günther Mark (Bad Rodach) and I use two 6-string classical guitars: the first was made in 1982 by Erwin von Grüner (Baiersdorf) and the second was created in 1936 by Richard Wolfram (Markneukirchen). Mentionable also a beautiful Eastman Archtop Jazz-guitar created in 2007.
But I play also contemporary oriental music. For study reasons inter alia I've transcribed all the compositions from the great Munir Bashir into modern notation-scripture. Actually a mission impossible as the density of the oriental maqâm improvisations with their micro tonality is incompatible with verbatim reporting. For this purpose I use an 'Ûd (6-course), constructed 2006 by the Syrian luthier Ahmed Ajaj from Damascus and an Iraqi 'Ûd, (7-course), made by Matthias Wagner in 2009 in Badenweiler.
Last but not least I play the piano and the trumpet.

What was your musical training, with which teachers have you studied and what impression they left in your music?

My musical education began on the trumpet, the instrument I love most after the guitar, and later on I studied this marvelous instrument together with the guitar. Breath control is such an important technique in the world of brass instruments and it makes you feel with the whole body how a musical phrase works. So this helped me a lot in creating my personal art of playing the guitar for my practice was never only technically oriented. I always kept the line in my mind. My trumpet Teacher was Prof. Wolfgang Siegert, Solo trumpet player at the Theater. Fortunately my professor at the Leopold Mozart Conservatory of Augsburg, Franz Mayr-Musiol had the same approach for playing the guitar, because his main profession was playing the double bass in several orchestras (amongst others at the Münchener Rundfunkorchester)! So also for him playing the guitar means to place the instrument into the service of the big picture that we call making music.

I know that you have studied with Sylvano Bussotti ... how it was to study with him?

The impact of Bussotti was enormous, especially his appreciation of arts. He's not only one of the greatest composers of the 20th century; he's also an extraordinary teacher. He has the rare gift to explain complex correlations in a pretty simple way (without banalizing them). Sometimes he could cut through the Gordian knot with a single word. Extraordinary! But being the student of such a charismatic personality implies the threat becoming the master's epigone. I'd like to say that the greatest effort during my time with M° Bussotti (and the biggest profit for myself) was manifesting myself as an independent artist. And he helped a lot to peak out.

Once, during an interrogation, I explained my score studies (at that time I worked intensively on the *Six Bagatelles for string quartet* by Anton Webern), Bussotti raised concerns not to exaggerate these studies:

"It's undoubtedly necessary to know what was and were we come from but remember, **every** hour of your life that you are working with the arts from others you do not push on your own! For this you have to weigh your worthy time; your main challenge is to create **art** not to study others!"

You have played Ermafrodito, one of his most famous guitar's score in world premiere in 2000, can you explain us this passage? I have seen the score and ... it's like a picture ... a piece of art...

Yes, in 1999 I decided to commission a new guitar solo piece by M° Bussotti and he agreed immediately, and he wrote "*Ermafrodito, fantasia mitologica per chitarra*" and beyond that he applied a notation on the score 'commissioned by Hans-Jürgen Gerung for his interpretation only'. Giving me the exclusive rights to be for about 10 years the only one playing that score was a great honor for me. I think if you want to play *Ermafrodito* (or lots of other scores) you should know some important things beforehand.

1st Bussotti's art often is embedded in Greek mythology. Not only as music's concerned also his poetry (for example the poem '*efebo, Febo lingua e abbronzatura*'), his numerous paintings that he did during his activities as art director, costume designer, regisseur etc. are filled with analogies. For this you have to be sure about Greeks aesthetics.

94

2nd Bussotti's music is (like Mozart's) written for stage! It's always dramatic in a scenic sense; even if the score is solo instrumental. For this you have to create a fictitious stage setting in your mind's eye at every phrase you play: you have to animate all the protagonists that you find in the piece.

3rd Bussotti's music has always to do with himself, regardless of persons, things, scenes (even long ago), for this you have to know a lot about his biography, or better you should talk to him as often as possible about the score you'd like to realize.

Ermafrodito arrived three weeks before an upcoming working session at Florence (**GAMO** = gruppo aperto di musica oggi) in late 1999 summer. Though we met there for composing together I was pretty sure that Bussotti would expect me to play the entire piece … and so it was! Fortunately I worked like a madman to get familiar with the score. At Florence I was confronted with the fact that Bussotti had already arranged a conference at the concert hall at the Conservatory Luigi Cherubini for an off-the-record presentation of *Ermafrodito*. The world première indeed was in May 2002 at the Teatro Carignano at Turin (together with the choreographer Luca Veggetti and Loredana Furno's dance company.)

I have seen the score... It's like a picture...

You said 'it's like a picture …' No, I wouldn't say so. Because the graphical notation, the pictography (often used in Bussotti's scores) is not applied in the entire piece. Bussotti uses rather let's say, dendritical notation. This kind of notation is place-saving and also very efficient. The musical impact indeed is a greater freedom of rhythmical expression as you have to play the notated notes in the determinate space of time but how you organize the length of each note is fairly free. Compared this with Bussotti's guitar piece *Ultima rara* written in 'millenocecensessantanove' for Siegfried Behrend,

Ermafrodito is more virtuosic and filled with poetical phrases, but I'd say it's less vanguard. *Ultima rara* uses a really dense score (one step ahead and Bussotti would have used the pictography by force to realize his musical thoughts. Look at his quintet *Rara eco sireologico*; there you'll find lots of phrases used in *Ultima rara*… and there you find also a large pictographical aria. *Ermafrodito* however picks some of the thoughts of these two early scores (especially in the **5th** movement "*Farinello"*) but the greatest deal of the score is to complete new material that you won't find neither in *Ultima rara*, nor in *Rara eco sireologico*, neither in the guitar score form *Nuovo Scenario a Lorenzaccio*, nor in *Circo minore.*

95

I'd like to say, **Ermafrodito** is somewhat a "pocket opera" for one guitar player and the theme is M° Bussotti on a walk through his life and through his garden in Genazzano, nearby Rome, it consist in seven movements:

1st movement: *E I fiori*: we enter the RARA-gate to his Villa and the scene of an overwhelming floridity interfused by glistening sunlight takes place.
2nd movement: *chitarronata*: gay-scene with some dancing and drinking[40] suddenly the thoughts went forty years back…
3rd movement: *dôme épais:* the scene changes. We see the young author in the audience of an opera; given is Léo Delibes, Lakmé: the flower Duet "Dôme épais".
4th movement: *Upupa*: suddenly the cry of the hoopoe is hearable and brings us back in the garden. The Wiedehopf, as we call him in Germany, was a permanent guest in Bussotti's garden as he told me often. With courageous steps we walk the line… but we loose in thoughts.
5th movement: *Farinello*: again an opera scene, Carlo Broschi detto *Il Farinello* is jumping in the picture, singing nerve-racking arias.
6th movement: *foto di me, fanciullo*: again drifting in the past, a picture appears with an young artist; the whole scene in a camera oscura.
7th movement: *statua*: immortal things appear, not just marble statues but also great Italian poetry. Guarini recites his famous poetry "*Lumi, miei cari lumi, che lampeggiate…*". And meanwhile the words reach Bussotti's ear he remembers an old melody from the Sicilian Renaissance Composer Gio. Pietro Flaccomini[41], and, still walking in the garden, he takes the melody, changes it, and, forceful, together with the melody he manipulates the Guarini Text and the recreation is the genial finale:

XXIII (because he finished the score on July 23) **lumimiei cari**
q'unsíveloceguardo
mirafugge Ch'oggetto mai   con
                    non verrete più   **cotanto vostro sia**
                              giustodesío   **quanto sonio**

Finally I'd like to highlight that Bussotti wrote **Ermafrodito** for my 10-string guitar (and its particular tuning) and only this instrument allows the necessary full sound and the sustain of the bass, basically in the 3rd movement.

---

40   may be similar to efebo, Febo lingua e abbronzatura cf. 'Non fare il minimo rumore' – Edizione del Girasole pag. 53

41   cf. Musiche Rinascimentale Siciliane (MRS) Bd. VI, Nr. XXIII.

Berio in his essay "A remembrance to the future," wrote: ".. A pianist who is a specialist about classical and romantic repertoire, and plays Beethoven and Chopin without knowing the music of the twentieth century, is also off as a pianist who is specialist about contemporary music and plays with hands and mind that have never been crossed in depth by Beethoven and Chopin". You play both traditional classical and contemporary repertoire ... do you recognize yourself in these words?

Playing contemporary music for me is normal, who else but we living artists should play it? Sure, sometimes the approach in solving problems during the realization of a contemporary score might be helpful for finding solutions in old scores but that is not the reason I'm playing the music of our times.
I always found it helpful to converge to a score (irrespective whether it's old or new) with all my knowledge, respect and heart and then, after I've done all my duties, I'll give my judgment. And sometimes the upshot was the decision not to perform the piece... after all the work I did! I think the question is not the *legitimacy* of the contemporary music but how to train the musical instinct to decide whether the new piece before you has extraordinary qualities or whether it's just new. There are no more rules. Anything goes and for this reason it has become so complicated.

I try to ask you a little bit provocative question about music in general, not just about contemporary or avant-garde. Frank Zappa in his autobiography he wrote: "If John Cage, for example, said, now I put a contact microphone on the throat, then I drink carrot juice and this will be my composition", then his gargling would qualify as a COMPOSITION, because he applied a frame, declaring it as such. "Take it or leave it, now I want this to be music." It's really good this statement to define a genre of music, just say this is classical music, this is contemporary and it's done? It still makes sense to speak about "genre"?

The classifications are very important. Not for us musicians of course, but for anybody else. Important for the music-market-industry, for concert-presenters, for the consumers, for the mass-medias, for the *Feuilletons, for the critic, for the postman for its wife and the Holy Ghost.*
Zappa by the way in his provoking statement referred to Cage's sentence 'If you open a door and celebrate it, it's art' so *celebrating* is the keyword. For Zappa Cage was extraordinarily important and Steve Lake wrote in his obit: "[...] anybody who's really interested in Zappa's music should at last know something about Edgard Varese, Strawinsky, Charles Ives, Schönberg, Webern, Cage, Boulez, Ligeti, Penderecki und Toru Takemitsu [...]"[42]

One of the things that I can honestly say about guitar is its ability and capacity to change its shape as a musical medium over the centuries and between the various musical and social forms, I think this incredible ability is due to several factors not least the fact that it can be realized both in industrial and artigianal forms, and the fact that we can choose between classical, acoustic and electric types suitable for different musical and social cultures. You have followed a very personal path inside the guitar, how did you develop this path and how are you developing it?

Let me say two words to the spread of the guitar and to the overwhelming estimation that this instrument has all over the world.

You mentioned Theodor W. Adorno and the Frankfurter School. The *"Kritische Theorie"* from Adorno and Horkheimer often is accused being in plain truth a romantic, intellectual and Neo-Marxian-protest against Western Way of Life. If the social-philosophers from the Frankfurt really would have been just angry because the youngsters of the 68-revolt obviously preferred the Rolling Stones and the Beatnik-Authors more than for example the second school of Vienna or the postmodern intellectual authors – if it really would have been like this, the guitar, as the protest-symbol itself, indeed would have contributed a big deal in crushing down this philosophical drift from Frankfurt ;).

You are right, the guitar is loved so much by so many and musicians and aficionados. But let's take a closer look at the appreciation that it really gets:

Search with Google: found	"Musikwissenschaft und Gitarre"	=>	**4**	matches
Search with Google: found	"Musikwissenschaft und Violin"	=>	**1.600**	matches
Search with Google: found	"Musikwissenschaft und Klavier"	=>	**39.900**	matches
Search with Google: found	"Urtextausgabe für Gitarre"	=>	**0**	matches
Search with Google: found	"Urtextausgabe für Violine"	=>	**945**	matches
Search with Google: found	"Urtextausgabe für Klavier"	=>	**2.850**	matches

---

If you insert 'Faksimile-Ausgabe für...' instead 'Urtextausgabe' you'll get quite analog results and if you do some research by browsing the pages of the most renowned and important music-publishing-houses for academic or critical guitar-music-editions you could remain disappointed.

Let's take for example the *Nocturnal after John Dowland op. 70* by Benjamin Britten. Till today the only legal original edition is the one from FABER ff MUSIC released in 1964/65. You'll not find a new critical edition including also the facsimile!

Let's search for example just for the famous *Sonata for Cello and Piano, op. 65.* Immediately you'll find (among various other things) the following:

Benjamin Britten and Chamber Music: Sonata for Cello and Piano, Op. 65: I. Historical Background And Perspectives II. Analysis of The Sonata In C, Op. 65 (Englisch) Taschenbuch – 25. Oktober 2012

Or, relating *Peter Grimes*:

The Making of Peter Grimes. Volume I: Facsimile of Benjamin Britten's Compositional Draft.

Volume II: Notes and Commentaries: Paul Banks, Philip Brett, Benjamin Britten, Eric Crozier, Donald Mitchell, Peter Pears, Philip Reed, Rosamund Strode. Edited by Paul Banks. Cambridge, 1996. Large 4°, 2 vols, 241 facs, 251 pp. Color facsimile issued for the 50th anniversary of the 1st *production. Conceived in California in 1941, Britten and the tenor Peter Pears made a number of draft scenarios while they waited for passage to England; after their return, Montagu Slater was asked to write the libretto. The compositional draft, begun in early 1944, is the single most important document in the creation of the work, showing the composer wrestling with text and music, and gradually fashioning the opera into its final version. Linen. $250 [item no.7177]*

and so on...

But maybe the *Nocturnal after John Dowland* is less important than the earlier (in 1960) written *Sonata for Cello and Piano* ;)

Years ago I found the following:

December 2009/February 2010 / Volume 17, Number 2

No Nocturnal?! *by Frank Wallace in:* **BCGS Artist Series, January 31, 2010** (pag. 4)

[...] Recently I received a call from famed Greek guitarist Eleftheria Kotzia. We discussed the possibility of her coming to Boston for a concert and I told her about Festival 21. I asked if she does much contemporary music. Would a full program of new works be of interest to her? Her response, "Well it depends on what you call 'contemporary'"? I explained that I am interested in presenting

99

performers who are actively commissioning works or writing their own music such as Dusan Bogdanovic, Atanas Ourkouzounov, Ernesto García de León, Gyan Riley and Andrew McKenna Lee. She said Stephen Dodgson, Carlo Domeniconi and others have written pieces for her, but she is mostly used to presenters telling her, "Please don't play the Nocturnal!" [by Benjamin Britten] I nearly fainted. Now I know we live in an extraordinarily conservative age and we rarely see the Nocturnal programmed. I have heard younger players gasp when I say that I think it is one of the most important and wonderful pieces ever written for guitar. But how can a presenter tell a great performer not to play an unquestioned masterpiece. Please don't show the Mona Lisa. Please don't play the Rite of Spring. What kind of absurd self-censorship is this? What kind of intellectual vacuum is being created and supported by guitar sponsors? This is sacrilege! [...]
wallacecomposer@gmail.com.

But let's turn to the guitar again. I assert that this marvelous instrument enjoys a great popularity but among the European intellectual circles I miss the appropriate appreciation. I feel it sometimes even still today – the resentful climate against the guitar. The guitar is *not always* considered being the ancestor from the noble Spanish Vihuela or being the honest contemporary advocate of the baroque Lute-compositions. The guitar is *not always* considered being the instrument that has fascinated Benjamin Britten and William Walton, Luciano Berio and Sylvano Bussotti and thousands of other great composers.

first dialogue:
Young guy to Aunt Elisabeth: "Auntie I'm studying the guitar!"
Aunt Elisabeth: "OK?" (eyebrows lifted)
second dialogue:
Young guy to Aunt Elisabeth: "Auntie, I've changed program, I'm studying the violin actually!"
Aunt Elisabeth: "WOW!" (grin like a Cheshire-cat).
first statement:
The guitar is the nasty thing in the hands from Jimi Hendrix playing the *The Star Spangled Banner* or *Purple Haze...* non-excusable!
second statement:
And still prejudice against the E-guitar, it's the evil itself! The big threat... and if we consider it an instrument at all so in any case less artificial than the classical guitar.
Crossover-projects between composers and instrumentalists out of various musical areas in Europe are still scarcely existent. This projects should become

obligatory subjects of study and should get an adequate financially support. A marvelous example from the United States is the album Guitar-Passions by Sharon Isbin & Friends.

Relating myself and the guitar:
I never considered myself being a guitarist though I love this instrument so much. In my self-conception I'm a composer and maybe because of this I had a different approach to all the instruments I have ever used.
I'm a sound- (and noise) prospector and while searching the *real-existing-pendant-sound* that fits exactly to the one I hear inside I have to do lots or experiments. These experiments are sometimes even unscrupulous (or let's say nonacademic) as far as traditional techniques are concerned, respective the common tunings, string material, number of strings and so on.
In these very important phases of searching and creating new sounds I try to become acquainted to the instrument in a totally new manner, maybe like children would do. This is extremely exhausting because I have to fade out everything I know and I have to keep it in mind at the same time.
Scarcely a composer will find an instrument that offers a cosmos as manifold as the guitar does.

Well I like to play both electric and classical guitars... you know... we electric bad guys love our dirty reputation. Do you think that the guitar, with its presence of very personal musicians at every musical level and genre would be a possible alternative to the distinction between high culture and popular culture and the affirmation of Schoenberg " if it is art, it is not for all, and if it is for all, it is not art."?

This would be a challenge too big for the guitar (and its players) and unfair as well. The overcoming of the class-distinction between the two camps high-culture and pop-culture will succeed if two things proceed:

1st: **The commitment in every moment to the music that I consume.**
Different life-styles established inter alia different kinds of music and therefore there is the risk that it's judged by the recipient just according to the aspect of whether it's socially correct (or helpful) or not. Who is totally free from this? Do I like what I consume or does the consumed item just belong to my habitués?
While watching the autumnal sheets falling, swayed by the wind, you're listening to the *string quartet bagatelles* from Anton Webern, it fits perfectly and you feel an infinite love for this music in this very moment... same day, later in the evening on the way to a party with friends, you're listening (and singing) *Seven Nation Army* by Jack White, you feel a deep love for this song in this

moment and you won't here anything else but this. So tell me why should be one of these compositions more precious than the other? Didn't both of them give you the deep awareness of life?

2ⁿᵈ: The capacity to preserve the childlike curiosity that genuine is laid in men.

Curiosity is the engine that produces happiness. If you're curious you might find something unexpected, something unknown or something that you do not understand yet ... and maybe it makes you uneasy and you start thinking ...

Do you know that curiosity is a swear word in German language, what nonsense!

I do not agree with Schönberg. If it's true that something that is for all is not art and if it's true that something that is for few we would posit the following: the artistic value is reciprocally proportional to its public appreciation. Supposing this is true it would mean that the less a creation is appreciated the more it matters. At the extreme, if I set its appreciation to zero, the artificial significance has reached its peak and viceversa. In fact there is no scale or measurement unit to count the worth of a creation. If the act of creating ennobles the very moment and gives a particular and extraordinary feeling to the creator it becomes precious for him in any sense and it has to be embraced with respect. This is the deeper sense behind Joseph Beuys sentence 'Jeder Mensch ist ein Künstler'[43]

We should not confuse between art and culture.

What does improvisation mean for your music research? Do you think it's possible to talk about improvisation for classical music or we have to turn to other repertories like jazz, contemporary music, etc.?

Improvisation is (and was) an important field of the music and every now and then I like doing it. The great denotation during the baroque-period and earlier was remarkable (remember the improvisation-meetings between Johann Sebastian Bach and Silvius Leopold Weiss) but unfortunately it lost more and more significance. In the world of Rock and Pop and Jazz music it's still alive but the results seem somewhat like interchangeable goods. Few instruments play on determinate scales and chord-patterns and so we see the results. If we understand improvisation as *creare musica al improvviso* we should liberate our music from all determinate systems. This could create something really new and this would ennoble these new and sudden creations as compositions born from a mastermind not born out of the fingers. But that is a great array, also our dodecaphonic system is a determinate one... isn't it?

---

43   Joseph *Beuys* in November 1985 in the Münchner Kammerspielen.

What's the role of the "error" in your musical vision? For "error" I mean an incorrect procedure, an irregularity in the normal operation of a mechanism, a discontinuity on an otherwise uniform surface that can lead to new developments and unexpected surprises ..

The horrifying error. I consider him being the Angelus. It always gave my scores the turn to a better level, even to its best.

Sometimes ago Elena Càsoli said to me "I improvise the interpretation of what you call encoded. Scored music requires an ethic of respect, attention, closeness and knowledge of its aesthetics, looking at the sign left by the author. But it's a moving, alive, elusive, intangible subject, which awaits the encounter with an interpretative act. And this meeting, in concert, has a space for improvisation, every evening new and different" What do you think about these words?

I agree. We instrumentalists are re-constructive artists. We have to finish the competition and with our spirit we have to awaken it every time new.

If you listen to a different interpretation of a score you already played and you want to perform this again do you keep it in mind listening or do you prefer to proceed in complete independence?

The second one.

If you had to choose, who is your favorite composer to play?

John Sebastian Bach.

I try to risk a reckless question. Bach composed sometimes without specifying instrumentation... maybe... maybe was he not interested in the "Sound of Music"? I mean maybe does the music in this case is hidden in a scheme, a structure capable of several realizations, several possible and different sounds? And the moment when the music reveals its true nature is contained in the exercise of its variations? Bach at this point would have composed something like jazz standards or pre Cage scores?

No I don't think so – Bach was pragmatist and composing without a specified instrumentation was common in his time, but he loved also the GEMATRIA[44,]

103

the cipher-mysticism that was pretty famous in baroque epoch. His works are full of cabalistic hints … too complicated to explain here. Anyway Bach was Bach, incommensurable.

I have, sometimes, the feeling that in our times music's history flows without a particular interest in its chronological course, in our discotheque before and after, past and future become interchangeable elements, shall this be a risk of a uniform vision for an interpreter and a composer? The risk of a musical "globalization"?

Yes it is, and what I mentioned above when you asked me what improvisation means for me applies here as well. The beats, the whole rhythm, the instrumental canon, the scales the lyrics, all seems more and more synchronized all over the world. Making music, or better making new music (and that should be our goal) means really very very strong efforts. Making music is always an extensive search, a search also to an own an individual language. By the way, it does not mean the search for commercial success.

Let's talk about marketing. How much do you think it's important for a modern musician? I mean: how much is crucial to be good promoters of themselves and their works in music today?

The knowledge in marketing is not only important for the modern musician – it was important all the time. After the birth of your artwork you have to look after it – help him to survive. There will never be one (no agent, no manager, no producer) that defends your art with such an enormous effort better than you. So your job is twofold: creating arts and defending arts. Too much for one life and for this we need helpful organizations that we can trust in. That's difficult because we all are a bit egomaniacal and egomaniacs scarcely affiliate.

What do you think about the discographic market crisis, with the transition to digital downloading in mp3 and all this new scenario?

There is a crisis but there is also some exaggeration. Sure, the Teens don't buy a lot of CDs, for the moment; they use Spotyfi and other suppliers. But I do not agree that they are lost for the market, or even ignorant. They are interested and later on they'll have the desire to own things like compacts or disks. The mass-media influence is enormous and to find your path is more difficult than it was. But the young consumers are getting orientated and I'm convinced we would

---

44   vgl. Helga Thoene in: Coethener Bach – Heft 6, 1994, pag. 15 ff

have acted like they do now. Sure, sometimes we find the user-opinion 'everything belongs to everybody', this we have to explain; and when explained it never happened that I faced incomprehension. Crisis means always also new chance.

Your musical career has been going on for several years, how have you seen the musical world changing around you? Do you note differences between the students you teach and you taught? How new technologies (new musical instruments, midi, social networks, forums) have influenced your choices and your musical form? How?

Teaching today is different than it was. I have to react immediately on various questions that students have and that occurred while watching videos in the web. Sure not all the influences are welcome but a great many are. I feel it healthy for me, it keeps me up to date. (laughs)

Which composer (or which historical movement) do you think is easiest for the non-musician listener to appreciate? Do you think they enjoy pieces that are more technically difficult or just more "flashy"?

I'd say the romantic period could be a somewhat easy door to open. This period offers an enormous amount of different music that still has strong connections to our times (apart form iPhone 6 and brave new world): it's talking about love and tragedy, about outrage and success, it's virtuous and flashy as well.

Please tell us five essential records, to have always with you - the classic five discs for the desert island ...

Carlo Gesualdo da Venosa: Responsoria, 2013   => collegium vocale, Gent,

Johann Sebastian Bach: Johannes Passion 1987   => Philippe Herreweghe,

Munir Bashir: IRAK – l'art du ûd 1971   => Munir Bashir,

Frank Zappa: The yellow shark, 1992/93   => Ensemble modern,

Hans-Jürgen Gerung: aus meinem Leben 2014   => Sampler,

What are your five favorite scores?

John Cage: => Sonatas and Interludes for prepared piano (1946-48), Ed.
Peters
Sylvano Bussotti: => ΦΑΙΔΡΑ / HELIOGABALUS (1975-81), Ricordi
Johann Sebastian Bach: => Aufs Lautenwerck, edition-gerung
György Ligeti: => Requiem (1963-65), Ed. Peters
Hans-Jürgen Gerung: => RITUS-Missa da Requiem (2002-03), edition-
gerung

With whom would you like to play? What kind of music do you listen to usually?

I'd like to jam with Naseer Shamma, Nigel North and Sting.
Usually I listen to chamber music, basically string quartets but also choir music, Dowland songs (I can't get enough of it) and of course my own music.

Your next projects?

new compositions and upcoming registrations:

piano cycles in 5 movements for the Japanese Pianist Mai Fukasawa, http://www.maifukasawa.com/english.html

music and poetry – collaboration with the Syrian Author Fouad El-Auwad. http://www.lyrik-salon.de/FOUAD-DEUTSCH/person.htm

When we will see you playing in Italy?

I'd really like to do a concert in Naples. I prepared a very interesting program that has a closer relation to this town because there are several pieces from the Neapolitan composers Luigi Esposito and Carlo Gesualdo da Venosa.

►Luigi Esposito, (*1962)
=> **nell'aria un madrigale** (written for H.J. Gerung)
▪ for guitar

►Hans-Jürgen Gerung (*1960)
=> **La Commedia dell'arte**
▪ for 10string guitar

►Carlo Gesualdo da Venosa (*1566-1613)
=> **Gagliarda del Principe**

• arranged for Renaissance lute by H.-J. Gerung

►Luigi Esposito:
=> **wanted** (written for H.J. Gerung)
• for guitar and electric guitar

►Sylvano Bussotti, (*1931)
=> **Ermafrodito** (written for H.J. Gerung)
• for 10string guitar

►Carlo Gesualdo da Venosa (*1566-1613)
=> **Canzon del Principe**
• arranged for Renaissance lute by H.-J. Gerung

►Luigi Esposito:
=> **Roseo velato** (written for H.J. Gerung)
• for guitar

But 'till now I have not found a festival organizer who was interested; maybe the year 2016 the 450th anniversary of Carlo Gesualdo offers a possibility, we will see .

SCOTT JOHNSON

Composer Scott Johnson has been a pioneering voice in the new relationship being forged between the classical tradition and the popular culture that surrounds it. An early advocate of using rock instruments and technology in scored composition, he has appeared as a virtuosic electric guitarist in many of his pieces. His early work introduced the idea of instrumental writing based on sampled speech, and later works continue to develop his musical gene-splicing, blending complex and intertwined chamber music with a rock band's hall-filling wall of sound.
Underneath the music lies a basic insight: the evolution of classical composition has always been shaped by its environments, and living composers are remaining true to that legacy when they draw on the ever-changing ecosystem of our own popular musics. Speaking the languages of contemporary culture will help us create a picture of our times, as composers of the past did with theirs. Johnson's music has been commissioned and performed internationally by ensembles such as the Kronos Quartet, the Bang On A Can All-Stars, and Alarm Will Sound, as well as his own groups. His three decades of effort have been recognized with numerous grants and awards, including a Koussevitsky commission, a 2006 Guggenheim Fellowship, and a 2015 American Academy of Arts and Letters Fellowship.

http://www.scottjohnsoncomposer.com/

The first question is always the classic one: how did your love and interest for guitar start, and what instruments do you play or have you played?

My real love in music is composing, but my first flirtation was playing guitar in rock bands as a teenager. Soon I learned more about harmony from an old-style jazz teacher, and then I became interested in classical music. The only older guitar music I felt attracted to were the Bach lute suites, and I never became a skilled classical performer, the sound of electric guitar was my world. Guitar is still the only instrument I play, although I always compose at the keyboard. But keyboard is only a writing tool for me.

What was your musical training, with which teachers have you studied and what impression they left in your music?

Although I studied general music theory in the university, I am self-taught as a composer. This has advantages and disadvantages, but on the whole I'm happy with the results. Gathering information is more difficult when you do it yourself, and you must be very self-motivated. But since I felt no need to please my teacher, I was able to take my music in an unusual direction.

How did your interest about the contemporary repertoire start, and what are the stylistic currents in which you recognize yourself most?

Like many people, my exposure to modern classical music began with Stravinsky. Then I discovered Varese, the European modernist line from Webern to Stockhausen, and American avant-gardists from Cage to Riley to the jazz avant-gard. But I didn't grow up with older classical music, so I never had to rebel against it. I have nothing against triads.
After studying both music and visual art in college, I had a musical crisis. My ears liked electric guitars and other sounds of American popular music, but my creative mind liked the skills and expressive possibilities of the classical tradition. I was afraid that my musical instincts would never be welcome in the world of composers, so I decided to quit music, and moved to New York City to be a visual artist. There I found a new musical world connected to the visual art world, the "downtown" mix of Minimalists, Cageans, improvisers, and experimental rock bands that were thriving at the time in Soho and the East Village. This encouraged me to return to music, and follow my own path, without belonging to an existing style.

One of the things that I can honestly say about guitar is its ability and capacity to change its shape as a musical medium over the centuries and between the various musical and social forms: we can choose between classical, acoustic and electric types suitable for different musical and social cultures. You have followed a very personal path inside the guitar, how did you develop this path and how are you developing it?

My early decision to combine electric guitar with contemporary, post-classical composition was unusual at the time, because the walls between High Modernism and the rest of the culture were very high. But although it felt like a personal decision, I think it was also part of some large cultural forces that were affecting many people. Modern composition needed to wake up to the real world, and my work still grows from those roots. Today this combination of classical and popular influences is a natural part of many young composer's paths. Trends like this are not completely personal. Much of our minds are created by our culture, so in some ways we don't completely own all of our own thoughts, they are part of the larger world.

Do you think that the guitar, with its presence of very personal musicians at every musical level and genre would be a viable alternative to the now tragicomic distinction between high culture and popular culture and the affirmation of Schoenberg " if it is art, it is not for all, and if it is for all, it is not art "?

Schoenberg was dead wrong about this. He is claiming that his area of the human artistic spectrum is the only one that deserves the name "art". This ignores the anthropological fact that all fine arts, including his particular corner, are the result of a long process of cultural evolution which began with very simple and direct emotional expressions. His own European classical tradition has had many moments when it spoke to all, or at least to most. Evolution never ceases, and today the process continues as other simpler expressions follow similar paths towards more sophisticated forms of expression. The recognized "fine arts" is where he made his living, and obtained his social status. He attempted to define his area as a special and separate category, rather than what it really is: part of a complex continuum which includes even the worst commercial song, which may be bad art, but it's still a kind of art. Schoenberg's clever statement reflects a professional's desire to preserve his high status by denying the historical, social, and psychological roots of his profession.

But back to guitars. Because they are part of a large family of plucked string instruments, which appear in nearly every culture around the world, in both folk musics and complex classical forms, they do offer pathways between high and low, east and west, north and south. I'm not a fan of purity, I think cross-influences are one of the interesting things about music.

Berio in his essay "A remembrance to the future, wrote: ".. A pianist who is a specialist about classical and romantic repertoire, and plays Beethoven and Chopin without knowing the music of the twentieth century, it is also off as a pianist who is specialist about contemporary music and plays with hands and mind that have never been crossed in depth by Beethoven and Chopin." You play a contemporary repertoire ... do you recognize yourself in these words?

Yes and no. It's true that the modern repertoire grows from the classical/romantic past, even when it sounds very different. Even a hardcore 20th century work that strongly rejects Romantic emotionalism can't be completely understood without understanding what it was opposed to.

But Berio was speaking from the inward-looking world of 20th century modernism, which was very concerned with the scholarly and historical side of music. There is another side of music which is missing in this quote, and in most modernism, but it was not missing in earlier periods. The founders of the European classical tradition borrowed freely from the living popular styles that surrounded them, transforming simple beginnings into complex results. In the 20th century, many composers focused only on past composers for inspiration or argument, and ignored our contemporary cultural environment. I believe this is a profound mistake. The great composers of the past were always looking around them, using living vernacular styles as starting points for more complex music. So Berio is correct as far as he goes. But he doesn't go far enough. A pianist who understands only classical, romantic, and modernist styles still doesn't understand our own age. This musician is ignoring the living musics which can be the basic building blocks of our own expression. Berio's ideal pianist is speaking only Latin and classical Greek, not Italian or English or Chinese.

Talking about living music, some years ago you wrote an interesting essay titled *"The Counterpoint of the species"*[45] *making interesting comparisons between biological evolution and music evolution. You wrote "But regardless of the damage done to the health of post-classical music by an oversimplified belief in linear progress, the basic perception that there are similarities between cultural change and biological evolution is no mistake. The same basic mechanisms and accidents of evolution which have granted us our survival and the ability to communicate with each other are also at work within seemingly unnecessary "luxuries" like music. They aren't at work because they were designed with music in mind. They are just unavoidably present in all that we do, because that is how people are put together. Once we've learned to be suspicious of the old triumphal stories of progress, contemporary evolutionary thought offers a set of ideas which work equally well on matters great and small, physical and intellectual." and "At this point all of the Darwinian requirements have been fully met: 1) inheritance, in the style of music; 2) variation, from the personal expression of the musicians or composers; and 3) differential success among the variants, from the assessment that we voted with our palms. Regardless of whether we have ever put much thought into examining our intuitions about evolution, any evening's concert or any trip to the record store both fit snugly within its definition."* Do you still agree with these ideas? Have you ever think about to write a following to it? Do you still compose "biological music"?

I still agree completely with those ideas and they were based on many years of observation and thought before I wrote them down. Human ideas evolve within the ecosystems of cultures and individual minds, and music is just one outgrowth

45   John Zorn, Arcana musicians on music, Hips Road and Granary Books, 2000, pag. 18

of our basic human tendencies and potentials. It's built upon the same basic biological foundations and brain functions as our other social behaviors, and it mutates and adapts according to the same basic Darwinian principles as other types of evolution, both biological and cultural.

I have thought about writing more essays, or perhaps expanding that paper into a less dense piece of writing that would be read by more musicians. But there is always music to compose, and never enough time. I needed to write "The Counterpoint of Species" at that moment, because my long-standing ideas about music had been clarified during the 90's by reading about Darwinism and evolutionary psychology. It was important to put it all on paper before my attention moved to other things, and I forgot all the details.

As a sort of metaphorical joke, I sometimes say that I write "biological music", as opposed to the "physics music" of 20th Century High Modernism, which often strives towards an otherworldly abstraction. I suppose another way of saying this would be to call myself a romantic composer, following unexpected paths and surprises as I write, as opposed to more mathematical or architectural composers who begin with a careful plan, and don't expect the listener to understand it without careful study.

Back to the guitar: Berlioz said that composing for classical guitar was difficult because the composer first has to be a guitarist, these words were often used as a justification for the limited repertoire of classical guitar compared to other instruments like piano and violin. At the same time I think that the growing interest for the guitar (classical, acoustic, electric, MIDI, etc) collected in contemporary music has changed the importance of Berlioz's words. As a guitarist and a composer do you think that these words are even true?

Berlioz's words are still true for complex chords, or solo classical guitar with polyphonic textures, because guitar fingerings and voicings are very idiomatic and difficult. But with amplified or electric guitar it is no longer true that guitar needs full voicings to be heard, and can only appear in small ensemble situations. Unamplified acoustic guitars are just not loud enough to be an equal player in large mixed ensembles, but with electric guitars this is not a problem: the opposite is the danger! And in these situations the electric guitar doesn't have to be used with complex idiomatic chords.

Like the arco and pizz of bowed strings, electric guitar today is an instrument with two distinct sounds, because distortion allows a single line with long sustained notes, and big noisy chords. You can now write a satisfying guitar part with no more special knowledge than it takes to write a violin or cello part with occasional double or triple stops and open strings. But for fully harmonized

112

passages, guitar is still difficult, much harder than one hand on a piano. So for dense polyphonic writing, Berlioz is still correct.

I have really enjoyed your record "John Somebody"... I think it's a minimalistic record that sound with the strength of a rock music, how much were you inspired by Steve Reich's early music?

Most people are not aware that Steve Reich and I influenced each other, first from him to me, and later from me to him. Steve and I have talked about it. His early speech loop pieces were one of three influences on me when I invented the idea of transcribing the pitches and rhythms of speech into instrumental lines, which began with "John Somebody" (1979-82). My other inspirations were Messiaen's transcription of the melodies of bird songs, and the call-and-response between singers and instrumentalists in the Chicago blues. Blues was very influential for most of my generation, I grew up in a university city north of Chicago, and played in a local bar where many of those musicians would come to perform.

So Steve's early pieces influenced "John Somebody", and then "John Somebody" influenced Steve to adopt my transcription idea in "Different Trains". It's like Manet's relationship to the younger generation of Impressionist painters: they were influenced by Manet's early work, and in his late work he adopted some of their techniques. This shows how influences can travel both ways. I now spend a lot of time listening to younger composers, and I hope that their influence will show up in my work. It's a sign of life and evolution.

I spent my early years in New York City in a post-modernist music scene dominated by minimalism, and "John Somebody" was probably my most minimalist-sounding piece. Most of my recent work has a fast rate of change and contrast, with very little of the suspension of time found in early minimalism (which they imported, I think, from African and Asian sources). But minimalism was very important to me at the time, because it offered a path away from the atonal modernism that still dominated the scene in the conservatories.

Minimalism was a revolutionary moment in modern music, but it was already fairly well-established when I began writing (in the late 1970's). It was important for me to find something more personal, and my experience with rock music provided my avenue. My idea was that earlier centuries of European classical music had always imported musical DNA from the folk musics around them, and rock was my folk music. So I used my natural cultural surroundings to make a music with a more narrative sense of time, and moved away from the stability of minimalism. If you listen to the later work of the first generation minimalists, like Philip, Steve, and Terry Riley, you can hear that they also felt the need to find a way towards a less static music.

Sometimes ago our friend Elena Càsoli said to me "I improvise the interpretation of what you call encoded. Scored music requires an ethic of respect, attention, closeness and knowledge of its aesthetics, looking at the sign left by the author. But it's a moving, alive, elusive, intangible subject, which awaits the encounter with an interpretative act. And this meeting, in concert, has a space for improvisation, every evening new and different" What do you think about these words?

I see what Elena means. A performer playing from a score is presented with a constant flow of large and small decisions... how to approach the shape of the piece, the shape of each phrase, and even individual notes. Much of this is prepared in rehearsal, but some happens at the moment, as with an improvisation. But of course the scale of available freedom is constrained by the score. A composer writing a piece is already doing much of the work that an improviser does at the moment. Sometimes I think of composing as extremely slow improvising.

One of your works, Americans, was played by Sentieri Selvaggi and Elena Càsoli in Milan, would you like to talk us about this experience?

I was very happy with the excellent work of Sentieri Selvaggi and their conductor Carlo Boccadoro, and I hope we will work together in the future. And I was impressed that Elena was able to give such a good performance of this piece using finger-picking technique. All of these guitar parts are very much based on rock pick technique, and I never thought of trying finger-picking. Although, among the great rock guitarists, Jeff Beck certainly gets a unique and impressive sound with his fingers.
The piece they performed, "Americans", is one of my most rock-influenced recent scores. I'm pleased that more European ensembles are beginning to be interested in "classical" music which accepts undisguised popular influences.

Tzadik is one of my favorite music label, how did you start working with them? Will you record again with Tzadik?

Tzadik is a project of John Zorn, and we share a common background in the New York "downtown" scene I mentioned above. Our paths have been very different, but I enjoy the feeling of comradeship. I released a CD of recent music for electric ensembles on Tzadik in 2010 which included "Americans", in a recording by my own musicians here in New York. It's a speech sampling piece, built around the voices of immigrants to America from China, Romania, and Afghanistan.

I try to ask you a little bit 'provocative question about music in general, not just about contemporary or avant-garde. Frank Zappa wrote in his autobiography: "If John Cage, for example, said, now I put a contact microphone on the throat, then I drink carrot juice and this will be my composition ", then his gargling would qualify as a COMPOSITION, because he applied a frame, declaring it as such. "Take it or leave it, now I want this to be music." Is this statement good enough to define a genre of music, just saying this is classical music, this is contemporary, and it's done? Does it still make sense to speak about "genre"?

Zappa was just restating Duchamp's provocative point about an artist's right to define their own intention in their own piece. When he made this point 100 years ago, with readymades like his urinal piece, he opened up the possibility of conceptual art. But an artist making this sort of point about their own work isn't the same thing as an observer defining someone else's work. Genre definitions like classical, minimalist, modernist, metal, or hiphop are all categories that are never clean, and never have definite boundaries. But the genres are still real, even if they are out of focus at the edges. Debate will always happen at the borders, and living genres are always mutating. Even an artist's statement is not always completely absolute. If John Cage says his gargling is a composition, we must accept it. But if he says it's reggae song, we are allowed to laugh.

What does improvisation mean for your music research? Do you think it's possible to talk about improvisation for classical music or we have to turn to other repertories like jazz, contemporary music, etc.?

There is no improvisation in my pieces, but my esthetic draws strongly on improvising styles like rock and jazz, and I prefer players who understand both written and improvised music. In early work like "John Somebody" I play some solos which began as improvisations, which I then I edited and wrote down. I think this was not so unusual for composers before the 20th century. Many baroque, classical and romantic composers were also famous improvisers, but that has mostly been lost.

It's certainly possible today to make mixed composed/improvised pieces. It's rare in contemporary classical circles, but some people specialize in it, Zorn is an example. I only use improvisation as an inspiration for completely composed scores, but that's just my personal habit, not an ideological position.

In 1968 Derek Bailey asked to Steve Lacy to define in 15 seconds the difference between improvisation and composition, the answer was "In 15 seconds the difference between improvisation and composition is that in composition you have all the time to decide what you say in 15 seconds, while in improvisation you have only 15 seconds". Was the Lacy's answer a little too much ironic or is it a true one?

The answer is funny, but not quite accurate. It's certainly true that a composer can take as long as they want to decide about 15". But an improviser is not really doing everything in 15" either. That 15 seconds was preceded by 15 hours or 15 weeks or 15 years of practice, and much of the hard work is finished before they go on to a stage. In the 15" of playing, the improviser's brain and muscles are creating a variation on existing pathways.

What's the role of the "Error" in your musical vision? For "error" I mean an incorrect procedure, an irregularity in the normal operation of a mechanism, a discontinuity on an otherwise uniform surface that can lead to new developments and unexpected surprises ...

For me irregularity is not incorrect, it's my normal method of operation. I was never completely comfortable with the preference for advance planning in many 20th century styles. Serialism and Minimalism both emphasize systematic thinking, even though Minimalism began as a rebellion against Serialism.
I write in a very intuitive way, and I always look for ideas that appear while I work. I begin with general structural plans, but if I have a better idea while working, I will usually change the system and follow the new idea. To me a system is a way to achieve a certain effect, not an ideal that I try to live up to. Technique should be the lieutenant, not the general.

It seems to me that there is a small music scene about classical guitarists dedicated to an innovative and contemporary repertoire, as well as you come to my mind the names of Marco Cappelli, David Tanenbaum, David Starobin, Elena Càsoli, Seth Josel, Marc Ribot who played John Zorn's music... shall I speak about a music scene? Are you in contact with these musicians? Are there other guitarists you know and that you can suggest us that they move on these innovative musical routes?

I know all but one of the guitarists you mention, and I've worked with several of them. Yes, there is a growing scene of guitarists, and also guitarist-composers. On my last Tzadik CD, I played my electric guitar duo "Bowery Haunt" with a young American guitarist/composer named Mark Dancigers. I also played this piece in your region in 2008, with Padova guitarist Marco Pavin. Dancigers also plays with the Now Ensemble, which like the Bang On A Can All-Stars has electric guitar in every piece. The All-Stars' guitarist Derek Johnson also plays on my CD. Here in New York the Dither Quartet is an all-electric group. Wiek Hijman[46] in Amsterdam has organized an electric guitar festival called "Output". Everywhere there is a growing list of young classically trained guitarists who play electric, and understand the idiomatic sounds and techniques of rock. I think this blending of influences will contribute to a healthy future for the classical tradition.

About "Bowery Haunt" some time ago you told me that this score was connected with the Bowery, Andy Warhol... it's a score for two guitars, how does it work?

It was connected to my memories of the CBGB-punk rock scene that I described above. CBGB's was on a street in NYC called The Bowery, and in 1976-77 I lived two blocks away on that street. I wasn't really part of the punk scene, because for myself I was interested in more complex music, but I enjoyed going out to hear the bands. Many images stayed with me, including the Ramones' strange and sometimes very funny recycling of American 60's pop. Maybe that's what I meant about Andy Warhol: the music doesn't refer to him, and we never met, but he certainly had an esthetic that used American pop culture as a source. The title "Bowery Haunt" has several meanings. Its main theme runs through rock "power chords" on all 12 chromatic notes, including a little chord progression that appears in a Ramones song (and in about 500 other old rock songs). When I wrote the piece, three of the four Ramones had died, and CBGB was going to close. In American slang, a "haunt" is a bar, the joke is that the regular patrons are like ghosts haunting the place. My title refers to the death of that old bar on the Bowery, and some of its musicians. "Bowery Haunt" also revisits many rock guitar gestures from my own youth, so the piece for me has a certain elegiac or nostalgic quality, and the title reflects that.

Talking about innovative composers, what do you think about John Zorn and the New York musical downtown scene, so ready to get and recode every musical language, improvisation, jazz, contemporary music, cartoon music?

I've known John, and others who work with both improvised and composed elements, for many years. Although our music sounds very different, I think that

---

46   http://wiekhijmans.wix.com/firste-attempt

in some ways we are working on the same underlying problem: how to make a new "art music" that accepts inspiration from anywhere, not just from academically accepted sources.

Talking about New York, you have been part of the whole scene, the '70's and '80's are something mythological, the No Wave, Sonic Youth, Ramones, Velvet Underground, Glenn Branca, Rhy Chatham, the CBGB, The Kitchen... what do you remember about those years and those music?

You would often see many of the same people at CBGB and at the Kitchen, although CBGB was a loud and crazy rock club, and the Kitchen, where my friend Rhys Chatham was the music curator, was an alternative art space with performance art and video as well as music. Early evening performance, late night club - I'm sure most young artists still have similar experiences. What was special about that time and place was that all forms of artistic activity were so focused in one small area of Manhattan, and, like being in Montparnasse in the 1920's, it included many of the greatest living artists. My work was always a little different from the noise-rock style you mention, but there was still a strong social connection between artists. Half of the rockers at CBGB were painters & sculptors & poets (no, they couldn't play very well, but it was fun).

Almost two year ago, October 27 2013, Lou Reed died. I know that you knew him and you know Laurie Anderson too, have you ever played with them?

I only talked with Lou towards the end of his life, when I would meet him with Laurie, or when they both played in a trio with John Zorn. I've known Laurie since the 1970's, when I was in her first band. Lou Reed was very unique, occupying a one-man bridge between the visual art world and rock. I think he was a big influence on that 70's-80's scene we are talking about.

How is the situation in USA and New York in these times? How much did the financial crisis hit the musical scene?

Support for experimental music began a slow decline in the 1990's, and so the 2008 financial crisis hit us at a moment of weakness. For most people the arts are a luxury, so if the Titanic goes down, we artists go into the water very quickly. But in recent years there is again a lot of activity,- partly because the US economy has improved, but also because a new generation of young musicians and composers are making their own ensembles, concerts, and recordings.

I have, sometimes, the feeling that in our times music's history flows without a particular interest in its chronological course, in our discotheque before and after, past and future become interchangeable elements, shall this be a risk of a uniform vision for an interpreter and a composer? The risk of a musical "globalization"?

It's true that today we have easy access to historical detail, and to many different cultures. And yes, if people lose themselves in this flood of information it can lead to imitations of the past, or to shallow borrowings like New Age. And the opposite reaction can lead to walled-off castles like High Modernism, as academic people try to fight against any lowering of standards. But creative artists will always find a way to make something interesting with whatever materials are at hand, including confusing globalization. I am not worried.
I don't see globalization as a risk. I see it as an opportunity for cross-fertilization, and the creation of hybrids. I don't like purity. And of course, some cultural traditions will die. Traditions always die and then something new grows. Can anyone speak Etruscan, or sing Etruscan songs? No, but the descendants of the Etruscans are having a perfectly nice time today in Siena.

Your musical career has been going on for several years, how have you seen the musical world changing? around you? Do you note differences between the students you teach and you taught? How new technologies (new musical instruments, midi, social networks, forums) have influenced your choices and your musical form? How?

I've never taught, but I do give talks at schools, and I'm always interested in the new generations who arrive in New York, ready to eat the world. The biggest change I see today is that the idea of using our culture's popular music as a "folk music" source for more complex composition, an idea which I've always held, is now very common and well-accepted among young composers. This was not true when I began. It seems that my big battleground as a young composer is now a peaceful territory for those who came after.
Early in my career, I did more pieces that involved new technologies, but later I found that a piece built around a particular machine often had little or no future life, because those machines can disappear. For example, I had five movements for solo guitar and Eventide Harmonizer that require a complex set of footpedals, and I need to find a laptop version of the old electronics to make it easy for performers. But of course, in 10 years that would have to be updated again! So new technologies have recently driven me towards old technologies, like basic electric guitar using only basic effects like distortion. A performance using that is just as easy to put together as acoustic instruments.

119

Non-Western instruments can also present challenges, sometimes because of notation. I wrote a piece featuring shamisen with electric guitar, piano, and cello, and it's very difficult to find people who have mastered both this traditional Japanese instrument and Western notation. Another argument for keeping it simple! So for the moment, I'm still enjoying the easily reproducible tools of scores and common instruments.

One technological system that I use consistently is my speech sampling technique, which began with tape loops in the 1970's, and has continued through various evolving sampling technologies, triggered via midi from a score program. These digital tools have been very stable now for more than a decade. I just finished an evening length piece using this technology together with a 16-piece sinfonietta, Alarm Will Sound, and I really enjoyed having the full range of orchestral instruments to play with. I'm having fun with these acoustic instruments, but I don't know where that will lead, or whether I'll discover a new electronic interest.

Let's talk about marketing. How much do you think it's important for a modern musician? I mean: how much is crucial to be good promoters of themselves and their works in music today?

Marketing is important for making a living, but I don't enjoy doing it. Sometimes I stop doing it for long periods of time, and then everyone forgets me until I start doing it again. It's also important to brush your teeth, take out the trash, and wash the dishes. Life is not always fun.

What do you think about the discographic market crisis, with the transition to digital downloading in mp3 and all this new scenario?

It's a paradise for the listener and a disaster for the creator. Now musicians must take time away from creating music in order to self-produce and promote recordings that will probably lose money. The situation is good for musicians who are charismatic performers, but I'm afraid that some of the best work by the quiet people will not be heard. The culture needs to solve this problem, and evolve a new system for paying musicians and protecting their rights.

Please tell us five essential records, to have always with you... the classic five discs for the desert island...

I can't really answer this. My listening habits in new music are constantly changing, because I'm curious. But of the older generation, I would listen to Louis Andriessen before I would listen to Boulez. And I like many of the young composers now appearing on the New Amsterdam label here in New York. My tastes in classical music are very ordinary, everybody likes Beethoven or Stravinsky. The same with popular music, it's easy to like a smart band like Radiohead. Wait, here's a band you might not have heard of: Dirty Projectors (try "The Getty Address"). Like most people, I like the popular music of my youth. But there are no essential records, I can get tired of anything if I hear it enough.

Yes you are right Radiohead are fine, I like Dirty Projectors too, they have nice ideas, but what are your five favorite scores?

Same as above, there is no handful of favorite scores, and if there were, it would constantly change, and would probably show no consistency. Much of the really great stuff is really obvious: who doesn't like "Sacre", or Beethoven the VII? I like Messiaen's "Illuminations of the Beyond" and Britten's "Sea Interludes", I like Ty Braxton's "Uffe's Woodshop" and Michael Gordon's "Yo Shakespeare". I like James Brown, and he had no scores. Different musics have different purposes, and different moments have different preferences.

With who would you like to play? What kind of music do you listen to usually?

Often I don't play for long periods of time, because I am happier with the solitude of writing. I want to sit in a chair while someone better than me plays my scores.
There are different types of listening, because different styles of music have different purposes. Music gives you instructions on how it wants you to behave. Music that tells me to sit down and focus can be irritating if I'm not concentrating on listening, and music which creates a good social atmosphere can be irritating if you listen carefully for too long. Even within the category of "serious listening", I have very eclectic tastes. I like variation.

Your next projects? When we will see you playing in Italy?

I have more concerts planned of "Mind Out Of Matter", my recent project based on the sampled speaking voice of American philosopher Daniel Dennett, and I hope to record it. I find a great sense of wonder in the complex world that Darwinian science reveals to us, and Dennett is a strong advocate of this in the philosophical community. "Mind Out Of Matter" focuses on his ideas about the origins and evolution of religion. He views it as a natural phenomenon, a result of the structure of the human brain and human cultures. When I move past that project, I'd like to do some smaller scale chamber pieces, and perhaps do a little performing again, just to change my daily habits for a while.

I've visited Italy several times in recent years, at a writing residency in Umbria, and also as an ordinary tourist, filling the streets and staring at history with the rest of them. I'd rather come as composer than a performer, but I'm always happy for any excuse to visit your beautiful country. Maybe I'll even practice guitar, if that will help.

A last question... my Blog[47] is read by several students... any good advices to give them?

Get a real job! And don't trust my advice.

This is really the last question... which is more a reflection: Luigi Nono said "Other thoughts, other noises, other sounds, other ideas. When we listen to, we often try to find ourselves in others. To find our mechanisms, system, rationalism, in the other. And this is a quite conservative violence."... Now... does experimentation free ourselves from the burden of having to remember?

Remembering is not the enemy of experimentation, as long as you remember that memory is a tool, not an authority.

If I understand Nono correctly, I think he is saying that we often listen not to hear what the other is thinking, but only to hear our own thoughts reflected. Unless he is saying that we often borrow our thoughts from others, which is also true. Yes, most people at most times are remembering themselves, and looking for support for their pre-existing thoughts. That's part of what culture is: a group of social primates in a circle, telling themselves that they all feel the same way. And sometimes that doesn't feel oppressive, often it's a comfort. Maybe a slightly lazy comfort.

But people also have moments when they are bored by comfort, and want adventure. Some people want this feeling more often, and they are the audience for new music. Experimentation will always be a minority interest. But many conservative people still have moments of curiosity, when they need something new, and we shouldn't just chase them away. Providing novelty is part of our job in the culture (sometimes we will be hired and paid for this job, sometimes not).

Evolution insures that culture will always need experimentalists. We serve the same function within culture that genetic mutation serves in nature: a source of unpredictable variation. Evolution cannot occur without a pool of variations to

---

47   http://chitarraedintorni.blogspot.com/

choose from. In nature, those genetic variations appear randomly. But in culture, we can consciously design the variations. This is what creative artists share with innovators in science or engineering: we design the prototypes, the early versions that become candidates for future change.

I promise this is the real last question. Sometimes ago in an interview Carlos Santana said "Some people have talent, some people have vision. And vision is more important then talent, obviously." I have listen to your music several times and I think you have a great talent but... what's your vision?

I think Santana was trying to get at the difference between technical facility and creative imagination. It's possible to have a lot of one, and less of the other, but most artists have both. He's defending creativity, which is obviously a necessity for serious artists, but the greatest artists have the talent and facility to make their creative vision into a reality, not just a hope.

Your question asks for a verbal description of my "vision", but any sentence like that might sound more like an advertising slogan than a vision. I don't think a single, easy-to-describe vision is the most admirable goal. As a composer I always had the hope of making a music that was capable of being subtle and complex like classical music, but was built out of the materials of the rock music that I loved when I was growing up. But that very general motivation can't describe the individuality of each piece, or the course of changing interests from piece to piece. I can't describe a single simple "vision" that would include all of those shifting factors, and without the more subtle qualities of each piece there is no body of work. So in a way I think this is not a productive way to think of things, even if Santana is a true guitar hero!

SETH JOSEL

Seth Josel - originally from New York, now residing in Berlin - has become one of the leading instrumental pioneers of his generation. As a soloist he has concertized in Belgium, Germany, Great Britain, France, Israel, Italy, The Netherlands, Switzerland, the US and Canada. He has performed as a guest with leading orchestras and ensembles of Europe, including the BBC Symphony Orchestra (London), the Rundfunksinfonie Orchester Berlin, the Deutsches Symphonie Orchester Berlin, the South German Radio Choir, the Staatskapelle Berlin and the Schönberg Ensemble of Amsterdam, and has appeared at several major European festivals including the Salzburg Festspiele, Ars Musica, Donaueschingen, The Holland Festival, Munich Biennale and London's South Bank Festival. After acquiring his Bachelor of Music degree at the Manhattan School of Music Seth Josel enrolled at Yale University and earned the Master of Music degree; he then went on to become the first guitarist at Yale to earn the Master of Musical Arts and the Doctor of Musical Art degrees. His teachers included Manuel Barrueco, Eliot Fisk and harpsichordist Richard Rephann; as well, he has participated in the master classes of Oscar Ghiglia and Andrés Segovia. He is recipient of numerous awards and prizes including a Fulbright-Hays grant from the United States government and an Artists Stipend from the Akademie Schloß Solitude, Stuttgart.

http://sethjosel.de/

The first question is always the classic one: how does it start, your love and interest for guitar? And what instruments do you play or have you played?

Well, my parents, who aren't musicians themselves, were certainly engaged and offered me the possibility of private instrumental lessons when I was a child. I wanted to start on drums, but they thought that might be too loud for the apartment we were living in at the time. A cousin had been studying piano, thus guitar seemed like the sensible "default" choice. My cousin was already studying the piano, so I wanted to study something different, so I chose the guitar.
I also studied viola in high school for a year when I was around 13. The school orchestra was desperate to fill the section, and my teacher had been highly encouraging, but I soon faced a dilemma commitment-wise: viola or guitar. I chose guitar, in hindsight certainly a poor practical choice, all things considered…

What instruments guitars do you play or have you played? I have seen a picture of you with a classical guitar with a curious guitar headstock…

My first hand-crafted instrument was built by Thomas Humphrey, a student model which I bought while I was studying at the pre-college division of MSM (Manhattan School of Music), that was back in the late 70's. I owned two other instruments of his during my conservatory studies, one spruce and one cedar. I played an instrument by Miguel Rodriguez (a spruce guitar from 1962!), which Pepe Romero had sold me, until I arrived in Germany and began playing ensemble regularly. While I really liked the way this guitar's spruce wood had developed and matured, I needed a more powerful instrument in order to compete with the surrounding forces and shifting contexts, and so I ordered a cedar "Special" from Yuichi Imai, which I still have to this day, and which can be heard on countless of my solo and ensemble recordings. A couple of years ago, I ordered an A-Series guitar – one, with a few rather unique design details, indigenous to this instrument solely, from Gary Southwell. the extraordinary English luthier. This is my primary instrument currently. Apart from my classical guitars, I have four electric guitars, a short-scale bass, a Dobro, an acoustic steel-stringed, a few banjos and quite an array of electronic gear.

What was your musical training, with which teachers have you studied and what impression have they left in your playing music?

While I am grateful to two teachers during my childhood who encouraged me to learn how to read music properly, my life changed radically when I enrolled at the pre-college division of Manhattan School of Music. Between my teacher there was someone who ostensibly dropped off the face of the planet, no need in mentioning his name herein, however he provided me with my wings, so to speak, and introduced me to a few folks who would then leave quite an imprimatur upon me, both personally and artistically: Manual Barrueco, as well as the Aspen Music Festival triumvirate, Eliot Fisk, Oscar Ghiglia and Robert Guthrie. In addition, Tom Humphrey, whose atelier on the upper west side of Manhattan at the time was buzzing with activity day and night, played a rather important role during my formative years. Anyhow, I did my Bachelors at MSM and then very happily left the city to begin my studies at Yale, which had a major impact on my development, on the way I thought about and heard music. I think it would be entirely fair to say that it was the Yale School of Music composition department, fearlessly led at that time by Martin Bresnick as well as the late Jacob Druckman, which was integral in providing me with the inspiration and motivation to pursue the path that I ultimately took, that is, as a specialist in the performance and dissemination of new art music. Mention must also be made of such stellar academic figures as Alan Forte, David Lewin, Larry Dreyfus,

Michael Friedmann and Paul Hawkshaw, all of whom contributed to introducing me to the beauties of artistic inquiry and scholarship.

You were born in New York, but you live in Berlin, why did you decide to come to Europe and why Berlin?

In 1988, I received a Fulbright Grant from the US Government, one of these luxurious one-year grants, to study in Cologne. I had been over here twice before in order to concertize, and I was fascinated, to say the least, in what I perceived to have been the different role that culture and the arts play here, as opposed to back home. I wished simply to immerse myself in such a seemingly culture-friendly society for a while. I was a so-called exchange student, having finished my Masters and pre-doctoral work at Yale, and was supposed to return to the States and spread the good news about the Germans per se, but I stayed instead. Believe me, it wasn't planned that way! I had always thought there was time to return and start teaching in the American University system. I didn't think it needed necessarily to begin at the ripe old age of 28. After struggling for a year or so, I received a grant in 1992 for a residency at the Akademie Schloß Solitude in Stuttgart. Upon conclusion of the grant, I moved to Berlin. This was a strictly personal decision at the time, having to do with a woman whom I had met at the Schloß. If we didn't meet, I would have returned to Cologne, since for the MusikFabrik was already on its way to establishing itself as a force in the German new art music ensemble scene and I had already been a permanent member.

One of the things that I can honestly say about guitar is its ability and capacity to change its shapes as a musical medium over the centuries and between the various musical and social forms: guitar seems to be the perfect instrument (not only by the musical but also logical, economic and philosophical aspect) to counter the theories of the Frankfurt School and Adorno...

Firstly, I agree with your preface. The guitar has a chameleon-like character and can bridge the seemingly unbridgeable gap between "high-brow" and "low-brow" music more effectively than any other instrument, really. My "path" as you refer to it, started out as a personal decision at a very particular moment in time (June 1989), firstly, to not participate in the Munich ARD competition that summer, whose required repertoire was almost fatefully tailored to mine, secondly, to devote myself to new art music exclusively and thirdly, to create my own "structure." (I was living at the time with someone who was deeply committed to Post-Modern theory and aesthetics, so we were talking a lot about

126

systems and structures.) That "structure" became a path of sorts, although it didn't really feel that way at the time! A couple of ideas and aims took shape in my mind: a) dramaturgical integrity and innovation, b) remaining open to the myriad streams which comprised new art music at the time, and c) honing further my chamber music and ensemble-performance skills. If we were to take "a" and look at my solo discography, we see programs that were very carefully designed, almost entirely comprised in premiere recordings. If we were to look more closely at "b" then we see that my taste has remained eclectic, but "catholic": I've played Niblock and Young, but I also played Lachenmann and Ablinger, as well as Berio and Kagel. For me, it's not about a school to which I need to be devoted, or follow religiously, it's simply about performing and recording the music with which I really feel an affinity, and which speaks to me in a particularly striking and personal way. If I need to play Dobro, then so be it (in the case of Marc Sabat's "Garden Songs"); or, if I need a MIDI-guitar to perform Manfred Stahnke's microtonally-oriented music, then so be it, I went out and purchased one. The "c" part has of course yielded tremendous fruit, and I am grateful for the opportunity to have performed with some of the leading ensembles and orchestras in Europe.

You have followed a very personal path inside the guitar, how did you develop this path and how are you developing it?

As a career path for a guitarist, that's been rather unique, wouldn't you say? Two other aspects are perhaps worth mentioning: a) I don't teach at the institutional level, which might appear odd since my training was preparing me for such a task, b) I remain somewhat on the fringe of the classical guitar community, which, I must say in all frankness, is a river that flows in both directions. Most of our colleagues are not interested, or actually turned off, by the music about which I am was passionate and therefore I felt like a persona non grata for a while; concomitantly, I went into reclusion for a long while, in part feeling as though I needed to strike out entirely on my own. That stance vis-à-vis the "community" has changed in recent years, as you probably know, and I've gravitated back to their fold a bit. Sometimes it feels like a homecoming. Writing the book had something to do with that sense of re-connection, no doubt.

Do you think that the guitar, with its presence of very personal musicians at every musical level and genre would be a viable alternative to the now tragicomic distinction between high culture and popular culture and the affirmation of Schoenberg " if it is art, it is not for all, and if it is for all, it is not art "?

127

Eliot Fisk once said to me, 'the guitar's primary function is to "democratize" the concert hall.' Does that answer your question?

How did you start your collaboration with Peter Ablinger? I was really surprised listening to your record "33-127", how did it start the idea for this particular record?

A friend from Los Angeles, whose taste I trusted implicitly, recommended that I have a closer look at his music; hence, I bought all the recordings that were available at the time, we're talking about 2002/2003 and I spent a certain amount of time listening to and thinking about Peter's music. It was an obsession for a while. In particular, I found the ensemble and orchestral pieces amazingly innovative, moreover completely void of compromise, a sort of relentless quality that I found, and still do find, rather appealing. I then initiated contact with Peter, sent him some recorded material, and he seemed intrigued by the idea of writing a piece for electric guitar. A few months later, unprompted, I received this huge package in the mail, and there they were: 127 miniatures! Brian Brandt from Mode had been interested in producing a disc by Peter. The piece was not conceived for presentation as a whole, neither in concert nor on CD; hence, the idea of doing a double CD, because its entire length is more than 80 minutes, never even crossed my mind. Peter thought 33 would be a good starting point, and so it came to be , and it was probably the most grueling learning/production process I had ever been involved in, for those middle sections with the ambient noise are fiendishly difficult and anything but idiomatic.

I have really enjoyed your "The Stroke that Kills", solo CD with works by Beglarian, Curran, Dramm, Fiday, Johnson, Matamoros, especially the Beglarian's music "Until it Blazes". Your version is quite different from the one of Emanuele Forni recorded in his "Ceci n'est pas une guitare", have you ever listened to it? How did you decide to realize this record?

Thanks for the compliment! I am embarrassed to say I haven't yet listened to Emanuele's version. New World Records is an American label, as the company name suggests; it was therefore clear from the start I'd need to design a recital of American new art music. Paul Tai, the executive producer, was keen to do a solo electric guitar CD, so it became simply a matter of developing a program. This took some time, I must say, because, as you well know, there isn't a deluge of repertoire available. One thread, which I hope the listener notices, concerns a textural motive, in terms of "electric guitar + …" – that is, multiples guitars, or guitar with delay(s), etc. In addition, there is a kind of post-minimalist strain therein. Lastly, I was interested in the American expatriate experience, being one myself, and so selecting music by David, Alvin and Tom became an important mission of sorts. In general, I tend to be allergic to buffet-like CDs, e.g. here one piece, there another, all thrown together rather haphazardly. It's been my experience as a collector and avid listener that if one is not doing a composer portrait CD, it's quite a challenge to come up with a compelling constellation of works. The dramaturgy has to make some sense to me, or else I am simply not interested.

You have created "Sheer Pluck[48]", a database of contemporary guitar music, would you like to talk about this work?

Well, I am not quite sure what to say except it is presently the "go-to" site for anyone interested in contemporary guitar repertoire. Klaus Heim, a professional programmer and guitar aficionado, and I worked very hard at the beginning, designing and conceiving the site, one which not only would be user friendly, but which would go beyond the mere surface of composer name and title. My experience in new music, as well as my musicological background, helped to provide for an integral academic foundation. We have received a tremendous response from both players and composers throughout the world. What more could one ask for?
Klaus is single-handedly running the show at present, and he's doing a magnificent job, a heroic effort really. I actually haven't worked actively on it since 2004, though I am feeding him data from time to time, especially involving premiere performances.

Berio, in his essay "A remembrance to the future, wrote: ".. A pianist who is a specialist of about classical and romantic repertoire, and plays Beethoven and Chopin without knowing the music of the twentieth century, it is also off as a pianist who is a specialist of about contemporary music and plays with hands and mind that have never been crossed in depth by Beethoven and Chopin. " You play both traditional classical and contemporary repertoire ... do you recognize yourself in these words?

Indeed, there is something very profound to which Berio was alluding, and I definitely am in agreement with his statement. In all frankness though, my concert appearances with traditional classical repertoire these days are far and few between. Certainly my musical training, not only as a guitarist, but with an extensive exposure to theory and musicology, provided me with a diverse array of analytic skills and exposure to a vast array of Western art music. I believe this

---

48   http://www.sheerpluck.de/

provided me with an excellent foundation, and it has been my goal to bring some of the experience and expressive qualities which I developed as I was studying and performing traditional repertoire to new art music performance. For instance, notions of precision, intensity, line, pacing, gesture, color: these are parameters equally worthy of consideration in contemporary music performance. It's a question mainly of context, and aesthetics of course.

Talking about Berio you have played his Sequenza XI? Would you like to talk to us about this score and your experience playing it?

Some might raise their eyebrows when I say this: I feel it would have been a great 8-minute work, but it unfortunately became 15 or 16, probably because of circumstances surrounding the commission. Why do I say this? Well, on an analytical level, we can see that every note comes from somewhere, has some distinct relationship to what preceded it. The piece is organic much in the same way that Beethoven's music is organic. I like to think of it as a spiral-like process. In my opinion, sorry for sounding pompous here, the work's basic material simply does not justify a 15-minute composing-out of that material. That's a highly subjective comment of course, but one that has been supported by some close friends of mine, composers of a high rank. My experience as both an audience member and performer has led me to believe that it's extremely difficult to capture and hold an audience's full attention during an airing of the work. This, in stark contrast to the way the trombone or viola Sequenzas. Regardless, it is a milestone indeed: that is, one of the most important composers of the 20th century composed a major work for the guitar.

After the exclusivity period expired, I was keen to study it of course, and it quickly became a central piece in my programs, even at the time when I started working with electronics and electric guitar, which in hindsight site was insane, given the work's inherent challenges. Anyway, I remember two performances in particular, one in Bonn for a very unprepared audience, as far as new art music is concerned, and one in Tel Aviv right before Gulf War I began. That was eerie indeed.

About performance, firstly, there are some important structural elements in the piece, including an array of symmetrical constructs on the foreground. Berio, from all accounts, and I know several composers who have consulted with him, was extremely meticulous. It seemed logical to me therefore to attempt to strive for a reading that would discern the subtle shifts in the organization of time, despite the "improvisamente" indication at the heading of the first section when the opening "chorale" comes to a conclusion. I also felt, in reference to my preparations for the recording, that it was necessary to adhere to his tempo indication very strictly.

The somewhat sad postlude to my Sequenza history is that Mode's boxed Sequenza set appeared almost immediately after Berio passed away. I had been planning to send him a copy.

Mode Records is one of my favorite music labels, how did you start working with them? Will you record again with Mode?

The new art music community is rather small indeed. I met Brian Brandt in the mid-90s through Ulrich Krieger with whom I went on to co-produce the Gavin Bryars portrait that explored Gavin's "experimental" music from the early 70s. In addition to that CD - as well as the aforementioned Berio, you are probably aware that Mode released Chaya Czernowin's Maim (a 50-minute work for 5 soloists and orchestra) two years ago; and, many folks have eagerly awaited my reconstruction of Feldman's The possibility of a new work for electric guitar, which is now available on iTunes. Brian and I speak regularly, and, although the CD/DVD business is in a miserable state presently, there is one portrait CD coming into view, on which I will have a fat-sized track collaborating with a world renowned group. I am not in the position to speak about this further, because the piece hasn't yet been written!

What does improvisation mean for your music research? Do you think it's possible to talk about improvisation for classical music or we have to turn to other repertories like jazz, contemporary music, etc.?

I have been involved occasionally in improvisational projects, a few years ago with Karlheinz Essl, and lately with some Berlin folks from the Electronica scene (Exercise One, Jacopo Carreras and DJ Dinky). These projects often provide me with the opportunity to explore some ideas and expressive elements, ones that I can't necessarily bring to my interpretations of notated music. This is particularly true when it comes to dealing with texture and sound, more specifically processing. I can integrate many more analogue pedals, which I prefer for their warmth, in an improvisational context and also devise somewhat unorthodox signal chains. When everything clicks in a live situation, it is a glorious, exhilarating feeling. By the way, someone whom I greatly respect, and who has an interesting take on all of this is Richard Barrett. I recommend that the readers have a look at his music, some of which is about capturing the spirit of improvisation, though with a notation that for most is unfortunately difficult to comprehend.

In 1968 Derek Bailey asked to Steve Lacy to define in 15 seconds the difference between improvisation and composition, the answer was "In 15

131

the difference between improvisation and composition is that in composition you have all the time to decide what to you say in 15 seconds, while in improvisation you have only 15 seconds" .. Was the Lacy's answer a little too much ironic or is it a true one?

I think you'd be best served by asking a composer, or someone such as Richard Barrett, who both composes and improvises. If I might be allowed to do some promo on his behalf: his duo "Furt", with Londoner Paul Obermeyer, has an unmatched visceral power and throws an interesting light on his compositional activities.

What's the role of the "Error" in your musical vision? For "error" I mean an incorrect procedure, an irregularity in the normal operation of a mechanism, a discontinuity on an otherwise uniform surface that can lead to new developments and unexpected surprises...

When I think about "error," inevitably I recall the Stravinsky anecdote. He said he liked to compose at the piano in case his finger slipped ....

If you listen to a different interpretation of a score you already played and you want to perform this again, do you keep it in mind listening or do you prefer to proceed in complete independence?

It depends, really. By and large, though, I try to remain in the present, since I know all too well that recordings are nothing more than a snapshot taken at a specific moment in time. Six months following the session, one could be thinking differently about such issues as tempi, articulation, phrasing, etc.

I try to ask you a little bit I'm going to ask you a provocative question about music in general, not just about contemporary or avant-garde. Frank Zappa in his autobiography he wrote: "If John Cage, for example, said, now I put a contact microphone on the throat, then I drink carrot juice and this will be my composition ", then his gargling would qualify as a COMPOSITION, because he applied a frame, declaring it as such. "Take it or leave it, now I want this to be music." It's really good Is this statement really a good way to define a genre of music, just say this is classical music, this is contemporary and it's done? Does It still makes sense to speak about "genre"?

I think Zappa was being rather cheeky in his description, firstly. I think we're talking about contextuality, and in this context the ACT action of drinking, not just the gargling sound, would be considered an integral part of the composition, which is important, not only in terms of the framing, but in terms of the interpretation. I personally find it extraordinarily difficult to define "contemporary music" for non-specialists; the term is so widely misunderstood and so angst-provoking in many circles. Anyway, the questions that require asking are: What's music actually? Is music simply organized sound, or organized noise? What about the temporal factors, on the micro and macro levels? What's perception? What's hearing? How can we deepen perception?

It seems to me that there is a small music scene about classical guitarists dedicated to an innovative and contemporary repertoire, as well as you come to my mind the names of Marco Cappelli, David Tanenbaum, David Starobin, Elena Casoli, Marc Ribot who played John Zorn music... shall I speak about a music scene? Are you in contact with these musicians? Are there other guitarists you know and that you can suggest to us that they move on in these innovative musical routes?

Yes, I have had dealings with most of these folks over the years, in different contexts and situations. They are all making significant contributions, in one way or another.

Well, Maurizio Grandinetti is a good friend. He plays very well and has done some extraordinary things, both as a soloist, but also as a member of Ensemble Phoenix. He's also someone who can elegantly travel back and forth between classic and electric guitar. The Swedish guitarist, Magnus Andersen, has had a number of extremely important works written for him, among them Brian Ferneyhough's Kurze Schatten. Recently, his student Stefan Östersjo has done some fantastic work, most notably tackling Rolf Riehm's monstrously difficult Toccata Orpheus, of which there is a video online. Of course, Jürgen Ruck is a towering figure in Germany, having been associated with Ensemble Modern since the early 90s. Tom Pauwels, the Belgian guitarist, is quite active. Lastly, someone who goes unrecognized, but who has premiered well over 100 works with the Nieuw Ensemble in Amsterdam, is Helenus de Rijke. I don't know of any living guitarist who has more ensemble experience, i.e. playing with conductor, than he.

Talking about innovative composers, what do you think about John Zorn and the New York musical downtown scene, so ready to get and recode every musical language, improvisation, jazz, contemporary music, cartoon music?

Frankly, I haven't spent a lot of time listening and thinking about John's music. I used to listen to Naked City CDs about 15 years ago; it was a revelation at the time. Eliott Sharp is tireless and has done some great things of course and, well there are countless others.

I'm a Rhys Chatham and Sonic Youth fan, I know that you have played with Chatham, can you tell us something about this experience?

I worked with him in two vastly different settings, one in NYC and one in Rome. The NYC concert, at Lincoln Center Festival Outdoors, was rained out unfortunately; the Rome concert went on as scheduled for it was in doors. I have fond memories of the way Rhys inspired and motivated a wildly diverse collection of players, from rank amateurs to seasoned professionals. The players varied in age, from 16 to 50 year olds. For me, it was mind blowing in a way. My ego was reduced to practically "nihil". I participated because I wanted to have the experience of being in this ocean of electric guitar sound in short, for the sheer thrill and ecstasy. In Rome we had the house shaking and the audience went beserk afterwards! Rhys has that thing we call magnetism and charisma. You can't teach that. It's either there or not and he's got it! Aside from that, the music itself is fairly simple in a way, lots of pulsating stuff, octaves, single notes, fairly conventional rhythmic figures, etc. Most of the players he assembles for his massive works with ca. 100 electric guitars can't read music, so he's forced to keep his musical gestures somewhat elementary. This is not to say that the sonic aggregate result is not rich, for it is and fantastically so!

Your musical career has been going on for several years, how have you seen the musical world changing? around you? Do you note differences between the students you teach and you taught? How new technologies (new musical instruments, midi, social networks, forums) have influenced your choices and your musical form? How?

Good question! Yes, it's changing, evolving in so many ways – some of which are highly lamentable, and some of which are quite amazing and startling. Take the digitalization of music for one: I grew up with vinyl, witnessed its slow demise, watched the concomitant rise of the CD (and DVD), and now students don't even buy a physical product anymore; instead, they store all their music on a hard drive, or have it streamed! Another part of the musical sociological firmament is the orchestral landscape: in the past two decades dozens of orchestras have folded, some notable ones included; some radio orchestras in Europe are dealing with very serious existential questions (see: fusion of SWR Stuttgart and Baden-Baden), some are now playing "staple" repertoire more regularly; lastly, the Berlin Philharmonic recently terminated its contract with Deutsche Grammophon, something utterly unimaginable 20 years ago! On the

134

other hand, let's consider the ensemble culture in the USA: 15 years ago there was no ICE, Chicago was a new music wasteland (now there's Dal Niente and a.pe.ri.od.ic, amongst others) and JACK Quartet was a remote dream. That's indeed revealing – and is indicative of a budding interest in new art music, both at the institutional and local level! Regarding pedagogy: I really can't comment on that with any sort of authority, except to say guitarists need to think about rhythm more carefully than they do.

I had two university students recently come to consult with me, both of whom brought Carter's "Changes" and both of whom couldn't execute comprehensible quintuplets and sextuplets. A conductor would have had them thrown out of rehearsal immediately with that kind of slovenliness. Regarding the last question: in part, I hinted at the answer above, in reference to the technology bit, but I would say that computer technology has spurred interest in performing works which involve interfacing, mostly facilitated by Max/MSP which was designed at IRCAM and was only available on a limited basis in the mid-90s due to the hardware restrictions and which has became a household item since!

If you had to choose, who is your favorite composer to play?

Oh dear, there are so many! How about a different question: who is my favorite composer whose music I have always dreamt of playing? The answer would be Brahms!

I have, sometimes, the feeling that in our times music's history flows without a particular interest in its chronological course, in our discotheque before and after, past and future become interchangeable elements, shall this be a risk of a uniform vision for an interpreter and a composer? The risk of a musical "globalization"?

Oh dear, that's complicated. I think there is music that stands outside of history, and I think there is music that takes history quite seriously and is commenting on past experience in some way shape or form. What I find now is through the internet and the concomitant facility with which information can be exchanged, that composers in the U.S. in particular are much more in touch with what is going on over here. I couldn't necessarily say that 20 years ago. You'd have traveled far and wide to find someone who could talk with authority about Helmut Lachenmann's string quartets, for instance. Today, they are almost part of the canon, and many of the American college the students know the scores intimately. That's noteworthy progress, I would say, and in that sense the world has indeed gotten smaller. In performance, I have noticed similar trends, also in respect to Helmut's music. There are actually ensembles over there that are now familiar with his playing techniques and sound world and who are performing his music. To get back to your question, though, I think that profound cultural differences still abound, and that affects directly the expressive and aesthetic content of any given score or performance. For instance, if one were to hear Ensemble Intercontemporain and Asko Ensemble play a major work by Louis Andriessen back-to-back, one would hear two very skilled performances, but two very different aesthetics in terms of sound and color. Most of this has to do with the instrumental schooling, especially as it applies to the woodwinds.

Let's talk about marketing. How much do you think it's important for a modern musician? I mean: how much is it crucial to be good promoters of themselves and their works in music today?

It's an unfortunate part of the business, a necessary evil of sorts. It often takes excessive amounts of energy from the real purpose of our lives, and that is music making. I find some of my colleagues highly offensive in that respect, and overbearing. (Also with reference to Facebook, the level of self-aggrandizement and self-promotion by some is tasteless and insufferable. I "hide" them….) I am committed to the light touch as it were, e.g. moderato. I find it works to a certain extent. Of course, I wish I had a manager, but I don't. Hence, promotion is a necessary component of my professional, irrespective of whether I like it, or not. On occasion I therefore have to send out spam in order to inform people that this or that disc has appeared. Only in rare situations, do I feel compelled to send out concert notices. If I do, it mostly concerns a local event; in that case, I use email as an ersatz invitation card. Anyway, right now a disturbing number of people are all consumed with Facebook, myspace and websites, whatever, and it's reached a level that is somewhat disconcerting.

What do you think about the discographic market crisis, with the transition to digital downloading in mp3 and all this new scenario?

I made passing reference to this above, when talking about Mode. I have one thing to say: stop the file sharing! It's as simple as that. My generation grew up buying vinyl; we spent our leftover cash purchasing records, listening to them together and talking about them endlessly. As for Gen X and subsequent ones, they could damn well do the same! They are living off the same restricted budgets that we were, so what's the difference? They spend more money on lattes and cappuccinos, I guess… The prevailing attitude is that they can have everything for free, whether it be music, news, TV, you name it. This is fundamentally corrupt!! In my discussions with students, I have often found them to be hopelessly clueless about the economics surrounding a CD

136

production, about cover and booklet design, text composition, studio costs, producer and engineer costs, etc, etc. In short, there's a micro-economic activity behind the scenes, so to speak, which needs illumination; and I am not even talking about royalties or honorarium for the performers! Perhaps if folk were better informed about the process, they would think twice the next time they download something illegally from Napster or equivalent, or copy a file from a friend.

My other rant is that the iPod has sounded the death knoll for the album concept. For instance, the second side of Abbey Road: it's a suite, really. If people's habits are mostly about downloading select songs, which group is going to be prepared to take such an enormous risk? Moreover, which label would actually support such a concept?

Which composer (or which historical movement) do you think is easiest for the non-musician listener to appreciate? Do you think they enjoy pieces that are more technically difficult or just more "flashy"?

Well, I think the whole "Bang-on-the-Can" movement has enjoyed great appeal to the non-specialized audiences and for very obvious reasons. They picked up though on an aesthetic thread which had been previously established by figures such as Steve Reich and Louis Andriessen, as well as Terry Riley or John Adams. Therein lies my answer: minimalism, and "post-minimalism." As regards the second part of your question, I think virtuosity still holds a kind of irresistible fascination for many audience members, but there are other "movements" and stylistic developments which enjoy notable followings, such as the "wandelweiser" group, who generally focus on quiet sounds, as well as silence. Their audiences are very interested in the more, say, contemplative aspects of the musical experience, as opposed to the extroverted pyrotechnics of a Ferneyhough or Xenakis.

I try to risk a reckless question... Bach composed sometimes without specifying instrumentation... maybe... maybe wasn't he interested about "Sound of Music"? I mean maybe does his music in this case is hidden in a scheme, a structure capable of several realizations, several possible and different sounds? And the moment when the music reveals its true nature, is it contained in the exercise of its variations? Bach at this point would have composed something like jazz standards or pre Cage scores?

Hmm...Yes, reckless indeed, as shall be my answer no doubt! I think Bach was primarily interested in form and rigorous counterpoint. (Not very reckless, yes, but objective, n'est pas?) While I like the question, I think the contexts are

137

entirely different, and thus I have difficulty drawing such an analogue! One point though worth bearing in mind: most concert musicians today know about improvisation, a highly refined and entirely normal practice in Early Music, as we know. The other point is that an overwhelming majority of composers currently are not involved in the performance of their own works today.

Please tell us five essential records, to have always with you. The classic five discs for the desert island ...

Only 5?!?! Oh dear ...

- Glenn Gould's first recording of Bach's "Goldberg" Variations
- Miles Davis – "Kind of Blue"
- Mahavishnu Orchestra – "Birds of Fire"
- Pat Metheny – "Bright Size Life"
- The Beatles – "White Album"

Each of them are epic in there their own special way.

What are your five favorite scores?

You like the number 5, don't you?

Beethoven - String Quartet op. 132
Schubert – Piano Sonata in Bb-major, op. posthumous
Brahms – Piano Concerto No. 2
Bartók – 5th String Quartet (or Music for Strings, Percussion and Celesta)
Ligeti – Atmosphères
(Sorry, this is self-indulgent, but I need to mention Wagner's Tristan and Isolde, as well as Stravinsky's In Memorium Dylan Thomas running closely behind the other five.)

Loads of guitar music therein, don't you think?

With who would you like to play? What kind of music do you listen to usually?

Hmm .... Dawn Upshaw and I were supposed to do the Argento cycle (Letters from Composers) while we were students at MSM. She got sick shortly before the concert and we had to cancel the appearance. I'd like to do something with her someday!

I've never had the chance to play under Peter Eötvös' baton. From what I have heard, that is a very special experience.
I must confess I have a difficult time listening to new art music at home – and, for that matter, most classical music. More and more I feel divorced from that whole ritual; I much prefer going to hear a concert, especially when you have the Berlin Philharmonie in your backyard! I mostly listen to indie Rock or Jazz, when I have the time. My taste in that regard is fairly catholic, I must say - from Sonic Youth to Yo La Tengo to Public Image Limited to Radiohead; from Miles Davis to Herbie Hancock to Bill Evans to Bill Frisell.

Your next projects? When we will see you playing in Italy again?

Well, as you know, the writing of "The Techniques of Guitar Playing" with Ming (Tsao) was a kind of monumental achievement for me, and in a way I am still dealing with it, in terms of giving book presentations and preparing colloquia, et all. Having said that, the most horrid portions of the season are now well behind me (two lengthy U.S. tours, Lachenmann's Schwankungen am Rand with RSB, Osvaldo Budón's installation/performance, etc.); coming up, though, is WDR's Witten Festival with knm berlin where we are performing works by Gorlinsky and Czernowin, I have a concert with Miss Moth in Berlin in early May, and am going to Oslo with ensemble zwischentöne also in May. I shall be revisiting Kagel's Unter Strom and Tactil next summer, and I will be giving the full-length first performance of Kirsten Reese's work for electric guitar and Fairlight CMI system here in Berlin in early July. After that, a well-earned holiday! Regarding Italy: no clue! Could you arrange a concert for me?

I wish I could, it would be fun.. you have mentioned your book "The Techniques of Guitar Playing[49]" written with Ming Tsao, I have read and I think it's a really powerful book, one of the most comprehensive and detailed collectionof styles and techniques applicableto the contemporary guitar. I think will be a great help for composers, how did you get the idea for this book?

The seed was planted, for the most part, ca. 23-24 years ago when I had a residency at Schloss Solitude near Stuttgart. The amazing New Zealand-born oboist, Peter Veale, who was also in residence there at the time, and the composer Claus-Steffan Mahnkopf were researching and writing what would eventually be the initial book in the Baerenreiter series. I was inspired by their dedication, rigor and spirit which they brought to the project - the incessant

---

49 https://www.baerenreiter.com/en/search/product/?artNo=BVK2243

sound of those multiphonics haunting the musician's wing of the Schloss!- , and thought the guitar might need such a book toward the new millenium. Apart from that, Frederic Rzewski once replied when I had asked him whether he had written fir the guitar: "Seth, the guitar is a preposterous instrument!" One could say that was the true genesis.

A last question... any good advices to give to your students?

1. Stop the file sharing!
2. Work hard and you shall be rewarded - sometimes, though, not in the ways you might expect!

This is really the last question .. which is more a reflection: Luigi Nono said "Other thoughts, other noises, other sounds, other ideas. When we listen to, we often try to find ourselves in others. To find our mechanisms, system, rationalism, in the other. And this is a quite conservative violence. "... Now .. does experimentation free ourselves from the burden of having to remember?

Oh gosh, no!

HEIKE MATTHIESEN

Heike Matthiesen is one of Germany's leading guitarists whose virtuosity and spirited performance, coupled with a charismatic stage presence, are regularly highlighted by the press. Born in Braunschweig, she received comprehensive musical training on the piano at an early age and only took up the guitar when she was 18. About a year later, she started studying at the Frankfurt Conservatory. Pepe Romero, who taught her for several years, was the formative influence on her playing.

Apart from her solo commitments, Heike Matthiesen regularly performs with chamber music ensembles, and since 1997 she has been closely affiliated with Villa Musica Mainz. She has appeared with Los Romeros and, in 2005, recorded a CD with the Spanish Art Guitar Quartet ("Bolero", NCA).

Heike Matthiesen has performed in many different countries, including the US, Russia, Japan, China, France, Spain, Italy, Poland, Iceland, Austria and Bulgaria, and is a very welcome guest at festivals and in guitar concert series.

https://heikematthiesen.wordpress.com/welcomeclassicalguitar/

The first question is always the classic one: how does it start your love and interest for guitar and what instruments do you play or have you played?

There is no this one moment when I fell in love with guitar, I grew up with piano and opera music, my parents working in the opera. But from early childhood I was fascinated by everything connected with Spain, I listened to Flamenco already as kid- and my first classical guitar recording were the Boccherini Quintets played by Pepe! We had an old simple guitar hanging on the wall which always attracted me.. like almost every beginner here in Frankfurt I started then with a Hopf guitar. Today my favourite guitar is my Gioachino Giussani which once belonged to Pepe, she is the guitar I feel safe with on stage, unbelievable projection but for many people not that convincing from upclose, so I started late to record on her. It is a dangerous temptation to follow your wish to collect every guitar you like because you just can play one at a time... For my guitar duo I bought last year a copy of a guitar by Thumhard from 1810 built by Herb. It is a great thing that you can choose your "voice" by having more than one instrument, but in the moment of truth you will always choose the same instrument you feel home with to have the biggest freedom for music on stage.

What was your musical training, with which teachers have you studied and what impression they left in your music? I know that you are... "devoted" to Pepe Romero...

141

I started late, my first guitar lesson when I was 18, and I immediately started with one of the best teachers available, Professor Heinz Teuchert, known from all his editions and his guitar school. I have played piano all my life, was surrounded by music, so Professor Teuchert later confessed that he wanted this "interesting case of a guitar beginner who already was complete musician". One year later I started to study at the Hochschule, then I studied with his son Michael Teuchert and finally made my artist diploma with Thomas Bittermann.

Already while being student I started to take super-regular masterclasses with Pepe. Before I met him I was a chamber musician, I played plucked instruments in the opera orchestra in Frankfurt and thought there is no way to make it into solo guitar world with my extremely late start. He changed me into what I am today!

There are many good teachers where you can learn to play guitar and to be a good musician, but there are few who can teach you to be a stage player, how to prepare for concerts, how to survive in this business and on stage, all this "mental" tools you can learn to feel home on stage. And he was giving this knowledge in public masterclasses.. sometimes students asked after a lesson they listened to: what where you talking about?

We talked about where to put you mind and your consciousness while playing, practising and performing...

One of the things that I can honestly say about guitar is its ability and capacity to change its shape as a musical medium over the centuries and between the various musical and social forms. This incredible ability is due to several factors not least the fact that it can be realized both in industrial and artigianal forms, and the fact that we can choose between classical, acoustic and electric types suitable for different musical and social cultures. You have followed a very personal path inside the guitar, how did you develop this path and how are you developing it?

The guitar for me always had a magic, almost nobody thinks negative about guitar no matter which style, so it is an instrument that really is crossing all borders. It has a magic in its sounds. And it's the instrument that gets you the closed to the making of sounds, except the voice of course, there is no bow, no mechanic things, you touch the strings directly... and I am sure this is one of the reasons for the magic of the guitar. And in a world where classical music in the "old" way with sometimes outdated routines guitar can have a great future, I strongly believe in that. Guitar concerts preserve the magic of visibly handmade music, of the unique moment when inspiration happens and it is the most friendly instrument to learn, everybody who learnt his first three chords know

142

this, and also because a guitar is affordable if it is made industrial. But one more aspect: in German romantic literature of the 19.century you have many times heroes who seek a truth beyond the visible and many times their Alter-Ego accompagning them on every journey is a guitar, the guitar as a mirror to yourself. So I answer your intellectual question in a spiritual way...

Do you think that the guitar, with its presence of virtuoso very personal musicians at every musical level and genre would be a viable alternative to the now tragicomic distinction between high culture and popular culture and the affirmation of Schönberg " if it is art, it is not for all, and if it is for all, it is not art "?

There will be always be the virtuoso- amateur gap, but for me it sounds simply arrogant to say, if it is for all, it is not art: popular classic then would be no art . And I have so much respect for people who make music at home at their level and enjoy it, sorry, Mr. Schönberg!!!
And the guitar could be the instrument that creates the new levels: good music, bad music, no matter if it was former pop culture or understandable for just some happy few, I have a lot of hope!

Berio in his essay "A remembrance to the future," wrote: ".. A pianist who is a specialist about classical and romantic repertoire, and plays Beethoven and Chopin without knowing the music of the twentieth century, is also off as a pianist who is specialist about contemporary music and plays with hands and mind that have never been crossed in depth by Beethoven and Chopin. " You play both traditional classical and contemporary repertoire ... do you recognize yourself in these words?

Of course.. I never stop learning and discovering music. I am mostly known for being specialists for Spanish music and my Mozart-pieces but of course I LOVE to play contempory music. My Dyens record was the first entire Dyens-CD not played by himself. And I just commissioned a nice collection of new pieces by guitarists/friends for a future program.
In German market it is very difficult to sell programs with living composers or those not longer dead than 70 years, the GEMA is protecting the rights of the composers so well that these kinds of programs can get quite expensive for smaller venues, so they ask for programs free of this charge. So I play much less new music than I would like too. I always felt being part of history and with this a responsibility: my teachers learned from theirs, and all our pupils will pass knowledge to theirs.. so I don't like the thought that I might have met the Beethoven of guitar from nowadays and not having realized it or even worse

ignored it. I would love to meet him/her... or maybe I already did? Future will tell!

What does improvisation mean for your music research? Do you think it's possible to talk about improvisation for classical music or we have to turn to other repertories like jazz, contemporary music, etc.?

I am terrible improviser... but my goal is to play on stage like if I am creating/composing/improvising this particular piece at the very moment. It is always like playing it the first time.
I have lots of respect for musicians who really improvise but many of them like we say in German "cook with water", you realize pre-prepared patterns etc... so what counts for me is how somebody jumps into music then it is not important which music it is. And we always can learn for example from blues players who can make you cry with three chords- we classical players always are in danger to try to impress and forget that music is about feelings. So this is something we can learn especially from many styles of world music!

Sometimes ago my friend Elena Càsoli said to me "I improvise the interpretation of what you call encoded. Scored music requires an ethic of respect, attention, closeness and knowledge of its aesthetics, looking at the sign left by the author. But it's a moving, alive, elusive, intangible subject, which awaits the encounter with an interpretative act. And this meeting, in concert, has a space for improvisation, every evening new and different" What do you think about these words?

Very wise words! On stage it is not about repeating something trained, it is about leaving your comfortzone. I never play a piece two times the same way, always tiny little changes, discoveries, always looking at the pieces like if I played them for the first time, so it is like an improvisation within the written score.

What's the role of the "Error" in your musical vision? For "error" I mean an incorrect procedure, an irregularity in the normal operation of a mechanism, a discontinuity on an otherwise uniform surface that can lead to new developments and unexpected surprises...

Errors on stage can open the door to magic, I am not afraid for errors. What I don't like if a mistake makes you leave music. Of course recordings changed our perception of music. Older great musicians left even wrong notes if the music was magic, today cleanness turned into a basic skill people seem to expect. I personally prefer errors to sterile perfection.

And in guitar technique I always tell when teaching: If it works, it is legal! I use barre-es across two frets, I allow my left hand to leave "correct" positioning to dance on the fingerboard, I move the guitar while playing (this is why I never playing with armsocks, leathers etc), I practice in all kind of position including playing on the right leg. What feels good for the body is legal.

If you listen to a different interpretation of a score you already played and you want to to perform this again do you keep it in mind listening or do you prefer to proceed in complete independence?

Before I work a piece I listen to the collegues, but when I start to work it the most important for me is to listen to nonguitar-music then, but fitting to my repertory. My goal is to go beyond the limitations of the guitar, so I have to have clear pictures of how it should be in my head- meaning phrasing like a singer, melody lines like a violin with crescendi and decrescendi in the longer notes, the structural clearness of playing piano with two hand etc. So when I work Sor, I listen to Mozart and Haydn, when I play Mertz I listen to Schubert, Rossini or Bellini etc

I try to ask you a little bit 'provocative question about music in general, not just about contemporary or avant-garde. Frank Zappa in his autobiography he wrote: "If John Cage, for example, said, now I put a contact microphone on the throat, then I drink carrot juice and this will be my composition ", then his gargling would qualify as a COMPOSITION, because he applied a frame, declaring it as such. "Take it or leave it, now I want this to be music." It's really good this statement to define a genre of music, just say this is classical music, this is contemporary and it's done? It still makes sense to speak about "genre"?

Of course it is an important question, especially for guitarists: If you see music composed of typical right hand patterns or collections of tapping sound effects you can discuss, but for me the solution is in the way of performing. Every piece I play on stage I meet with respect in a humble way, the attitude of the performer towards the piece can create art. And not every guitar piece has the level of late Beethoven, but also mediocer pieces treated with respect can turn into great music if the performer has the right attitude. Plus the next point: where does the performance happen? In the right surrounding (which does not always mean a concert hall) it is so much easier to create art. Plus an audience that is prepared to meet some crazy things happening! The borders of classical guitar are already so much more open than in other instrument, but I guess for presenters and audiences labels of how it is called ,will stay important.

145

Your musical career has been going on for several years, how have you seen the musical world changing? around you? Do you note differences between the students you teach and you taught? How new technologies (new musical instruments, midi, social networks, forums) have influenced your choices and your musical form? How?

There has been unbelievable progress in technical abilities, but all this attempt to play clean and perfect took away personal language and risks. In blind tests I hear for example Bream, Segovia, the Romeros at the first notes they pluck but many of those multicompetition-winners sound very much alike, clear consequence of being trained to play clean and so much mainstream that no judge can say anything against his interpretation. And there are nowadays so many competitions, it is much easier to collect a dozen or 20 prizes... This can give those players a nice income as long as they compete but it will never naturally mean a successful career as concert player afterwards. And today the possibility to listen to players around the world, also to see them and how they manage the difficult spots are immense and it is so much easier to learn about music and not just about fingers. I remember how much it meant to choose a record to buy as poor student before youtube! But today everybody has all possibilities at home in his computer and is not using it enough...
For myself I choose music that means something to me, not to impress somebody and I realize sometimes I play super-mainstream, another time music people never heard about...
I spent evenings sigh-treading stuff from Rischel or Boije bibliotheques, in search for repertory I use youtube. Before starting to work a piece I listen to a lot of different interpretations, then I do mine in my head, then I start to work.

If you had to choose, who is your favorite composer to play?

I guess it is evident that I feel a strong connection to the music of Mozart. A wise man once said that Mozart hides his depth directly underneath the surface.. and I like the perfect balance of Apollo and Dyonisos. What a pity that he did not write for the guitar!
From the guitar composers I fall more and more in love with Mertz, I am romantic girl!

I have, sometimes, the feeling that in our times music's history flows without a particular interest in its chronological course, in our discotheque before and after, past and future become interchangeable elements, shall this be a

risk of a uniform vision for an interpreter and a composer? The risk of a musical "globalization"?

When I studied with Pepe he always asked me for all kind of background knowledge, not just about the composers but about the historical setting in which those pieces where written. Art, literature, political facts etc, that is for me clear that I should know as much as possible. Then you learn about the style as much as possible and then you let the audience see it through your eyes within your personal style. I am a belcanto girl, I love to let the guitar sing, so this will be present no matter if I play Bach or Dodecaphonic music, but it will have gone through a strong process of background knowledge before.

This is something I am not happy to see nowadays with these super-short bachelor and master studies, you don't have time to "waste" to gain all kind of extra-knowledge. On the same moment more knowledge than ever is accessible through the web but you know less when you know where to search for it.

Let's talk about marketing. How much do you think it's important for a modern musician? I mean: how much is crucial to be good promoters of themselves and their works in music today?

It is crucial, but there are many possible styles of promotion. Business is changing so much, there are still the super-powerful major labels, if you are with them it is another story.. and for the "middleclass" it gets more and more difficult because many presenters like to do more and more few"events" instead of regular concerts, so also in the paradise-looking arts world Germany there is big erosion happening. So the number of indie-classical-musicians is constantly growing. You can be wordwide avaible today without a major label or agency, but the people have to know you, so they can find you... or you have to make them find you!

And for this the internet can do magic!

And I believe the times are gone where a musician had to be an iconic hero or genius, not talking to normal people, you should communicate... then it depends on your personality how you deal with it, you don't need to be extroverted to be a good ambassador for your music, but it helps. When I am using all those social media platforms I more think about being ambassador for classical guitar than doing promotion for myself.

Which composer (or which historical movement) do you think is easiest for the non-musician listener to appreciate? Do you think they enjoy pieces that are more technically difficult or just more "flashy"?

Guitar is a magic instrument, almost nobody has negative associations to it, it is an instrument of romantic, cosy mood, dreams of holidays etc.. so I believe that especially those not too long romantic pieces can attract people to listen to classical music.

How many people love guitar because they once heard Asturias, Alhambra, our beloved Spanish Romance- or Cavatina??

Some people get overwhelmed if their first opera are the Soldaten by Zimmermann.. but that is the exception I guess.

And it would depend of the taste of these newbies: A methal fan can easily connect to medieval music, one who loves ballads might love Chopin, world musiclovers - that is the easiest, Techno fans might feel attracted to minimal.. so there is not just one answer to this question.

I try to risk a reckless question... Bach composed sometimes without specifying instrumentation... maybe... maybe wasn't he interested about the "Sound of Music"? I mean maybe in this case hismusic is hidden in a scheme, a structure capable of several realizations, several possible and different sounds? And the moment when the music reveals its true nature is contained in the exercise of its variations? Bach at this point would have composed something like jazz standards or pre-Cage scores?

Did Beethoven ever really write for an instrument? No, instrumentalist says his music is nicely made for fingers or voice, his music is always beyond what feels in the idiomatic of any instrument. In Bach's time everything was transcribed so for me it sounds logical to write for no instrument and leave it to the performers. Or maybe one more thought: was it written for brain pleasure just to read and visualize sounds?

Please tell us five essential records, to have always with you .. the classic five discs for the desert island ...

Fritz Wunderlich singing Schumann's Dichterliebe
Emil Gilels playing Liszt b-minor Sonata
Nathan Milstein playing Bach Chaconne
Tzimon Barto playing Chopin
Martha Argerich never sure which record to choose and can I add Casta Diva by Maria Callas too?

Of course you can... what are your five favorite scores?

My favorite operas: Don Giovanni, Der Ring des Nibelungen, Falstaff, Carmen and I love Puccini! (I first thought should I give an "impressive" answer or just say the truth... so here is the truth!)
In guitar I just can give the common philosophical answer: always the piece I am playing at that moment.

With who would you like to play? What kind of music do you listen to usually?

I would have loved to play duo with Mozart to convince to write something for me...
Being a little bit superstitious it would feel strange to put some "real names" here, so yes, there is a wishlist!
Mostly I listen to nonguitar-music, piano music, worldmusic, Flamenco... but I also enjoy the silence after all these hours I am busy with plucking strings. It is very difficult to listen to classical music, my brain immediately starts to work, so it is not really relaxing... and the worst: If friends invite you and play your own CD as sign of respect, my brain can't stop commenting my work!

Your next projects? When we will see you playing in Italy?

Right now I am working on two new solo programs, one entirely dedicated to female composers which I will record next spring, the other one will be a wide range of contemporary music, some not yet composed. And my "normal" life, concerts, masterclasses.. so a lot of practicing waiting for me.
And no dates fixed for Italy right now, but I hope to come back to Italy soon, I would love to improve my Italian and there is so much love for guitar in Italy, it was always a very special atmosphere with good audience in beautiful places, spero che ci vediamo presto!

I promise this is the real last question. Sometimes ago in an interview Carlos Santana said "Some people have talent, some people have vision. And vision is more important then talent, obviously." I have listen to your music several times and I think you have a great talent but... what's your vision?

I am sure that my vision must be bigger than my talent (laughs), I was never a child prodigy, I was not the superstar at the Conservatory, I never won a competition, but I am here! I want to be on stage and I want to share music, I want to give hope and some happiness, the biggest compliment for me is when the people tell what comes to their mind when they listen, their dreams, their phantasies... In our loud chaotic world there is a strong need for calmness and

149

awareness of the presence (also for silence) and what else can bring this better to the people than the fragile sounds of a guitar?

AMANDA MONACO

Since moving to New York City, Amanda Monaco has performed with a variety of musical groups, from jazz chamber ensembles and big bands to regular appearances with her own groups at such venues as Birdland, Joe's Pub, and The Blue Note, to name a few.
Amanda's current projects includes her quartet (aka Deathblow), a jazz and improvisational music ensemble that combines free-bop sensibilities with through-composed pieces equal parts textural, adventurous, and whimsical. Amanda is currently working on a series of compositions inspired by her love of Formula One racing.
Amanda also co-leads the quintet "Playdate" with old friends Noah Baerman (piano) and Wayne Escoffery (tenor saxophone) and new friends Henry Lugo (bass) and Vinnie Sperrazza.
Amanda is also a resident musician at Congregation B'nai Jeshurun in New York City, and appears on both of their recordings, *Halailah Hazeh: The music of Pesah* and *Teki Yah: The High Holy Days*. In 2011, Amanda released a CD of music accompanying text from the *Pirkei Avot*, a collection of rabbinical teachings compiled in the third century C.E., sung in Hebrew and Aramaic by Israel vocalist Ayelet Rose Gottlieb and accompanied by Monaco on electric guitar, with Daphna Mor on recorders and nay, Sean Conly on bass, and Satoshi Takeishi on percussion. The Pirkei Avot Project recently played the Boston Jewish Music Festival with vocalist Tammy Scheffer.
An educator since 1990, Amanda has served on the faculty of New School University, and is an Assistant Professor at Berklee College of Music. Her book, *Jazz Guitar for the Absolute Beginner* (Alfred Publishing), is available worldwide.

http://amandamonaco.com/

The first question is always the classic one: how does it start your love and interest for guitar and what instruments do you play or have you played?

I come from a very musical family. My father played guitar, and he was in a band with his three older brothers when he was a teenager. My grandmother would book them gigs! They were called the Monacats, then they changed their name to the Pat Williams Four (my grandfather's name was Pasquale William). I come from a large Italian family, and they will spontaneously break into song at family functions. Every member of the Monaco family sings in tune! I know it doesn't sound possible, but it's true.
I played French horn in high school, but since age 12 it's been all about the

151

guitar. I keep saying I'm going to start playing French horn again, but when I have an extra time (which is almost never) I always give that extra time to the guitar. I also play a little piano but not very well.

I know that you play a Brian Moore guitar, how is this instrument?

I love it! It's got a warm tone and it's small and light. The neck is just thick enough to have some weight to it, not too skinny.

I know you had a Klein guitar some time ago; how was it?

It was great, but after I got the Brian Moore I realized that I missed having a guitar with a traditionally shaped body and a headstock, so I sold my Klein to Kenny Wessel, who still plays it today. The Klein was perfect for me for a long time: it was small, it was ergonomic, and it was versatile.

I noticed something in the young people who want to play an electric guitar today, compared to 20 years ago it seems to me that there is less a search on tone, on instruments with a particular sound and a greater focus on pedals and effects... sometimes I wonder if today the guitars are actually becoming platforms for electronic wizardry and alchemy. I noticed that this also happens in the context of contemporary composers, few (and they are almost all Americans and especially New Yorkers) work with the "pure" guitar tone, otherwise it's a race to the effects and pedals, I think this is fine for people like Adrian Belew and the Edge... but otherwise aren't we exaggerating? Or is it an excuse to skip the traditional learning process based on the playing of the old classics?

I think that for a lot of people today, using effects and pedals with their guitars is a logical evolution of the instrument. There are still guitarists who use pedals extensively, however, that embrace the natural tone of the guitar itself; Mary Halvorson and Nels Cline are two that come to mind.
Regarding the question of whether or not people are trying to skip the traditional learning process, that's a topic that comes up in discussion frequently. When it comes to my students [at Berklee College of Music] I am sure to teach them the fundamentals of music as well as the basic vocabulary of whatever style they are focused on. Even if a student is an avid fan of more modern, avant-garde jazz guitarists, we still study Charlie Christian, Grant Green, Wes Montgomery etc. as that is the foundation.

What was your musical training, with which teachers have you studied and

152

what impression they left in your music? I asked for it because, I don't know if it's true, but listening to your music I immediately though about Jim Hall...

I <u>love</u> Jim Hall. I had the good fortune to attend his very last concert in November 2013 at Jazz at Lincoln Center. I must have heard him play 100 times over the years, and every time was just incredible. I once bumped into him on the street in Greenwich Village and we took a lovely, slow walk together, talking about Charlie Christian and Oscar Moore. I'll never forget it.
In high school I studied with a wonderful guitarist named George Raccio. He was an incredible teacher who always taught things in a very simple, accessible way; even when it was really difficult material, George had a way of making everything seem simple. In college I studied with the great Ted Dunbar, as well as pianist Kenny Barron, bassist Rufus Reid, pianist Harold Mabern and saxophonist Steve Wilson, all big influences on me. After college I studied with guitarist Wayne Krantz, and in graduate school it was Gene Bertoncini and Adam Rogers.

The first time I met you it was on Ralph Gibson's book "State of the Axe: Guitar Masters in Photographs and Words[50]", there are two pictures of you on that book ... how do you meet Gibson and... do you still have problems with club's owner who play your guitar without asking it to you?

I met Ralph Gibson through Tina Pelikan of ECM Records. He is a phenomenal photographer, taking those pictures in under five minutes during a sound check. As for my essay about being treated differently for being a woman, it still happens, but a lot less. Maybe it's because I'm over 40 now. (laughs)

What does improvisation mean for your music research? Do you think it's possible to talk about improvisation for classical music or we have to turn to other repertories like jazz, contemporary music, etc.?

Improvisation is everything. I'm currently serving as Artistic Director of Convergence Arts, Inc., a non-profit 501(c)(3) organization committed to sharing the art and fun of improvisation with the community at large. Classical music used to have improvisational sections - the cadenza of a concerto was traditionally used for that - and I think there's room still for that today. Improvisation is an important tool in all aspects of life; it gives you flexibility and resilience.

---

50   Ralph Gibson, State of the Axe: Guitar Masters in Photographs and Words, The Museum of Fine Arts, Houston, 2008, pag. 92

Sometimes ago my friend Elena Càsoli said to me "I improvise the interpretation of what you call encoded. Scored music requires an ethic of respect, attention, closeness and knowledge of its aesthetics, looking at the sign left by the author. But it's a moving, alive, elusive, intangible subject, which awaits the encounter with an interpretative act. And this meeting, in concert, has a space for improvisation, every evening new and different." What do you think about these words?

Elena has a point, but I think it's a matter of semantics. I don't think I would call it "improvising the interpretation" so much as internalizing the interpretation, which is a personal act as well as an artistic one. It's true that every evening is new and different, but not in an improvisational matter as much as a personal, respectful one.

If you listen to a different interpretation of a score you already played and you want to perform this again do you keep it in mind listening or do you prefer to proceed with complete independence?

I think it depends on the interpretation. The more esoteric the arrangement, the more I might be listening for something familiar.

In 1968 Derek Bailey asked to Steve Lacy to define in 15 seconds the difference between improvisation and composition, the answer was "In composition you have all the time to decide what you say in 15 seconds, while in improvisation you have only 15 seconds." Was the Lacy's answer a little too much ironic or is it a true one?

I think it's brilliant.

Shall we enter a bit 'more into the technical details of your playing? Listening to your solos I don't think you're a guitar player tied to "licks"; what kind of "vocabulary" do you use in your music? Do you use special scales? Do you ever find that you use a phrase that you've played before? Do you ever feel the need to stop using something you already know that would work? Do you ever use some "filling phrases"?

I believe that by learning one's instrument thoroughly, the chords, scales, and arpeggios, one achieves a level of ear training that allows one to play what she is hearing in her head on the instrument. So many times musicians are unable to execute what they are hearing in their heads simply because they lack the technique and the comfort with their instruments.

I was never one to play licks. I've done a lot of transcribing, but even more than that, I've done a lot of listening. It's like learning a language, and being able to navigate its vocabulary and grammar as opposed to simply repeating cliches.

I will admit that when I run out of melodic ideas, I start playing block chords. I was a huge Wes Montgomery fan in college, and learned a bunch of his block chord solos. My husband makes fun of me whenever he hears me start playing block chords at the end of a solo; he knows when I mean it and when I don't.

Your record "The Pirkei Avot Project Vol. 1" really surprised me. I like Jewish music, I'm a fan of John Zorn and Tzadik, and I really like it. Can you tell us more about this recording? How much important is your religion for you and your music?

I discovered the Pirkei Avot when reading through a prayer book at my synagogue. I looked for music that had been written to some of its verses, but found nothing, so I decided to write some, and record it with some of my favorite musicians.

Since 2000 I have been a resident musician at Congregation B'nai Jeshurun on the Upper West Side of Manhattan. Music is a very big part of the spiritual life there, and I play Shabbat services with myriad ensembles that include cello, piano, recorder, percussion and/or mandolin. There are seven resident musicians in total.

What's the role of the "Error" in your musical vision? For "error" I mean an incorrect procedure, an irregularity in the normal operation of a mechanism, a discontinuity on an otherwise uniform surface that can lead to new developments and unexpected surprise.

Some of the greatest discoveries are made through mistakes. I welcome them and embrace them.

I have met your drummer, Satoshi Takeishi, two years ago in a concert closer to my home in Mestre, he was playing with Marco Cappelli, I really enjoyed him, he is a great drummer and percussionist. How did you meet him?

I met Satoshi in 1999 through a mutual friend, guitarist Adam Levy. We played for a few years together, then life took us in different paths and we started playing together again in 2008. I'm so glad we're working together again!

I have, sometimes, the feeling that in our times music's history flows without a particular interest in its chronological course, in our discotheque before and after, past and future become interchangeable elements, shall this be a risk of a uniform vision for an interpreter and a composer? The risk of a musical "globalization"?

I think that it's important to have a history of the music even if you're not going to play it the way it used to be played. Some of my favorite avant-garde jazz musicians are incredible straight-ahead players when asked to play that way. I love it when I can hear the entire history of the music come out of someone's horn. Otherwise it sounds like a lot of noise.

Let's talk about marketing. How much do you think it's important for a modern musician? I mean: how much is crucial to be good promoters of themselves and their works in music today?

I think it's essential in this day and age of accessibility to carve out a niche for oneself in order to get noticed. There are so many musicians out there it's easy to get lost in the mix. Today's modern musician needs to have a story to tell, something that sets him/herself apart from the rest of the pack.
Since 2012 I've been working with a business consultant named Marty Khan. He has a blog on his web site www.outwardvisions.com, and has written a great music business book called *Straight Ahead* that stresses the importance of the collective as a way to move ahead in the music business as well as the 501(c)(3) non-profit organization as a vehicle for doing business (the way almost every other arts organization does it; for some reason it hasn't caught on as much in jazz).

What do you think about the discographic market crisis, with the transition to digital downloading in mp3 and this new scenario?

There's so much magic that's gone because of digital downloading. I loved going to the record store and poking around the stacks of vinyl and CDs, and it makes me sad that a lot of people have never had that opportunity.
The fact that so few people actually pay for their music anymore says so much about the state of humanity and its loss of respect and understanding for others. I know this sounds exaggerated, but I do believe that we have lost our way in terms of how we relate to the artist; we take for granted the heart and soul that he puts into his work. Come to think of it, we treat everyone that poorly, not just the artist; the difference is that at least with other jobs there's a guaranteed paycheck,

but often that paycheck is not enough and one needs to work two, three jobs to make ends meet.
On the flip side, I have fans all over the world because of digital downloading. If I can ever figure out how to get it all together, I'll be booking gigs in far-flung places because of mp3s, which is pretty exciting.

Your musical career has been going on for several years; how have you seen the musical world changing around you? Do you note differences between the students you teach and you taught? How new technologies (new musical instruments, midi, social networks, forums) have influenced your choices and your musical form? How?

As far as teaching, everything is different because of technology. It's so much easier for students to research artists and find their music, which is great. I also feel like the generation that's in college now is pretty tough considering that they're choosing a career in music at a time when hardly anyone pays for music anymore.
I used to sell a ton of CDs, but now they are more like a "business card" than anything else. On the flip side, there are still promoters who want to see that you have a CD out, and my husband is a jazz journalist who receives hundreds of CDs a month for review.

I try to ask you a little bit 'provocative question about music in general, not just about contemporary or avant-garde. Frank Zappa in his autobiography he wrote: "If John Cage, for example, said, now I put a contact microphone on the throat, then I drink carrot juice and this will be my composition ", then his gargling would qualify as a COMPOSITION, because he applied a frame, declaring it as such. "Take it or leave it, now I want this to be music." It's really good this statement to define a genre of music, just say this is classical music, this is contemporary and it's done? It still makes sense to speak about "genre"?

I think that as long as there are people who are interested in music, there needs to be some sort of classification. I think that people need a springboard to get them started on exploring different types of music.

Talking about innovative composers, what do you think about John Zorn and the New York musical downtown scene, so ready to get and recode every musical language, improvisation, jazz, contemporary music, cartoon music?

157

I think it's great, and it's healthy. There's tons of creativity everywhere, and people are digging it. Music will always bring people together.

One of the things that I can honestly say about guitar is its ability and capacity to change its shape as a musical medium over the centuries and between the various musical and social forms: guitar seems to be the perfect instrument (not only by the musical but also logical, economic and philosophical aspect) to counter the theories of the Frankfurt School and Adorno. Its incredible ability to spread is due to several factors not least the fact that it can be realized both in industrial and artisanal forms, and the fact that we can choose between classical, acoustic and electric types suitable for different musical and social cultures. You have followed a very personal path inside the guitar, how did you develop this path and how are you developing it?

Developing a personal path came naturally to me. I learned from those who came before me, and I took the information and created my own music from it. I feel that it's important to study those that came before, because it's how the tradition of the music evolves.

Which composer (or which historical movement or genre) do you think is easiest for the non-musician listener to appreciate? Do you think they enjoy pieces that are more technically difficult or just more "flashy"?

This is a tough question because I think that all music is accessible, but jazz has been given a bad rap. There's been too much discussion of how "intellectual" it is, or how you have to be "sophisticated". But truth be told, I think the gateway is always a steady beat. The music can be super avant-garde, but if there's a groove nobody seems to notice.

Please tell us five essential records, to have always with you... the classic five discs for the desert island...

OOH! That's a tough one!
"The Bridge" - Sonny Rollins
"Extrapolation" - John McLaughlin
"Cannonball Adderley and the Poll Winners"
"Coltrane's Sound"
"James Brown's 20 All-Time Greatest Hits"

With whom would you like to play? What kind of music do you listen to usually?

There's so many musicians I'd love to play with, but I'm really happy with the ones I'm playing with now. I am very blessed in that regard. What I listen to depends on where I am. I commute four hours from NYC every week to teach at Berklee College of Music in Boston, so I usually listen to guitar music (Ralph Towner's album *Travel Guide* with Slava Grigoryan and Wolfgang Muthspiel is amazing, you must hear it, you'll love it!) or stuff like Tony Bennett/Bill Evans. When I go for a run it has to be soul music/Motown. My husband is the Editorial Director of *The New York City Jazz Record*, so we listen to a lot of new jazz of all styles in the house as well as the re-issue classics.

Your next projects? When we will see you playing in Italy?

Currently I am writing music inspired by Formula One racing. I am a huge F1 fan and recently discovered that my great-uncle Walter E. Monaco was heavily involved in the racing scene, as well as a good pal of Sir Stirling Moss. I'm also writing music for Volume 2 of my Pirkei Avot project, as well as music for my classical/jazz guitar duo, Canterbury Guitar Duo (with classical guitarist Kim Perlak).

And I would LOVE LOVE LOVE to play in Italy! Where do I sign up?

PABLO MONTAGNE

Guitarist, composer, improvisor, Pablo Montagne was awarded the highest marks in classical guitar at the "A. Casella" Conservatoire of L'Aquila (Italy).
Following this, he studied with M.Felici and M.Grandinetti at the "N.Rota" Conservatoire of Monopoli (Italy), receiving the Master degree in guitar solo performance along with the mention "con Lode".
During this period he also studied improvisation with G.Lenoci obtaining the Diploma in "Jazz Music" with the mention "con Lode".
Furthermore, he studied electronic music with M.Lupone, meanwhile working with the CRM (Centre of Musical Research).
Over the years, Pablo Montagne has dedicated much time to the practices of improvisation and composition, which he conceives also as de-composition and re-composition,with a leaning towards diverse and multiple aspects of performance in both solo and group playing.

http://www.pablomontagne.com/

The first question is always the classic one: how did your love and interest for guitar start and which instruments do you play or have you played?

I've started with the violin, but I stopped since my teacher was too severe.
Later I've begun playing the electric guitar; a dear friend of mine was passionate about Metallica and was able to play several pieces of the band, this inspired me at the point that I took the guitar practicing very seriously.

What was your musical training, with which teachers have you studied and what impression did they leave in your music?

Music has always been a constant and uninterrupted background in my family life: my mother being a pianist and my father a violin maker.
Through my childhood I've always heard and almost learned by heart my mother's favourites pieces that she used to play at home by Debussy, Chopin, Messiaen, Bach etc...
In the following years me and my brother, viola player, gave our contribution to this daily musical background.
Later I've studied electric guitar with Luigi Candelori, Malo Vallois (Paris) and Italo de Angelis, and classical guitar with Massimo Felici and Maurizio Grandinetti.
There are many things that I've learned from these teachers, an entire book wouldn't be enough to list them all.

In sum through electric guitar I've learned to visualize and use the musical material technically (scales, chords, intervals) in order to improvise.
From the classical guitar I've learned how to see music from different points of view through interpretation. I've also developed a taste for sound production in relation to a wooden and acoustic instrument. Later I've learned to transfer this relation between instrument and sound to the electric guitar (electricity, metallic sound, volume, distortion).
Many sources of inspiration have been: the musicians I've played with through my career, my students, bad concerts that I've assisted to (things not to do), myself writing music... artists from other disciplines.

One of the things that I can honestly say about guitar is its ability and capacity to change its shapes as a musical medium over the centuries and between the various musical and social forms: guitar seems to be the perfect instrument (not only by the musical but also logical, economic and philosophical aspect) to counter the theories of the Frankfurt School and Adorno. You have followed a very personal path inside the guitar, how did you develop this path and how are you developing it?

Its in the nature of the guitar player to look for new and innovative solutions from the instrumental and technical point of view since he literally loves to "stick his hands" into the sound production.
The musician himself had always influenced new solutions in relation to the guitar construction, obtaining substantial modifications of the original instrument.
The sound research in its various aspects lies in the guitarist's DNA.
Personally the search for a sound that I've never heard interests me particularly and pushes me to look for creative instrumental, structural and musical solutions.

Do you think that the guitar, with its great virtuosos musicians at every musical level and genre would be a viable alternative to the now tragicomic distinction between high and popular culture in relation to Schoenberg's affirmation " if it is art, it is not for all, and if it is for all, it is not art "?

Honestly I think that these distinctions are created by those who are in charge of the festivals programs and of cultural and musical events management, and has the power to decide who will play or not.
If they have the entitlement to decide what's to be considered high culture, then Schoenberg was right...
I think that music can manage itself, finding its path and way out trough unexpected forms and places.

Berio in his essay "A remembrance to the future,"wrote: "... A pianist who is a specialist about classical and romantic repertoire, and plays Beethoven and Chopin without knowing the music of the twentieth century, is also off as a pianist who is specialist about contemporary music and plays with hands and mind that have never been crossed in depth by Beethoven and Chopin. " You play both traditional classical and contemporary repertoire .. do you recognize yourself in these words?

It is true that the more we know, the better we play... I've know great musicians with whom I could have spoken about Chopin as well as about Dire Straits, Bach or Zappa.
However I've encountered very cultivated musicians that knew a lot of things but could not express themselves deeply with their instrument.
In the other hand I've met musicians without a particular cultural background who were extraordinary expressive and inspiring.
It's difficult to find a good balance between these two approaches, I suppose that the truth lies in how genuinely the musician feels the music.

What does improvisation mean for your music research? Do you think it's possible to talk about improvisation for classical music or we have to turn to other repertories like jazz, contemporary music, etc.?

Improvisation is the most natural thing we could do, if a musician doesn't practice it (even just for amusement) he looses something.
In the past I've met classical musicians that could improvise their own repertoire more than an improviser, to my opinion what makes the difference is in our musical sensibility, our ideas and our ability to communicate. What we perform is finally a secondary aspect.

Sometime ago my friend Elena Càsoli said to me "I improvise the interpretation of what you call encoded. Scored music requires an ethic of respect, attention, closeness and knowledge of its aesthetics, king at the sign left by the author. But it's a moving, alive, elusive, intangible subject, which awaits the encounter with an interpretative act. And this meeting, in concert, has a space for improvisation, every evening new and different" What do you think about these words?

Improvisation is a composition that uses the moment, the instant as a protagonist, it's a tribute/sacrifice to the music that happens "Now".

This thing is also valuable for the written repertoire, since, however the material is already being established, the musician has to let things happen, to generate musical meaning instantly, "Now".

Many times during performances of classical repertoire we tend to neglect this element which is so vital to the music itself. Even worse, we try to create the standard repertoire always in the same way, producing a music which is always similar to itself.

What's the role of the "Error" in your musical vision? For "error" I mean an incorrect procedure, an irregularity in the normal operation of a mechanism, a discontinuity on an otherwise uniform surface that can lead to new developments and unexpected surprises .

Indeed the "Error" suggests alternatives paths, other solutions, realities, and sounding dimensions. However it's up to our sensibility to be able to recognize the new paths and signs that these errors are showing us. Having the courage to follow these paths and to cope with the eventual consequences of our choices is the real challenge.

If you listen to a different interpretation of a score you already played and you want to perform this again do you keep what you've heard in mind or do you prefer to proceed in complete independence?

Most of the times I try to avoid listening to, or I even hate listening to a piece that I'm supposed to perform... actually, in certain cases, I should do it since it would help me to observe the piece from different points of view. Fortunately I play my "stuff" basically 80% of the time...

I try to ask you a little bit 'provocative question about music in general, not just about contemporary or avant-garde. Frank Zappa in his autobiography wrote: "If John Cage, for example, said, now I put a contact microphone on the throat, then I drink carrot juice and this will be my composition ", then his gargling would qualify as a COMPOSITION, because he applied a frame, declaring it as such. "Take it or leave it, now I want this to be music." It's really good this statement to define a genre of music, just say this is classical music, this is contemporary and it's done? It still makes sense to speak about "genre"?

It is hard to define a musical "genre" within the historical period which we are living in, for instance Claude Debussy was not aware of the genre of his own compositions, perhaps he didn't care about it at all. The idea of "genre" itself

trough history of music it's very flexible, for example 30 years ago Debussy was classified as an impressionist composer whereas nowadays he's considered as a symbolist!
The artistic production of a musician is always in relation with the musical attitude of the period he's living in. This relation can modulate in different directions, it can either follow the main stream or it can be in a total rupture with it. Personally I'm not against the definition of "genre" itself, it can define a tendency, but certainly I think that the quality of a musical production exists regardless to the genre it belongs to.

Your musical career has been going on for several years, how have you seen the musical world changing? around you? Do you note differences between the students you teach and you taught? How new technologies (new musical instruments, midi, social networks, forums) have influenced your choices and your musical form? How?

Regarding the new recruits, I think that the general level had considerably risen, thanks to youtube and the easy access to music material compared to 20 years ago. Nevertheless this great amount of information had led to a certain homologation in the musical approaches and results.

If you had to choose, who is your favorite composer to play?

In general I prefer to play composers with whom I can exchange ideas and try to find various solutions... in this way I feel myself more involved.

I have, sometimes, the feeling that in our times music's history flows without a particular interest in its chronological course, in our discotheque before and after, past and future become interchangeable elements, shall this be a risk of a uniform vision for an interpreter and a composer? The risk of a musical "globalization"?

The risk exists, but what I'm the most concerned with is the way the music is being listened to through cds, mp3 players, youtube, smartphones etc., at the expense of live music.

Let's talk about marketing. How much do you think it's important for a modern musician? I mean: how much is crucial to be good promoters of themselves and their works in music today?

Knowing how to promote ourselves is fundamental and vital for the professional and financial aspect of a musician. However, when these two aspects are working properly, the artistic and creative part of a musician may often suffer. It's a very delicate balance and compromise, as if we should choose whether to force our hand to take advantage personally or let the music lead our career.

Which composer (or which historical movement) do you think is easiest for the non-musician listener to appreciate? Do you think they enjoy pieces that are more technically difficult or just more "flashy"?

It is undeniable that challenging pieces are more easily appreciated by non-musicians. This is due to the fact that a virtuoso piece is in itself a form of show (acoustic and visual), moreover it brings in itself a communicative and energetic side which is quite easy to understand.

I try to risk a reckless question... Bach composed sometimes without specifying instrumentation... maybe... maybe wasn't he interested about "Sound of Music"? I mean maybe does the music in this case is hidden in a scheme, a structure capable of several realizations, several possible and different sounds? And the moment when the music reveals its true nature is contained in the exercise of its variations? Bach at this point would have composed something like jazz standards or pre Cage scores?

It occurred to me to listen to some Bach music played by some self phones or in some musical software's file. It is curious that many aspects of his music are being preserved even in these versions and maintain a certain beauty.
Bach manages to work with the pure note's pitch creating relations between them trough tensions and resolutions, without adding any expressive ingredient. The result is a music that we could define "not terrestrial".

Please tell us five essential records, to have always with you... the classic five discs for the desert island

- Master of Puppets (Metallica)
- Vingt regards sur l'enfant Jesus played by Yvonne Loriod (Olivier Messiaen)
- "Thrak" or "Three of a perfect pair" (King Crimson)
- Joe Henderson "The State of the Tenor" Vols.1&2, live at the Village Vanguard
- Keith Jarrett "My Song" of the "European Quartet" with Jan Garbarek, Palle Danielsson and Jon Christensen.

What are your five favorite scores?

Playing some Bach Suites, at home by myself, give me a great pleasure, without really practicing them, just reading and enjoying the sound which is coming out of them.
I had great fun playing the Fred Firth's pieces for guitar quartet. However there are no pieces that I'm particularly attached to. In fact I love playing my friend's music or mine.

With who would you like to play? What kind of music do you listen to usually?

I wouldn't know, I wouldn't like to be disappointed, sometimes you dream about meeting a musician you like and playing with him, but sometimes it doesn't work, I rather prefer to keep dreaming.
However, if I really have to tell name, I would choose for Bill Frisell, it seems to me a reliable person and a great musician.

Your next projects?

At the moment I'm publishing 12 Studies for Legato Technique, with a particular attention to the independence of the two hands, with a preface by Massimo Felici.
I'm planning to publish some pieces for two classic guitars, for solo electric guitar and for electric guitar quartet.

You have published the two volumes of Mirrors, two study books for electric guitar and delay, why did you choose only the delay pedal? How do you program it? Do you use it only as a delay or as a loop as well?

The decision to use the delay was a challenge, I just wanted to create interesting passages for electric guitar by using a very simple effect like the delay, for doing this I pushed everything to the extreme:
a) The delay stays the same all over the passages: you just set it before you start to play the study as it's written (es: 1000 milliseconds or 800 milliseconds).
b) The delay repeats the minimum amount of possible repetitions, that is just one repetition, in most cases you play a whole bar which is repeated while you play the next one, so that the "chase" (the canon) goes on without interruption.
c) I did not want the delay to be stopped, so it continues to postpone the phrases you play until the end of the song.
There are no other effects as loop or any others, even though the rhythmic joints sometimes sound as if there were other effects.

166

*The delay is a common pedal used in rock n' roll since the rockabilly's days...
then it was back in the 80's thanks to guitarists like The Edge of U2, who made
it his trademark style, but also by Adrian Belew and Bill Frisell... did you think
about those player in your compositions?*

No, because in Mirrors the delay is not really used as an effect, but as a second
guitar.
Perhaps in these works I have been influenced by Robert Fripp and Adrian
Belew, I think of King Crimson for example, in my predilection for rhythmic
twists because of the great ability they require both musically and technically.

*The songs are quite long. How did you manage their development, I mean ..
You seem to move on a well-defined and planned path, how did you define
their structure?*

Mirrors are compositions based on "repetition", it is therefore inevitable to find
characteristics typical of the "minimalism", like for example composers such as
Steve Reich and Terry Riley, and so the passages, since they are based on small
changes, need time to develop (approximately by 6 to 8 minutes each).
Composing Mirrors was a bit like playing tennis against a wall, where every shot
is sent immediately back to the player, they are almost like a boxing match
against the Delay Box, since the pedal has no intelligence, it simply refers back
to you what you are playing and this challenge/combat aspect generated songs
with a certain duration. Another aspect that I have re-evaluated at the end of this
talk, is that Mirrors, I would say, are intended more for the delay itself rather
than the guitar... we could call them "music for a delay pedal."

*One last question, I promise. Sometime ago Carlos Santana said during an
interview: "Some people have talent, some people have vision. And vision is
more important then talent, obviously." I have heard you playing several times
and I think you have a great talent but... could you tell me what's your vision?*

My vision is.... Keep changing VisiOn

JOE MORRIS

Joe Morris was born in New Haven, Connecticut, United States in 1955. He started on guitar in 1969 and played his first professional gig later that year. With the exception of a few lessons he is self-taught. The influence of Jimi Hendrix and other guitarists of that period led him to concentrate on learning to play the blues. John Coltrane's Om inspired him to learn about Jazz and New Music. He worked to establish his own voice on guitar in a free jazz context from the age of 17. After high school he performed in rock bands, rehearsed in jazz bands and played totally improvised music until 1975 when he moved to Boston.

Between 1975 and 1978 he was active on the Boston creative music scene. In 1983 he formed his own record company, Riti, and recorded his first Lp Wraparound.

Between 1989 and 1993 he performed and recorded with his electric trio Sweatshop and electric quartet Racket Club. In 1994 he became the first guitarist to lead his own session in the twenty-year history of Black Saint/Soul Note with the trio recording Symbolic Gesture, and he has continued to record extensively for many labels such as Leo, Knitting Factory, AUM Fidelity, Hathut, Clean Feed, ESP and RogueArt. In addition to leading his own groups, he has recorded and performed with among others: Matthew Shipp, William Parker, John Zorn, Joe Maneri, Rob Brown, Ivo Perelman, Ken Vandermark and DKV Trio, Jim Hobbs, Steve Lantner, Daniel Levin, Petr Cancura and David S. Ware.

He has lectured and conducted workshops through the US and Europe. He is a former member of the faculty of Tufts University Extension College and is currently on the faculty at New England Conservatory in the jazz and improvisation department.

http://www.joe-morris.com/

The first question is always the classic one: how does it start your love and interest for guitar?

The Beatles are the cause of my interest in guitar. I started playing when I was 14 years old. Later it was blues, Jimi Hendrix and the rest of the rock guitar material. I began improvising after hearing Coltrane, Albert Ayler, Cecil Taylor, Anthony Braxton. I learned to play standards and then began a self-directed course of study in guitar and improvisation. I've only had a few guitar lessons, otherwise I am self-taught. I played trumpet for about a year when I was 12 years old. I began playing double bass in 2000 at age 45. I am a decent improviser on piano and drums, but I have never performed on either one, yet.

I noticed something in the young people who want to play an electric guitar today, compared to 20 years ago it seems to me that there is less a search on tone, on instruments with a particular sound and a greater focus on pedals and effects... sometimes I wonder if today the guitars are actually becoming platforms for electronic wizardry and alchemy, I noticed that this also happens in the context of contemporary composers, few (and they are almost all Americans and especially New Yorkers) work with the "pure" guitar tone, otherwise it's a race to effects and pedals, I think this is fine for people like Adrian Belew and the Edge... but otherwise aren't we exaggerating? Or is it an excuse to skip the traditional learning process based on the play the old classics?

For decades I plugged my Les Paul directly into the amp. I did that because it gave me a more personal sound, which was then affected by my articulation and overall touch. Effects and electronics take away the subtleties of phrasing, intonation and articulation on the guitar. I noticed that the guitar players before effects were popular all had their own sound and no one sounded the same. People criticized me for having what they called a "clean sound" like it was an insult. I couldn't have done what I did with playing that way. I had to defend it all the time. To me using effects with the guitar is another instrument with different challenges. Now I use some effects in suitable situations. The understanding of the different situations gives me more sonic options. Direct is different than effected. Either way demands close attention to maintaining a personal sound. So I never use effects in a known way. I improvise the configuration of the pedals too. In one situation I combine the acoustic sound of my archtop with effects using a mic on the instrument and the pickup through a volume pedal, which is connected to the pedals. With this configuration I can blend the acoustic timbre with the electronic one.

You have released a new album with Chris Cretella, called Storms. How did it start this collaboration e and why did you choose to play classical guitars?

Chris was my student at New England Conservatory of Music. I knew him before he enrolled and knew that he was a very strong player. So our lessons were very advanced, about improvisation, technique etc. Since his graduation we have worked together in a few settings. We decided to work on this duo quite deliberately. Once we began we knew quickly that we had to record it.

I have enjoyed a lot your book "Perpetual Frontier[51]", shall we try a game? I ask you the same questions you have asked to the musicians who you

interviewed in your book, I'm curious to read your answer: "What were and are your main musical influences?

On guitar, Jimi Hendrix, Django Reinhardt, Charlie Christian, Derek Bailey, Rene Thomas, Blind Lemon Jefferson, John McLaughlin, Baden Powell. More broadly, blues, jazz, West African kora music. African fiddle music, Gnawa music, Gamelan, Tibetan Chant Music, Indian Music, Messiaen, Cage, Elliott Carter, Charles Ives, Ornette Coleman, Coltrane, Duke Ellington, Miles Davis, Evan Parker, Braxton, Fred Hopkins, Monk, to name a few.

How do you express your "musical form" both in execution and improvisation, whether you're playing "in solo" or together with other musicians?

For years I composed. My technique emerged partly due to my compositions and also due to serious study of the methodologies of improvised music. gradually I began to understand that I didn't need composition, that the way I played was the composition. My use of what I call *the properties of free music* functioned in ways that shaped every aspect of my performances solo, and in groups, by providing me with many points of reference in the process of making the music.

Do you develop a "form" by default making adjustments as necessary or leave the "form" itself to emerge depending on the situation, or exploits both creative approaches?"

Some of my work is organized prior to the performance. But most of it is what I call a *resultant form.* It is formulated in the process of being made. However I use very specific materials in process to shape the music in a way that varies within each duration of performance.

Sometimes ago Elena Càsoli said to me "I improvise the interpretation of what you call encoded. Scored music requires an ethic of respect, attention, closeness and knowledge of its aesthetics, looking at the sign left by the author. But it's a moving, alive, elusive, intangible subject, which awaits the encounter with an interpretative act. And this meeting, in concert, has a space for improvisation, every evening new and different" What do you think about these words?

---

51   Joe Morris, Perpetual Frontier The Properties of Free Music, Riti Publishing, 2012

I agree. All music can be made more of a personal expression if the performer commits to that premise and engages his or her creative ideas. That takes courage and more regard for expression that for approval.

Berio in his essay "A remembrance to the future," wrote: "..A pianist who is a specialist about classical and romantic repertoire, and plays Beethoven and Chopin without knowing the music of the twentieth century, is also off as a pianist who is specialist about contemporary music and plays with hands and mind that have never been crossed in depth by Beethoven and Chopin." You play both traditional classical and contemporary repertoire... do you recognize yourself in these words?

Although I actually don't play classical, I am an improviser, I do see myself in these words. I study music all the time searching for an understanding of the design and expression. And I don't believe that contemporary music should be devoid of the qualities of classical music. However I do believe that those qualities need to be rendered in ways that express our time, our world now. And I believe that rigor in music extend itself to an expression speaks of the deepest and most searching view of existence.

What does improvisation mean for your music research? Do you think it's possible to talk about improvisation for classical music or we have to turn to other repertories like jazz, contemporary music, etc.?

I use improvisation to make music. I never make "an improvisation" and I think musicians who do are terribly naive. Improvisation enables me to configure music in subtle and complex ways on a spontaneous platform. The work in preparing to make music this way is in the study and understanding of how improvisation can be used to achieve this goal. But the result has to be heard as music and not as mere process.

In 1968 Derek Bailey asked to Steve Lacy to define in 15 seconds the difference between improvisation and composition, the answer was "In 15 the difference between improvisation and composition is that in composition you have all the time to decide what you say in 15 seconds, while in improvisation you have only 15 seconds" .. Was the Lacy's answer a little too much ironic or is it a true one?

Maybe was a bit too clever? I think improvisation, when it's done well, doesn't declare form or design, it allows those things to be rendered by the players and deciphered by the listeners in whatever way they hear it. Composition declares form and design and demands that the performers and listeners contend with it.

Shall we enter a bit more into the technical details of your playing? Listening to your solos I don't think you're a guitar player tied to "lick", what kind of "vocabulary" do you use in your music? Do you use special scales? Do you ever find that you use a phrase that you've played before? Do you ever feel the need to stop using something you already know that would work? Do you ever use some "filling phrases"?

I don't use lick, filling phrases, scales or practiced phrases. I do have what I call my "default" material. The stuff that I have used that is in my head, ears and hands. Always I am trying to overcome that and make something brand new. I expect that on a good performance I will invent something whice will then become part of my default. I reach for a rarified "melodic" expression all the time. The kind that requires concentration by me, my fellow players and the audience. The kind that must be deciphered in the process of playing it and hearing it. The original, surprising kind. There is a lot of thought and effort that goes into this process. My life is in this process as well as a lot of very specific knowledge of the use of methodology in the process of making music spontaneously.

What's the role of the "Error" in your musical vision? For "error" I mean an incorrect procedure, an irregularity in the normal operation of a mechanism, a discontinuity on an otherwise uniform surface that can lead to new developments and unexpected surprises .

Great question! In my work, an error occurs when there is an attempt to compose something within the performance, using improvisation that is meant to provide more order than is actually needed. As if someone tries to insert material meant to formally organize the process with identifiable material. That kind of attempt inhibits the process with too much control and so that is what I think would be an error or wrong, in the negative sense.
Otherwise, the configuration of ideas/materials/decisions when encountering a contingency that may not be what is hoped for, or expected, is to me, an opportunity to create a new result.
The one exception to these situations would be when I personally just cannot accurately play what I am attempting to play. In which case I attempt to utilize what I get and carry on either with another try, a variation using what I got, or a shift to something else.

I have, sometimes, the feeling that in our times music's history flows without a particular interest in its chronological course, in our discotheque before and after, past and future become interchangeable elements, shall this be a risk of a uniform vision for an interpreter and a composer? The risk of a musical "globalization"?

This doesn't bother me. I am not a linear thinker so I enjoy tracking the ontological framework of everything. As an artist in the world, I am generally in a state of mind that is a combination of contemplation, inspiration, fear and horror. The world is amazing and terrifying to me. No matter what art and music have done to evolve us and civilize us, humans continue to devolve in new horrifying ways all the time. So it is necessary for us artists to remain open to what is a new no matter where it comes from, and try to be as inclusive as possible. I think this is a very exciting time for the area I work in because it has grown to be Global and new things; techniques, ideas and communities of musicians are popping up all over.

Your musical career has been going on for several years, how have you seen the musical world changing around you? Do you note differences between the students you teach and you taught? How new technologies (new musical instruments, midi, social networks, forums) have influenced your choices and your musical form? How?

Some students expect that they will just jump on the career train and do the kind of thing that I did or Braxton and Zorn did. They don't realize that we all built the entire thing for ourselves, and they are not happy to learn that they must to it this way. Other students are very happy to know this and many know it before I meet them.

I think the Do-It-Yourself artist is helped greatly by the new social media. Always we have had to build our own communities, networks and infrastructure to do our work, and that is much easier to do now. The use of the internet has helped my artistic life in ways that are extraordinary. I can connect with new people, musicians, promoters, writers, students, listeners over the internet. I sell books and CD's. I can post sounds and videos. It's fantastic for me the do-it-myself musician.

Let's talk about marketing. How much do you think it's important for a modern musician? I mean: how much is crucial to be good promoters of themselves and their works in music today?

I am not sure. There are facets of the music business that stagnate rather than generate a future forward sensibility and so old things always do better than new things. Therefore it's necessary to know your own market and to build it yourself if one that welcomes you doesn't already exist. The parts of the music scene that support me are mostly grassroots or musician run with some exceptions.

What do you think about the discographic market crisis, with the transition to digital downloading in mp3 and all this new scenario?

My area of music has always been held back by the big music industry. I am happy to see it go away. Meanwhile my business is thriving. It's done on a small and workable scale. I never cared to be a millionaire by making horrible music. I only want to live and make music. Things are fine for me.

I try to ask you a little bit provocative question about music in general, not just about contemporary or avant-garde. Frank Zappa in his autobiography he wrote: "If John Cage, for example, said, now I put a contact microphone on the throat, then I drink carrot juice and this will be my composition ", then his gargling would qualify as a COMPOSITION, because he applied a frame, declaring it as such. "Take it or leave it, now I want this to be music." It's really good this statement to define a genre of music, just say this is classical music, this is contemporary and it's done? It still makes sense to speak about "genre"?

I will only say that I honestly think that it's less important to argue about what is this or that than it is to expand how we all think, feel and experience sound, music, life, and our existence. We need more challenges with sound, music and art to happen. The world is full of horror and more musical challenges are one kind of antidote to that horror. Who cares what is composition? We need more kindness, peace, love and beauty and less arguing about unimportant things.

Talking about innovative composers, what do you think about John Zorn and the New york musical downtown scene, so ready to get and recode every musical language, improvisation, jazz, contemporary music, cartoon music?

John is a genius. He's a deep, generous and adventurous high artist. I appreciate every effort he's made. He's sees a challenge and he tried to conquer it. He's amazing.

One of the things that I can honestly say about guitar is its ability and capacity to change its shape as a musical medium over the centuries and between the various musical and social forms: I think this incredible ability is due to several factors not least the fact that it can be realized both in industrial and artigianal forms, and the fact that we can choose between classical, acoustic and electric types suitable for different musical and social cultures. You have followed a very personal path inside the guitar, how did you develop this path and how are you developing it?

Guitar really is a perfect "peoples" instrument. The beauty of the modern guitar is that it is only about invention. There is no correct way to play it. There is no pedagogy for it. The future of the guitar is the same as it's past. It will require that its players use it in a unique and innovative way. For me, it's been the means of an incredible life adventure. I struggle with it every time I touch it, but it's helped me to understand myself, to see myself and to literally see the world. I guess I saw the value of the guitar for these possibilities by seeing what it did for the blues, jazz and rock musicians before I started playing it. I had a realization as a teenager when I was trying to play the guitar like another player. It dawned on me that I admired his originality and therefore in order to really play like him I should play like myself. Immediately I stopped practicing his material and focused on my own, which I was already playing but trying to ignore. For that moment it's been just about speaking my mind with the guitar.

Do you think that the guitar, with its presence of virtuoso very personal musicians at every musical level and genre would be a viable alternative to the now tragicomic distinction between high culture and popular culture and the affirmation of Schoenberg " if it is art, it is not for all, and if it is for all, it is not art "?

I guess that depend on who gets to decide what art is? High culture knows absolutely nothing about me. I don't exist to that part of culture, and yet I make art all the time and I am free of all the constraints of their opinion and oversight. Popular culture knows nothing about me either. The expectations of Pop culture are not my problem. I am free from that burden too. I am exactly where I want to be. I am happy, thriving, free and moving forward.

Please tell us five essential records, to have always with you .. the classic five discs for the desert island...

I don't know if this list is *the* 5. But it would do:
Albert Ayler *Spiritual Unity*

175

Alhaji Bai Konte *Kora Melodies from the Republic of The Gambia, West Africa*
Jimi Hendrix *Band of Gypsies*
Jimmy Lyons/Sunny Murray *Jump up/What to do about*
Evan Parker/Barry Guy *Obliquities*

What are your five favorite scores?

Five that I love. Not sure what are my absolute favorites. All chamber or orchestral:
Olivier Messiaen *Sept Haiku*
Charles Ives *Calcium Light Night*
Elliott Carter *1st String Quartet*
Sofia Gubaidulina *Concerto for viola and orchestra*
Witold Lutoslawski *String Quartet*

With who would you like to play? What kind of music do you listen to usually?

The only person I wanted to play with who I haven't played with yet is Ornette Coleman. He's very old so I doubt it can happen[52]. The people I enjoy playing with or would like to work with more are Anthony Braxton, Barry, Evan Parker, John Butcher, Peter Evans, Agusti Fernandez, Mat Maneri, Chris Cretella, Yasmine Azaiez, Brad Barrett, Nate Wooley, Ken Vandermark, Alex Ward, Andria Nicodemou, Jim Hobbs, Mat Maneri, Taylor Ho Bynum, Tyshawn Sorey, and a few others.
I drive a lot. Most of my listening for enjoyment is in my car. It's normal for me to listen to Mozart, Bob Dylan, Brian Ferneyhough, Scodanibbio, Ornette Coleman, Rev Gary Davis, Derek Bailey, some traditional African music and some noise improvisation or any similar mix during a drive.

Your next projects?

New Cds. II have realized a new solo guitar recording last winter[53], a new electric trio called Mess Hall, duo with the bassist Brad Barrett, trio wth Nate Wooley and Evan Parker, duo with Evan Parker and a 5 piece chamber work called Ultra with feature Agusti Fernandez on piano.

When we will see you playing in Italy?

---

52   This interview was made before Coleman died in 2015.

53   Joe Morris, Solos Bimhuis, Relavive Pitch, 2015

Soon I hope.

MARCO OPPEDISANO

Marco Oppedisano (born November 20, 1971 in Brooklyn, New York) is an American guitarist and composer whose compositions focus on the innovative use of electric guitar in the genre of electroacoustic music. His musique concrète/acousmatic music compositions have utilized multitrack recording and extended performance techniques for electric guitar, nylon string guitar andelectric bass. In addition to musique concrète, compositions by Oppedisano also consist of "live" electric guitar in combination with a fixed playback of various electronic, acoustic (specifically female voice courtesy of Kimberly Fiedelman) and sampled sounds.
Oppedisano has also composed works for solo classical guitar, solo electric guitar and mixed ensemble.

http://www.marcooppedisano.net/

The first question is always the classic one: how does it start your love and interest for guitar and what instruments do you play or have you played?

My father played guitar and sang at home, so there was that influence and sound growing up. At around the age of 12, I seriously picked up the guitar and fell in love with it immediately. I was not interested in singing though. I grew up a teenager in the 80s, so I was very influenced by the technical guitar playing in the rock/metal music of that time.

What instruments do you play or have you played? I see you have a beautiful Stratocaster, I love those guitars...

I have not had many guitars in my life, mainly because I've seen myself more a composer than guitarist for quite some time now. I have two electrics that are my main guitars. I have a Guild nylon string guitar from my days studying classical guitar in the conservatory. I also play some banjo. I have a modified 1979 American hardtail Fender Stratocaster and a 90's Ibanez AS-120, (semi-hollow). I cover a lot of sound with those two electrics. I like that each guitar almost forces me to play differently.

I noticed something in the young people who want to play an electric guitar today, compared to 20 years ago it seems to me that there is less a search on tone, on instruments with a particular sound and a greater focus on pedals and effects... sometimes I wonder if today the guitars are actually becoming platforms for electronic wizardry and alchemy, I noticed that this also

happens in the context of contemporary composers, few (and they are almost all Americans and especially New Yorkers) work with the "pure" guitar tone, otherwise it's a race to effects and pedals, I think this is fine for people like Adrian Belew and the Edge.. but otherwise aren't we exagerating? Or is it an excuse to skip the traditional learning process based on the play the old classics?

As much as I have explored the world of processing and effects, I still want to hear what the guitar in its purest state has to offer. Much of the time I simply play a guitar plugged into an amp. I've never obsessed about tone and always looked to be more original in my compositions, not my in my guitar playing.
I agree with the less emphasis on tone these days. At one time, you could identify a player by their tone. Guitar solos in pop music now are non-existent and so many of the great guitar tones were on popular songs, or at least in songs by popular bands.
It's important to understand the relationship between the guitar and amp without effects and then work from there. Don't get me wrong, effects are great, but the use of an effect should be musically compelling and not just a gimmick.

What was your musical training, with which teachers have you studied and what impression they left in your music?

I had six months of lessons with a family friend during the second year of playing guitar and then was self taught right up until I started college. I had learned enough knowledge of harmony and theory on my own to get in to the conservatory and was admitted as a classical guitar performance major. I studied classical guitar with Michael Cedric Smith at the Brooklyn College Conservatory of Music for two years and realized that I did not want to devote my studies to being a professional classical guitarist. At that time, Charles Dodge had recommended that I study composition. It turned out to be a better direction for me.
As an undergraduate at Brooklyn College, I studied composition with Noah Creshevsky. Charles Dodge, and Tania Leon. As a graduate student at the Queens College Aaron Copland School of Music I studied with Thea Musgrave and Henry Weinberg.
Later on when returning as an alumnus to work at the Brooklyn College Center for Computer Music, I learned so much from George Brunner about composing electroacoustic music and working in the recording studio. Much of my debut compilation CD, Electroacoustic Compositions for Electric Guitar (with the exception of Time Lapse, Karmicom and Three Short Electronic Pieces) was created at the Brooklyn College Center for Computer Music.

179

I must say that my perspective on studying with a teacher now is from someone who has not studied with anyone for over 10 years. It was a good experience having worked with composition teachers who each had different teaching methods, philosophies and styles. They offered many invaluable perspectives on all aspects of being a serious composer.

I have the book "State of the Axe" made by the photographer Ralph Gibson... and you are in the book, like Andy Summer, Bill Frisell, Nels Cline and several other guitarists, how it happened that Gibson made a photo of you?

A few years ago, I received a message from Ralph asking me if I would like to be in a book of guitarists he was working on. When I found out who was in State of The Axe, I was blown away. Half the guitarists in the book were influences for me growing up. It is a great honor for me to be included with such distinguished company in a beautifully put together collection of photographs.

Berlioz said that composing for classical guitar it was difficult because the composer have first to be a guitarists, these words were often used as a justification for the limited repertoire of classical guitar with other instruments like piano and violin. At the same time I think that the growing interest for the guitar (whether classical, acoustic, electric, MIDI) collected in contemporary music has changed the importance of Berlioz's words. As a guitarist and a composer do you think that these words are even true?

First, it is important to understand that Berlioz came from a very different time. Composing for any instrument is difficult. In regards to guitar, the fourths (with the major 3rd between the 3rd and 2nd strings) make standard guitar tuning slightly unusual compared to the fifths used in string instruments. I've found that contemporary composers who are not guitarists are often intrigued with the standard tuning, often using it as a chord (low to high: E-A-D-G-B-E). Alternate tunings are also an option, as they make the guitar resonate differently too - but anything more involved than a drop D becomes more difficult to sightread.
I think it is still easy to forget that the classical guitar is capable of so much. Six strings offer many polyphonic and harmonic possibilities; requiring composers have a strong understanding of guitar fingerings. I think a composer who is just starting to write for classical or electric guitar, should work closely with a trained guitarist. Another issue with the classical guitar is volume. Amplification has come a long way now in getting the classical guitar to be easily heard in larger ensemble settings. This obviously was not possible in Berlioz's time.

Since I am a composer who plays guitar, I've found that the physical aspects required to play an instrument can be hindering to creativity due to the tendency on relying on familiar fingerings and tendencies.

My composition, Primo Volo[54] (composed for Oren Fader) was composed without having picked up the guitar once. I couldn't have composed that particular piece otherwise. Also, I wasn't composing it for me in mind as performer.

I enjoyed very much the $100 Guitar Project. It was an amazing idea: buying a $100 guitar and giving it to 65 different guitar players so that everyone could express himself on this guitar, the result is an excellent double cd. I was amazed by how each one of you have left his own style still using the same cheap guitar, How did you join this project and... how was this guitar?"

The $100 Guitar Project[55] was started by guitarists, Nick Didkovsky and Charles O'Meara in October 2010. I found about the project a month later and quickly decided this was something I wanted to be a part of. In January 2011, I picked up the guitar from Elliott Sharp in downtown NYC, had it for a week in Sunnyside, Queens and then dropped it off with Ron Anderson (PAK) in Park Slope, Brooklyn.

I've always believed that the player makes the guitar. My first impression of the $100 guitar was that, yes, it was a real cheapo, but found that it had a good amount of resonance, was a bit quirky and a lot of character.

So, I plucked around and thought, what kind of sounds can I get on this thing? After some thought, it came to me to compose a piece that incorporated all kinds of sounds from the instrument. This approach is not too far off from what I've done in the past. But with writing a short piece (a little over 2 minutes), I had to find a compelling way (at least to me) to demonstrate these sounds in a short amount of time without coming off contrived.

So, I plugged it in and with the help of a Boss GT-6 multi effects processor, and some alligator clips, I got to work. Recorded a few improvisations and grabbed a bunch of samples…

My piece is called Red Cent. The title inspired by it being a $100 red guitar. Cent means a hundred in French. And the phrase, "Not worth a red cent."

The $100 Guitar Project was released on Bridge Records, Inc. in January 2013.and royalties on every sale are paid directly to CARE, a leading

---

[54]   http://www.youtube.com/watch?v=C7yL0PPRAmM

[55]   Www.100dollarguitar.com

humanitarian organization fighting global poverty. The 2CD set contains such a wonderful variety of music. I enjoy visualizing that guitar being passed around having traveled over 30,000 miles and hearing all the great sounds coming from it. I'm still amazed me that it remained in one piece

What does improvisation mean for your music research? Do you think it's possible to talk about improvisation for classical music or we have to turn to other repertories like jazz, contemporary music, etc.?

Improvisation for me is one means of generating material for my electroacoustic music. Outside of that, improvisation is a nice way for me to perform with friends.

If we are talking about students learning classical pieces in the conservatory, there isn't much room for improvisation there. Some people may not realize that the classical masters , Beethoven, Mozart, Handel and Bach for example, were all excellent improvisers themselves.

In 1968 Derek Bailey asked to Steve Lacy to define in 15 seconds the difference between improvisation and composition, the answer was "In 15 the difference between improvisation and composition is that in composition you have all the time to decide what you say in 15 seconds, while in improvisation you have only 15 seconds"... Was the Lacy's answer a little too much ironic or is it a true one??

Sounds to me like a clever response by a great musician. There are various forms of improvisation. For example, one must make a distinction between free improvisation, in comparison to improvisation rooted in more tonal/harmonic languages. It's not a simple or clear cut matter.

What's the role of the "Error" in your musical vision? For "error" I mean an incorrect procedure, an irregularity in the normal operation of a mechanism, a discontinuity on an otherwise uniform surface that can lead to new developments and unexpected surprises...

As far as "errors" that occur unintentionally, I prefer to call them happy accidents. Some people believe in divine intervention, I don't. Maybe they aren't mistakes and were intended all along without realizing it? While working many hard hours on composing, I always leave room the unexpected. The more you work, the more things happen. An unexpected occurrence can easily direct me to a different place within a composition.

Shall we enter a bit 'more into the technical details of your playing? Listening to your solos I don't think you're a guitar player tied to "lick", what kind of "vocabulary" do you use in your music? Do you use special scales? Do you ever find that you use a phrase that you've played before? Do you ever feel the need to stop using something you already know that would work? Do you ever use some "filling phrases"?

Growing up a rock player I learned many licks, especially being a teenger in the 80's where I was very influenced by rock and metal. I'm very careful about the use of guitar in my electroacoustic compositions. I've spent a lot of time thinking about how to incorporate guitar in a way where it does not become the focus of the piece. I like to think that my use of guitar serves the composition. In this regard I don't think of licks even though my phrases may be brief. There are never "filling phrases" and I rarely take extended guitar solos in my work. I've become more melodic in my note selection, but I'm still open to letting anything happen. And that means dissonance, noise, free improvisation and extended techniques. I do like to deliberately change things up with my guitar playing.

My first album, Electroacoustic Compositions for Electric Guitar (2007) utilized the guitar more as a sound source. Later releases, demonstrate more of my playing and recent work seeks to find a balance between conventional guitar playing, guitar sounds and sounds in general (electronic, virtual instruments and samples).

It seems to me that there is a small music scene about classical guitarists dedicated to an innovative and contemporary repertoire, as well as you come to my mind the names of Marco Cappelli, David Tanenbaum, David Starobin, Elena Casoli, Maurizio Grandinetti, Marc Ribot, etc. Are there other guitarists you know and that you can suggest us that they move on these innovative musical routes?

The late Hans Reichel has released albums of wonderful solo guitar music. He is a personal favorite of mine. I am familiar with the names you mention – some of whom I admire - but to be quite honest, contemporary classical guitar music is not something I listen to as much as I used to. My primary work now deals with electric guitar in the genre of electroacoustic music. My solo classical guitar piece, Primo Volo (2003), was recorded by New York City based guitarist Oren Fader and included on a CD in 2005 that I also produced and edited called First Flight[56].

---

56   http://www.cdbaby.com/cd/orenfader2

Also, another composition that might be of interest to readers here is a four movement work I composed for solo electric guitar called, <u>Urban Mosaic</u>[57] (2002). It was composed for and performed by Kevin R. Gallagher.

How is the situation in USA and New York in those times? How much the crisis hit the musical scene

Isn't there always some sort of crisis in regards to the arts? Don't the arts always suffer because they are not funded enough? Well, I can say that whatever "scene" exists in New York is not only in Manhattan anymore, there are still a few places to play and still some great music to catch there, but I've noticed that lots of stuff is now happening in Brooklyn (my hometown). I've done a lot less performing and concert attending the last few years, so maybe I'm not the best person to ask about this. I've become more of a studio composer. I haven't ruled out consistently performing live ever again, it just hasn't been a priority for a little while now.

I'm a Rhys Chatham, Sonic Youth and Glenn Branca fan, I know that you have played with Branca, can you tell us something about this experience?

I never actually performed with Branca. My first experience performing Branca's music involved playing el. guitar in a US premiere of a 3 el. Gtr., el. bass and drums piece called <u>Guitars D' Amour.</u> This was back in 2004 in New York City. Branca supervised a rehearsal and we played 2 performances of the piece - a 15 minute sightreading beast of a work. A very different piece than one is accustomed to hearing from Branca and at the same time intense and also fun. Then I performed once in Branca's well known 100 guitar symphony (80 electric guitars, 20 el. basses and drum set) as part of a recording session in Queens, NY back in late 2004. It was a memorable experience. One vivid memory was taking off my earplugs off out of curiosity and lasting only a few seconds before putting them back on. It was violently loud and nothing like I had ever experienced before. It was great.

I have, sometimes, the feeling that in our times music's history flows without a particular interest in its chronological course, in our discotheque before and after, past and future become interchangeable elements, shall this be a risk of a uniform vision for an interpreter and a composer? The risk of a musical "globalization"?

---

57   http://www.youtube.com/watch?v=JddbW5Y2eb0

We've reached a point now where anything goes in music. I think that it's important that there are people out there who along with listening to music also want to think deeply and form opinions about it. A problem I hear these days with much experimental/electronic music is it seems disposable. It makes no real attempt to be memorable and I hear so many of the same, sometimes recycled, gestures and sounds.

Maybe there is no more musical history to be made. I think it's OK if the lines are blurred or simply nonexistent. If anything, technology seems to be making more history. Then again, technology could be at fault too for making artists and listeners lazy.

Your musical career has been going on for several years, how have you seen the musical world changing around you? Do you note differences between the students you teach and you taught? How new technologies (new musical instruments, midi, social networks, forums) have influenced your choices and your musical form? How?

As a guitar and band instructor for the last 22 years, I've seen so many changes. There is so much more available to students then when I was first starting. With an iPad and a wireless internet connection you have a world of information and music at your fingertips. I still marvel at that. Actually, I think there is too much easily available. One of my best memories as a young guitar player, was how I couldn't wait for the new issues of guitar magazines to come out each month.

As far as music technology is concerned, I know that without the use of a home studio I wouldn't have been able to create the amount of electroacoustic music I have now. I never had to splice tape and know some of my present compositions would have taken forever to compete this way.

I used a computer music studio to create some of my early works, but having a home studio has made all the difference. The drawback to the popularity of the home studio, is it has also resulted in so many people independently releasing their own music making it harder for some people to stand out and be heard.

Social networks have been good for me because I've made connections I would have not made otherwise. It also has turned me on to a lot of independent musicians and artists I might have not discovered. I'm grateful for that. Spending time on social networks and forums can be a big time waster too. I have nice memories of life without the internet.

Let's talk about marketing. How much do you think it's important for a modern musician? I mean: how much is crucial to be good promoters of themselves and their works in music today?

It depends on what you are trying to achieve with music. A good label can help get your music better exposure, but there is less emphasis these days with getting on a label because of independent/DIY releases. Self-promotion is easier with the internet now, but nowadays it is so saturated with people trying to get known, that it can be difficult to get noticed. If one can afford management, that is always useful. A service like Kickstarter has been useful for many artists in generating funding for their projects.

What do you think about the discographic market crisis, with the transition to digital downloading in mp3 and all this new scenario?

Physical CD releases are important for artists because most reviewers or radio station programmers won't bother with mp3s alone. Then again I hear vinyl is making a big comeback. Anyway, real fans of a group or an artist are mostly likely to purchase a physical release... with the availability of many free mp3s online, the younger audience feels entitled to music without having to pay for any of it. Younger people have no idea what it's like to go to record store and never will. The availability of music has made listening more fragmented and taken for granted. I know artists, including myself, who still think of the track order as an important part of the listening experience. That is lost much of the time with free downloading and purchasing from digital stores.
Unfortunately with bit torrent, music piracy is very difficult to control. Although with streaming sites like Spotify and Pandora, artists do get some royalties, but the amount is still very small. I don't think I'll ever get used to the idea of being able to listen to practically anything with few clicks of the mouse. It's easy to get swept up in the new technology, but I always make it a point to remember where I came from.

I try to ask you a little bit provocative question about music in general, not just about contemporary or avant-garde. Frank Zappa in his autobiography he wrote: "If John Cage, for example, said, now I put a contact microphone on the throat, then I drink carrot juice and this will be my composition ", then his gargling would qualify as a COMPOSITION, because he applied a frame, declaring it as such. "Take it or leave it, now I want this to be music." It's really good this statement to define a genre of music, just say this is classical music, this is contemporary and it's done? It still makes sense to speak about "genre"?

I know the Zappa quote. Art for most requires that there be some craft involved. For example, a work of art can't be as simple as recording one drinking carrot juice. I hear sound organized in a "frame" as a composition. Whether I think it is good or not is another story. I've had quite a few involved discussions about this. People can get very protective of what they think is art.

One of the things that I can honestly say about guitar is its ability and capacity to change its shape as a musical medium over the centuries and between the various musical and social forms: guitar seems to be the perfect instrument (not only by the musical but also logical, economic and philosophical aspect) to counter the theories of the Frankfurt School and Adorno. You have followed a very personal path inside the guitar, how did you develop this path and how are you developing it?

It took me a bit of time to get where I am. When I started studying classical guitar in the conservatory in the late 80's/early 90's, the electric guitar hadn't quite crossed over in to the contemporary classical music concert world. I did not think of using the electric guitar in my compositions until the mid 90's. And by the late 90's when I was out of school, I was using electric guitar in almost all of my compositions: solo, quartet, mixed ensemble or electroacoustic. Now electric guitar is everywhere. I use it in all of my compositions and always think about trying new things.

Do you think that the guitar, with its presence of virtuoso very personal musicians at every musical level and genre would be a viable alternative to the now tragicomic distinction between high culture and popular culture and the affirmation of Schoenberg " if it is art, it is not for all, and if it is for all, it is not art"?

I think at one time the classical world didn't even consider the electric guitar a real instrument. I don't see guitar as alternative to "high culture," but it is the sort of instrument that can adapt to more musical situations than any other.

Please tell us five essential records, to have always with you... the classic five discs for the desert island...

Lists like this are always challenging because they could get very long. Anyway, I'll try to have some fun with it although I will be leaving out many recordings that I love:

1. The American Stravinsky, The Composer, Vol. 4 - Igor Stravinsky (cond. Robert Craft). Love it mostly for Agon. So much of why I love that piece cannot be put to words.

2. The Rite of Spring: CBS Great Performances – Igor Stravinsky (cond. Pierre Boulez: Cleveland Orchestra). I've heard many recordings of this piece and this Boulez recording is my favorite.
3. Band of Gypsys (live at The Fillmore East) – Jimi Hendrix and The Band of Gypsys. I loved it when I was younger and still do. Something as incredible as Hendrix's Machine Gun from that 1970 release is still mindblowing.
4. Absolutely Free – The Mothers of Invention. Everything about Frank Zappa that I love is on that album. I'm a big fan of the original Mothers and I never tire hearing that band and those early albums.
5. Sonatas and Interludes – John Cage. I immediately fell in love with this music. It inspired me to explore preparing my guitars.

With who would you like to play? What kind of music do you listen to usually?

I would like to play with anyone who can inspire me to play better. I listen to all kinds of music. I'll listen to some electronic music and then may throw on some metal or jazz. I don't listen to as nearly as much guitar music as I used to. I particularly like to listen to music by people that I know. Sometimes, I'll even listen to my own stuff. And a good size portion of my free time is spent not listening to music, especially after a long day of teaching music.

Your next projects? When we will see you playing in Italy?

I've contributed to a few compilations within the last few years and plan to release an album of electric guitar driven music sometime in 2015. I have a four and half year old daughter that keeps me very busy. Most of my time is spent teaching and being a freelance musician.
I would love to come to Italy to play. I've been there a few times on vacation. Unfortunately, I don't expect to be there anytime soon.

A last question... my Blog is read by several students... any good advices to give them?

It's obvious that one has to work hard in order to be successful. There's no question that music schools churn out many competent musicians, so what can you do to make yourself stand out? What makes you unique? Focus on your strengths and worry less about your weaknesses. Learn as much as you can, respect tradition, be versatile, professional and never be a music genre elitist. All great players have something distinct about them that make them stand out from

the rest. One must experience life outside of music too. It is important to be a well-rounded individual.
Also, avoid getting into serious debt and if you are able to, get yourself a job with flexible hours... (laughs)

Ok. This is really the last question... which is more a reflection: Luigi Nono said "Other thoughts, other noises, other sounds, other ideas. When we listen to, we often try to find ourselves in others. To find our mechanisms, system, rationalism, in the other. And this is a quite conservative violence."... Now... does experimentation free ourselves from the burden of having to remember?

I know my sense for experimentation started as a young teenager and was based simply on wanting to be different, call it rebelliousness. I eventually learned a lot, and as I grew older, focused on what I thought to be useful in my own music. I allow for influences to get in my music in one way or another and I don't think there is anything wrong with that. Conservative violence? I think that's a bit drastic. I do think it takes a bit of courage to follow your own path. I try to genuinely tap into how I see the world and find my place in it through my art. Experimentation is freeing, but why should it require that we forget? What's wrong with remembering? I don't even mind being a bit nostalgic too, but that's just me.